Nelson against Napoleon

Nelson against Napoleon

From the Nile to
Copenhagen, 1798 – 1801

Edited by Robert Gardiner

CAXTON EDITIONS

In association with
The National Maritime Museum

Contributors

Roger Morriss
Introduction 1798-1801
Part I: The Battle for the Mediterranean
Part II: The Channel and Ireland
Part III: Colonial and Commerce Warfare
Part IV: The Northern Threat
The Hero of the Nile
Forcing the Sound
The Battle of Copenhagen

Stephen Chumbley
West Indies 1798
West Indies 1799-1801
The Black Ship
The Caribbean commerce war

Robert Gardiner
The *élite* of the navy of England
Bonaparte's oriental adventure
Malta and the Knights
The French landings in Egypt
Nelson's pursuit of Bonaparte
Leander and Généreux
The capture of Minorca
Nelson and Naples
The Neapolitan navy
The Cadiz station 1798-1799
The Defence of Acre
The French stranded in Egypt
The seige of Malta
The Mediterranean fleet under Keith
The loss of the Queen Charlotte
The invasion of Egypt – an opposed landing
Victory in Egypt
Ships of the Royal Navy: the 44-gun two-decker
Cochrane and the Speedy
Ships of the Royal Navy: experimental vessels
Popham's attack on Ostend
Ships of the Royal Navy: the Second Rate`
Anglo-Russian invasion of the Netherlands 1799
Tightening the blockade 1799-1800
Watching the Biscay ports
Captain Schank's Q-ship
Invasion threat
The birth of a new naval power
America's 'quasi-war' with France
Ships of the Royal Navy: the Sixth Rate
East Indies 1798-1801
Red Sea operations
'Dangers of the sea': dismasting
Indian Ocean raiders
Ships of the Royal Navy: bomb vessels

David Lyon
The Battle of the Nile – the attack
The destruction of *L'Orient*
Pressing home the victory
The Battle of Algesiras
Saumarez's revenge
Mars versus Hercule
Rehearsing the invasion: attack on St Marcouf
The Destruction of Bompart off Lough Swilly
The wandering army
Cutting-out attacks in the Channel

Julian Mannering
Notes on artists

EVE Sharpston
French naval bases: Le Havre
One against the odds

FRONTISPIECE
For the Royal Navy, what historians call the War of the
Second Coalition might be said to start and finish in Egypt,
with Nelson's great victory of the Nile in 1798 reflected in
the successful conquest of Egypt in 1801. The landings in
March of that year were a tribute to the Navy's expertise in
amphibious warfare, although as de Loutherbourg's typically
dramatic representations shows, they were fiercely contested.
NMM neg 1738

Copyright © Chatham Publishing 1997

First published in Great Britain in 1997 by
Chatham Publishing, an imprint of Gerald
Duckworth & Co Ltd

This edition published 2001 by Caxton Editions
an imprint of The Caxton Publishing Group
ISBN 1 84067 3613

British Library Cataloguing in Publication Data
A catalogue record for this book is available
from the British Library

Designed and typeset by Tony Hart, Isle of Wight
Printed and bound by C.T.P.S.

CONTENTS

Thematic pages in italic

PREFACE

ALTHOUGH THE eighteenth century lacked the kind of mass, and instant-aneous, media so familiar in the late twentieth, the earlier age was just as interested in news and current affairs. This was largely satisfied by the written word—at increasing chronological distance from the events themselves, newspapers, journals and books. But even in the 1700s, the written medium was not the only source of information. A sophisticated printselling industry evolved, producing relatively cheap, and sometimes tasteless images of a nature that even modern tabloids would eschew, purporting to depict recent happenings of public interest. However, among them were also to be found fine engravings based on the works of well known artists, including remarkably detailed maps and charts of land and sea engagements, which often stand up in point of accuracy to modern research.

In this fashion the public was provided with an image of the great occurrences of the time, and the 'Chatham Pictorial Histories' are intended to recreate this impression in the naval sphere, which for an island nation like Britain was a paramount concern right down to recent decades. Of course, besides the public prints, there were also more formal representations like the oil paintings commissioned by those involved, but by their very nature they are celebratory and, although often the result of the most meticulous research by the artist, they lack immediacy. They are also quite well known, and another of our concerns has been to seek out the less familiar, and in some cases the never previously published, so while we do use some finished paintings, we have preferred the artist's own sketchbooks where available; they reveal not only the lengths the painters went to get details correct, but often cover occurrences that are not otherwise represented, or where the art world has lost track of the finished work.

In the search for original and, if possible, eyewitness depictions, we have also dipped into some of the logs, journals and contemporary manuscripts. Naval officers, in particular, were encouraged to observe closely, and part of the training process involved making sketches of everything from coastal features to life on board. To a lesser extent, this was true of army officers, who were often fine mapmakers—especially those in the technical branches like the engineers and the artillery (today most people in Britain are unaware of why the best official mapping of the country is called the Ordnance Survey).

However, the series was inspired by the Prints and Drawings collection of the National Maritime Museum at Greenwich, on the outskirts of London. Reckoned to comprise 66,000 images, it is a surprisingly under-used resource, despite the fact that an ongoing copying programme has made three-quarters of it available on microfilm. While this forms the core of the series, we have also had recourse to the Admiralty Collection of ship draughts—itself running to about 100,000 plans—as well as some reference to the charts collection in the Navigation Department and logs and personal journals kept by the Manuscripts Department. This last is a very substantial holding with no easy mode of access to any illustrations it may contain, so although some work has been done in this area, it must be said that there is probably far more to discover if only time were available for the task.

The series is intended first and foremost to illustrate the great events of maritime history, and we have made little attempt to pass artistic judgement on any of the images, which were chosen for content rather than style. The pictures are grouped, as far as practical, to show how events were presented at the time. Since this is not primarily a work of art history, for the technical credits we have relied on the Maritime Museum's extant indexing, the product of a massive and long-running documentation programme by many hands with some inevitable inconsistencies, depending on the state of knowledge at the time each item was catalogued. We have reproduced what infor-mation there is, only correcting obviously wrong attributions and dates, and quoting the negative number or unique reference number of each illustration for anyone wishing to obtain copies of these from the museum or archive concerned.

Following *Fleet Battle and Blockade* in chronology, *Nelson against Napoleon* is the second of five titles covering the whole of the period of the great French wars from 1793 to 1815, including America's 'quasi-war' with France and the conflict with the Barbary states. The series follows the order of the original events, except that the War of 1812 fills a single volume of its own, and each otherwise covers its period completely. However, the thematic spreads are cumulative in their coverage, because we are keen to illustrate many general aspects of the weapons and warfare of the period which stand outside the chronological structure. Therefore, we devised a single programme of such topics and simply positioned each at an appropriate point in the series. The best example is provided by the many features on individual ship types and their roles, which will add up to a complete analysis of the function of the Navy's order of battle by the end of this five-volume set. Similarly, *Fleet Battle and Blockade* looked at the life of commissioned officers, while later volumes will do the same for seamen; and there will be ongoing picture essays on themes like the perils of the sea, and on individual ports and harbours. This, we believe, avoids predictability and gives every volume variety and additional interest.

Acknowledgements

The project would have been impossible without the co-operation of those at the National Maritime Museum's publications division, initially David Spence and latterly Pieter van der Merwe, who negotiated and set up a workable joint venture. I received generous and friendly advice from Clive Powell on logs and journals and from Brian Thynne on charts, while the staff of the library were endlessly patient with demands for myriads of photocopies and frequent requests to put right snarl-ups in the microfilm readers. The volunteer 'Friends' of the museum showed similar forbearance in the Picture Research Room.

With the minimum of fuss and bureaucracy Jane Costantini organised the numerous visits to the outstation where the original prints and drawings are stored, and I am grateful to the Ladies of LTE for their tea and sympathy during these long and rather gruelling days. Gael Dundas deserves particular praise for the spirit of co-operation that suffuses her outpost of empire: large numbers of heavy boxes were cheerfully hauled out and reshelved without a hint of complaint, and any queries were pursued with persistence and real enthusiasm.

However, our greatest thanks must be reserved, as previously, for Chris Gray, Head of Picture Research, and his assistant David Taylor, who organised and executed the massive programme of photography that was demanded within our very unreasonable time-scale. This volume presented them with a number of particularly elusive problem images, and the fact that the book includes everything that we requested is a tribute to their efforts.

Outside Britain my debts are less extensive, but I would thank the staff of the Peabody Essex Museum of Salem, Massachusetts and Sigrid Trumpy of the Beverley R Robinson Collection at Annapolis who helped with material on the American 'quasi-war' with France.

Robert Gardiner
London, May 1997

INTRODUCTION 1798-1801

IN 1797 William Pitt at the head of the British government despaired of concluding the war against Revolutionary France successfully for Britain. That July, in recognition of Britain's inability to prosecute war further, Pitt sent Lord Malmesbury from the Foreign Office to offer the French recognition of their control over the Netherlands, including the coastline from Dunkirk and the mouths of the River Rhine. By so doing, he virtually abandoned the principle upon which he had gone to war: in 1793 hostilities between Britain and France had broken out after French forces, already fighting Austria since April 1792, had overrun the Austrian Netherlands and, in defiance of international treaties dating back to 1648, opened the River Scheldt to navigation and permitted naval vessels and troops up the river to take Antwerp from the sea. Combined with their offer of fraternity and assistance to all peoples desirous of gaining their liberty, the invasion had threatened both the sovereignty of the Austrian emperor over Belgian provinces and the ruling House of Orange in Holland, whom Britain was bound by treaty to defend. The subsequent decapitation of its monarch by Revolutionary France brought the whole British establishment behind Pitt. Yet, four years later, he was prepared to abandon the territories at the heart of his war policy.

What had gone wrong? In the first place, France seemed insuperable on land and her continental enemies shattered. In 1793 Pitt had woven a formidable net of alliances with Russia, Prussia, Austria, Piedmont-Sardinia, Naples, Spain and Portugal, surrounding and checking the expansionist impulses released by revolutionary fervour in France. One by one, however, the allies had been defeated or neutralised: Prussia in April 1795, Holland a month later, Spain in July 1796. The invasion threat posed by France's control of the three greatest navies in continental Europe now forced British withdrawal from the Mediterranean. Unsupported, the forces of Austria, already driven out of Italy, were forced to treat for peace in October 1797.

The neutralisation of Austria, the strongest of Britain's continental allies, raised expectations of further invasion attempts. There was ample evidence of French determination in the pursuit of this objective. Only the weather had prevented a French landing in Bantry Bay in December 1796. Only the interception and defeat of the Spanish Cartagena fleet off Cape St Vincent in February 1797 had prevented a huge reinforcement of the French Brest fleet that might have easily overwhelmed British defences. Only the defeat of the Franco-Dutch Texel fleet off the Dutch coastal village of Camperdown in October 1797 reduced the threat of intervention in the English Channel from the north. This victory had proved the effectiveness of the British North Sea fleet in spite of the mutinies at Spithead and the Nore that summer. Nevertheless weaknesses in defences remained. Disaffection was widespread. Rebellion threatened in Ireland where great hopes were attached to the expected French invasion. For this purpose, indeed, an army remained poised along the French Channel coast where France's most successful general, Napoleon Bonaparte, fresh from victories in Italy, was placed in command at the end of the year.

Strategic weakness on the continent reflected also Britain's financial weakness, for the allies, and Prussia in particular, had depended on the generous provision of British subsidies. However, hitherto the war had been largely financed on government credit rather than taxation. This was of two sorts: bills issued by the Navy and Treasury in payment for contract supplies and services, saleable at a discount depending on the date of encashment; and loans subscribed by the investing public whenever a new influx of public funding was necessary. Loan money always seemed available: a 'loyalty loan' of £18 million was subscribed in sixteen hours in December 1796. Yet this form of finance was heavily inflationary. By 1795 unfunded navy bills in circulation amounted in value to £9 million; by the end of 1796 loans worth £108 million carried interest nearly doubling their value. By 1797 the lack of sufficient gold to back the currency, combined with the landing of a French raiding expedition at Fishguard in February, precipitated a run on the banks and the suspension of cash payments by the Bank of England.

The issue of paper money proved even more inflationary. Only after 1798, with the enlargement of assessed taxes to three or four times their former level, did the government realise they had stumbled upon a new method of war finance. Following a survey of national income in 1798, Pitt financed further loans by the introduction of a rudimentary tax on incomes that aimed to divert nearly one-tenth of private income into government revenue. Although this aim was not fully realised, the tax was again to be used at the outbreak of the Napoleonic War in 1803 and to prove fundamental to ever-greater non-inflationary expenditure.

Pitt's financial expedients were soon tested, for in 1797 France did not want peace. Members of the French Directory only wanted a complete British surrender, with the return of all Dutch, Spanish as well as French colonial territories taken earlier in the war. Pitt and his government had no option but to continue hostilities. While enrolling thousands of amateur soldiers in regiments of 'volunteers' for the defence of southern England, new schemes were contemplated to resuscitate a European coalition. One option was for a new effort in the Mediterranean. In the event, it was a French initiative that paved the way for a new alliance. Early in 1798 Napoleon persuaded the French Directory that an immediate invasion of England was impossible. Instead he argued for 'the necessity, in order really to destroy England, to seize Egypt' from where bases could be maintained in the Middle East to attack British strength in India. In consequence, the French army of invasion was disbanded, and an expedition mounted for Egypt. On its way, the expedition seized Malta, incensing Tsar Paul I, aspirant protector to the Maltese Knights of St John of Jerusalem, and bringing Russia into the conflict. Eventually the Turks also declared war in response to the French occupation of Egypt, hitherto a province of the Ottoman Empire. The entry of Russia and Turkey, combined with the defeat of the French fleet at Battle of the Nile, revived

Austria. Encouraged by Nelson, the Kingdom of the Two Sicilies stimulated Piedmont-Sardinia, whose warlike preparations brought the French plunging deep into Italy, deposing the Pope and bringing Portugal into the war. By the beginning of 1799 French aggression had everywhere raised enemies. Furthermore, early that year French threats against Austria effectively cemented a second European coalition, for Austria was allied to Russia, who accepted British subsidies to maintain troops in the field.

However, to oppose France was not to defeat

her. The invasion of the Helder region of north Holland by a combined Anglo-Russian force in August 1799 was withdrawn in October, the victim of bad weather and non-existent Dutch assistance. The expedition nonetheless had the good fortune to take almost all that was left of the Dutch fleet. After significant successes, the Russians were defeated at Zurich in Switzerland later that year, and in June 1800 the Austrians were defeated at Marengo in northern Italy, later at Moesskirch in southern Germany, and in November 1800 at Hohen-

For Britain the collapse of the First Coalition seemed to mark an end to the immediate prospect of defeating revolutionary France, and in a morale-boosting gesture the government decreed a service of thanksgiving for the naval victories of Howe, St Vincent and Duncan. The King and Queen led a 'Grand Royal Procession' to St Pauls on 19 December 1797, where French, Spanish and Dutch colours taken at the Glorious First of June, St Vincent and Camperdown were paraded. Etching published by G Thompson and J Evans, 20 January 1798.   NMM ref PAG8673

1. the King
2. the Queen
3. the Marchioness of Bath
4. the Countess of Harcourt
5. the Colonel of the Life Guards
6. the Officers of Lord Howe's Fleet

7. the Seamen bearing the Colours taken by Lord Howe 1st of June 1794.
8. the Marines of Lord Howe's Fleet
9. the Officers of Lord St Vincent's Fleet
10. the Seamen bearing the Colours taken by Lord St Vincent the 14th February 1797

11. the Marines of Lord St Vincent Fleet
12. the Officers of Lord Duncan's Fleet
13. the Seamen bearing the Colours taken by Lord Viscount Duncan the Eleventh of October 1797.

14. the Lord Mayor bearing the City State Sword
15. the Two Sheriffs
16. the Yeomen of the Guards
17. the Gentlemen of the London & Westminster association

18. Lord Duncan's Coach
19. Lord Howe's Coach
20. the East and West London Militia
21. the East-India and Islington

Published Jan 20, 1798 by J Evans No 50 Long Lane West Smithfield.

linden. By early 1801 the Second Coalition was at an end.

In this uneven contest, France was everywhere successful on land. In the main French thrusts of the war, those into Italy, into Egypt, and against the Austrians in southern Europe, the outstanding commander at decisive encounters was Napoleon Bonaparte. By contrast, the allies were on the whole successful at sea, permitting Minorca to be seized and Malta to be retaken; and in Nelson, they too had their national hero. At Aboukir Bay, close to the mouth of the River Nile, it was he who destroyed the French fleet, isolating the French army with Bonaparte on shore. He was to be used again early in 1801 against the Armed Neutrality of the North, formed by Russia, Denmark, Sweden and Prussia, to resist the British blockade of their trade with France. Following the defeat of Austria, Napoleon courted the northern powers, especially Russia, with whom he agreed a peace settlement. However, the power of the northern coalition depended on their combined naval strength. Nelson's destruction of the Danish fleet at Copenhagen in 1801, along with the murder of Tsar Paul, resulted in the dissolution of the Armed Neutrality and effectively assured the supply of naval stores to Britain from the Baltic.

In this rivalry between land and sea powers, popular acclaim surrounded the two national champions. Their achievements seized the public imagination. Both Nelson and Napoleon became internationally known, the focus of media attention. More than that, their successes fuelled the will of each side to maintain the war. Their contribution to these years was thus far greater than their immediate military functions. Nelson remained a vice-admiral as the Revolutionary War dragged to a close, the instrument of politicians who slightly scorned his private *amours*. Napoleon, on the other hand, at the end of 1799 made himself First Consul of France and virtual dictator.

When the preliminaries of peace were discussed in 1801, it was Bonaparte who took the initiative in opening negotiations. The British government, deprived of leverage on the continent by the defeat of Austria, abandoned almost all its colonial gains from France, Spain and Holland, and even allowed Napoleon the opportunity to capitalise on British conces-

sions to Britain's further disadvantage. The terms of the peace, as finally signed at Amiens early in 1802, were so unacceptable in Britain that they served only as the basis for a truce. At heart, British politicians knew that British strength and achievements warranted greater gains. It was a view justified with hindsight by the economic and logistical trends in the contest at sea which favoured Britain.

The policy pursued by the British government during these years was in many ways similar to that developed by Pitt's father during the Seven Years War. It has since been termed a 'blue water policy', on account of the importance it gave to maritime operations. After 1793, however, the militant fervour of revolutionary France demanded that the policy was pursued with far greater determination and logic.

Awareness of the need to protect British trade and colonies, and at the same time destroy those of the enemy, led to the development of the close blockade to a higher level than had ever before been achieved. The blockade of Brest, Rochefort, Lorient, Cadiz and Toulon deprived enemy fleets both of practice at sea and of the capacity to sail forth at will. The Egypt expedition from Toulon in May 1798, the escape of Bruix from Brest in April 1799, and the escape of Ganteaume from Brest in January 1801 all demonstrated that French fleets could and did escape. Nevertheless, it is also clear that without special reason to send squadrons to sea, the French government refrained from doing so on account of the almost certain knowledge that they would soon meet a closely matched force brought into action by signals from frigates of observation.

Although executed by the admirals commanding at sea, the logistics of the blockade were organised by naval lords at the Board of Admiralty. These probably made similar calculations to those of Sir Charles Middleton in 1794-95. He worked from accounts of the supposed numbers of the enemy in each port and the size of the British force required effectually to oppose it. The squadrons inside and outside were weighed in terms of gunpower – frigates being distinguished from ships of the line – the ideal blockading force set against the actual number of ships available, the number always to be kept outside, and the number that could be away refitting.

The effect of this policy on French naval forces was apparent in the derogatory comments made by British naval officers like Nelson about the ship-handling of French and Spanish crews once they escaped from port. Their sea training was undoubtedly affected. After 1794 the French officer corps became more stable both in numbers and in morale, but those of French seamen did not. Their morale was severely affected by the loss in livelihood from the decline in French shipping, and by the legacy of 'revolutionary' insubordination to central authority. John Nichol, a British seaman who helped to save survivors from *L'Orient* at the Battle of the Nile, noticed a marked difference in French attitudes from those two decades earlier. During the American War, prisoners had been philosophical: '*fortune de guerre* – you take me to-day, I take you to-morrow'. In 1798, however, they were thankful for kindness 'but were sullen and as downcast as if each had lost a ship of his own'.

The French seamen may have appreciated better than their superiors the damaging effect on their numbers of war with Britain. In 1790 a survey of French seamen indicated an availability of 85,000. Yet by 1798 British domination of the seas had severely reduced this number. Early that year, 30,265 were registered as prisoners-of-war in British hands. Losses at the Battle of the Glorious First of June in 1794 had accounted for 3500 taken prisoner with 1500 killed and 2000 wounded. The Battle of the Nile was to add another 3225 to the prisoners, with another 1400 killed and 600 wounded. By then only about half of France's original strength in seamen were still available for service. Little wonder, therefore, that the morale of those captured was low.

Their morale also reflected the loss in French naval vessels. Between 1793 and the beginning of 1798 234 French vessels were lost by wreck, battle damage or capture; 35 of these losses were ships of the line. By the end of 1798 France had lost another 49 vessels, including 14 of the line, the Nile accounting for 11 of the line and 2 frigates. Losses were to continue, so that by time the preliminaries of peace were under discussion 371 French naval vessels had been lost including 55 ships of the line. This amounted to 67 per cent of her battlefleet at the beginning of the war.

Reacting to these losses, the French naval

dockyards did not remain idle. But under British blockade, deliveries by sea to these yards of bulk cargoes of timber from Italy and naval stores from the Baltic was severely reduced. The replacement of ships of the line in particular was difficult and costly. France was able to employ subject or allied navies to supplement her own, but both Holland and Spain lost more than they gained in naval force during the war: Holland 95 vessels including 18 ships of the line, and Spain 77 vessels including 10 ships of the line.

Payment for French naval materials also presented problems. French army expenses far exceeded those of the navy, especially as military forces had to be maintained in the Low Countries, Italy, southern Germany, and to defend France's Channel coastline. Loans and debt serviced naval expenditure, but the capability of funding these costs were handicapped by declining revenues from trade.

The effect of Britain's 'blue water' policy was particularly apparent in the inability of France to retake colonies lost earlier in the Revolutionary war—especially Tobago, Martinique, St Lucia and Guadaloupe, all taken by Britain in 1793-94—or repair her commerce with St Domingue (modern Haiti), racked by insurrection and partly occupied by British forces between 1794 and 1798. These islands had provided almost a third of France's foreign trade in the 1780s, and the impact of their loss on French revenues is indicated by the virtual annihilation of France's imports of sugar and coffee, large proportions of both of which had been re-exported within Europe. A decade earlier 90 per cent of Europe's sugar came from the West Indies, 43.3 per cent from the French West Indian islands of which between 1785 and 1789 France re-exported 69.4 per cent. (Only 36.7 per cent came from British islands, and Britain consumed most of its imports.) Before the war French West Indian coffee imports were only slightly less valuable than sugar, and with 88.9 per cent re-exported were the most valuable of all her imports that were sold on. Yet all such sales virtually disappeared with the loss of her island colonies.

If France's capability to wage hostilities by sea declined as the Revolutionary War progressed, the reverse was true of Britain. In spite of the war, her foreign trade underwent considerable growth, especially after 1797. During the first half of the war her re-export of colonial goods increased by 81 per cent over their average values between 1788 and 1792, with domestic exports rising only 8.6 per cent and her imports 15 per cent. Between 1798 and 1802, however, imports increased by 58.5 per cent over 1788-92 values, more than half the increase on account of West Indian produce: sugar imports nearly doubled while coffee imports underwent a ninefold increase over the 1792 figure. Domestic exports rose 57.7 per cent in the same period, with re-exports growing a remarkable 187.2 per cent over their 1788-92 values.

On this rising tide of trade, Pitt and Addington were able to increase import duties, and after 1798 maintain even greater quantities of funded and unfunded debt than had ever before been thought possible. Growth in trade also enlarged numbers of merchant ships and of seamen. Between 1798 and 1802 British shipping rose from 14,631 vessels (1,494,000 tons) to 17,207 vessels (1,901,000 tons), a growth that was to continue throughout the Napoleonic War.

So too with the stock of British seamen. In 1792 there were an estimated 133,000 in the country: that is, 16,613 in the Navy, 118,286 in registered merchant vessels, with probably another 30,000 in unregistered vessels. By 1801, with the help of the Quota Acts of 1794-95, there were 126,279 men in the Navy, and 144,558 in registered merchant ships. With perhaps 30,000 in unregistered vessels, by 1801 there were in total around 300,000 seamen available for service. Of these, moreover, very few were French prisoners-of-war: only 4000 in 1798.

These resources permitted the British government both to fund and man its navy. British losses were significant. Over the whole war, 1793-1802 they amounted to 200 vessels precisely: 20 ships of the line, 60 frigates, and 120 other vessels. But captures on the scale achieved permitted the purchase of warships from the agents of captors to far exceed new construction as the main means of supplementing the existing force—27 French ships of the line, 17 Dutch, 5 Spanish, and 1 Danish ship of the line found their way into the Royal Navy over the course of the whole war. In consequence by 1801 as much as 35 per cent of the British navy was foreign-built. Many of the captured ships, in need of repair, were immediately placed in reserve. Nevertheless, by the end of 1801 they permitted the margin of superiority of Britain over France in ships of the line alone to stand in the ratio of 169 to 126.

Of the British vessels at the end of 1801 only 104 were in commission for service at sea, with 17 on harbour duties. Nevertheless their crews were well supplied with fresh provisions and anti-scorbutics. The order of 1795 to supply lemon juice to the fleet ensured that scurvy in the second half of the war was kept to a minimum, and that warships could maintain sea blockade duties for months at a time. In spite of the Spithead and Nore mutinies, morale in battle was never higher. Indeed, the achievement of some of the mutinies' aims probably did much to lift morale. Furthermore, the mutinies accentuated the necessity for professionalism in crew management. Long years at sea had the effect of honing that professionalism in the officer corps. Never was a sailing fleet better prepared, supported and lead than the British fleet at the end of the Revolutionary War.

Only the dockyards, where in 1801 a movement for higher basic rates of pay coincided with riots against the imprisonment of food rioters and the impressment of yard employees, threatened to weaken that organisation. However, discontent there did not for long impair the naval war machine. With its logistical superiority, and a buoyant economy permitting persistent funding, British sea power offered a marked contrast to the difficulties being experienced in maintaining continental alliances against the might of the French land forces.

Had Pitt in 1797 been able to foresee the advantages to Britain's underlying economic trends, and the relative disadvantages that would handicap France, he might not have been so despondent. Her colonial gains and economic buoyancy—food supplies apart—gave critics of the peace in 1802 every reason to feel that Britain had not gained all that was possible. However, in these divergent responses to the problems of waging the French Revolutionary War lay the resolution of ways and means by which hostilities would be maintained from 1803 for another twelve years. The period 1798 to 1801 was a learning experience which would lay the foundation of a naval ascendancy that would last not just for another decade but in certain respects for another century.

Part I

THE BATTLE FOR THE MEDITERRANEAN

HAVING withdrawn the Mediterranean fleet to Gibraltar, virtually abandoning that sea to the enemy early in 1797, the British government was prompted to re-enter it again in 1798 on hearing rumours of preparations for a massive expedition from Toulon. The Admiralty directed Lord St Vincent, commanding the Mediterranean fleet off Cadiz, to detach a few ships, preferably under Rear-Admiral Nelson, to ascertain where the expedition was intended. Having convalesced in England from the loss of his right arm, Nelson rejoined the fleet under St Vincent on 29 April and sailed for Toulon with three 74s, two frigates and a sloop on 2 May. Just north of Cape Sicie, however, between 19 and 21 May the squadron encountered gales in which Nelson's ship, the *Vanguard*, lost her main and mizzen topmasts, her mainmast and sprang her bowsprit. Crippled and taken in tow, he was forced for repairs into the bay of St Pietro, Sardinia, from where the squadron only emerged to reach Toulon on 31 May.

By then the French expedition had sailed — on 19 May. Gathering strength as it sailed, from Marseille, Civita Vecchia, Genoa and Bastia, by the time it reached Malta the fleet totalled seventy-two warships, including thirteen ships of the line, two 64s and fourteen frigates, escorting an estimated 400 transports containing 36,000 troops. The fleet was under Vice-Admiral Brueys, but Napoleon Bonaparte commanded the whole force, his appointment dated 5 March. Indeed, though appointed and instructed by the French Directory, the expedition was the inspiration of Napoleon himself who, on 23 February had decided that direct cross-channel invasion of England was impossible. Instead, he proposed that Britain be destroyed by seizing Egypt, from where bases could be maintained in the Middle East to launch an attack on British territories in India. It was an inspiration perhaps sown by books on Egypt in the Ambrosian Library that Napoleon had brought back to Paris from Milan in 1797

after concluding his campaign against Austria.

It was also perhaps linked to soundings taken by the secretary to the French legation at Genoa with the Knights and Grand Master of the Order of St John of Jerusalem, as to their inclination to permit the French navy to use the island. In March one of a squadron under Brueys repaired at Valletta while the remainder of his force charted the coastline. On 10 June 1798 the French were consequently able to make landings in seven places to enforce the surrender of the main island with its dependencies Gozo and Comino. Seizing church treasures worth three million francs, Napoleon left a garrison of 4000 men and pressed east for Egypt. Having delayed barely a week at Malta, he reached Alexandria on 1 July. By 22 July he was also in possession of Cairo.

Nelson meanwhile had been desperately hunting for the expedition. On 7 June his juncture with reinforcement from Cadiz brought Nelson's fleet to thirteen 74s and one 50-gun ship. Having parted company with his only two frigates in the storm of 21 May, his powers of reconnaissance were limited. Thinking the Kingdom of the Two Sicilies was a possible objective, Nelson looked first into Naples, before being directed east by a sighting of the French by a Ragusan brig. On 28 June Nelson was off Alexandria. But with no sighting, he sailed north and west, to stand on 19 July into Syracuse, Sicily. Gathering all the information available, he established the French were not west of him and on 25 July resumed his search to the east. Here he found them on 1 August, in Aboukir Bay near the mouth of the Nile.

With evening approaching, Brueys did not expect the British to enter the bay where his fleet of thirteen of the line (nine 74s, three 80s and the 120-gun *L'Orient*) was anchored in a defensive line in shallow waters. At six o'clock, however, Nelson signalled for his fleet to stand into the bay, where battle commenced twenty minutes later. One of his vessels, the *Culloden*, stuck on a ridge of rocks skirting the island of

Aboukir. But for the others, the French were unprepared. The French were spaced sufficiently wide apart for British vessels to penetrate their line. They were also anchored by the bow only, and the British captains realised that, where the French could swing to wind and current, there was depth of water enough for their own ships to go inside and 'double' the French line. The tactic enhanced surprise. Hundreds of the French seamen were ashore getting water and their guns were cleared only on the seaward side. Capitalising on this initial advantage, through the night the British ships moved along both sides of the French line, systematically destroying the moored ships. About ten o'clock the French flagship, *L'Orient*, blew up, stunning the combatants into ten minutes fatigued wonder before the cannonade recommenced. Of the French battleships nine surrendered, and one went ashore and was wrecked; only two escaped. No British ship was lost, although some were badly shattered.

The victory had far-reaching consequences. At a stroke, it restored command of the Mediterranean to the Royal Navy, and encouraged participants in forming the Second Coalition of European allies against France. No longer commanding the sea, French garrisons throughout the Mediterranean were isolated, to be reduced as allied forces permitted.

While the prizes were despatched to England, and a force left off the Egyptian coast, Nelson, with two of the line, fell back on Naples. At Malta in September, Sir James Saumarez with the prizes joined with a Portuguese squadron under the Marquis de Niza and was approached for assistance by the Maltese who claimed the French garrison in Valletta were distressed for want of supplies. The French refused to surrender. However, the Portuguese were left to blockade the island, and were reinforced in October by three 74s under Captain Alexander Ball, who was soon joined by Nelson with two more. The garrison on the neighbouring island of Gozo fell on 28

October, but that in Valletta was to resist a blockade that eventually lasted another two years.

Meanwhile, early in October 1798 the Turks had reinforced the Albanians to drive French garrisons from former Venetian colonies in Albanian territory that had been occupied by the French. A Turko-Russian fleet also retook all the coastal islands except Corfu. From 20 October the French garrison on that island was besieged, to fall eventually in March 1799.

As with Malta and Corfu, so with the Spanish island of Minorca. With the re-entry of the British fleet into the Mediterranean, a naval base was required in the western basin from which to maintain the blockade of Toulon. On 7 November 1798 a squadron commanded by Sir John Duckworth landed troops under General Charles Stuart which within two days overran the island, with the exception of the

After an absence of a year, Royal Navy ships of the line again became a common sight off the Mediterranean coasts of Europe. Although the actual location is unidentified, the tower-style lighthouse and the defensive gun-tower on the headland are characteristic of the south of France and northern Italy. The ships represent the classic battlefleet vessel of the time, the 74-gun Third Rate. Black and wash, grey pen and ink by Piedagnel, c1806. NMM neg A5840

town of Cuidadella. That town, and with it the whole island, surrendered on 15 November.

While British and allied forces took advantage of France's weakness at sea, French land forces continued to assert their superiority in Italy and Egypt. At Naples Nelson urged the King of the Two Sicilies to abandon his neutrality. Early in December, hostile preparations on the part of Charles Emmanuel of Piedmont-Sardinia resulted in the French occupation of

the former principality and the forced retirement of the monarch to his remaining island territory. At the same time, in a movement concerted with Charles Emmanuel, King Ferdinand of the Two Sicilies advanced north to occupy and drive the French out of Rome where the Pope had been deposed. However in mid-December the French rallied, retook Rome and marched on Naples, Ferdinand's capital. Nelson was there enjoying the hospitality of the British ambassador and his wife, Sir William and Lady Hamilton. Four days before Christmas he was forced to embark the suites of both the Sicilian royal family and the British ambassador on board the *Vanguard* and to evacuate them all to Palermo in Sicily.

At Palermo, infatuated by Lady Hamilton, Nelson remained. In April 1799 a fleet of twenty-five ships of the line under Admiral Bruix escaped from Brest and entered the Mediterranean, followed by seventeen Spanish ships of the line from Cadiz. Lord Keith, who had been blockading Cadiz, demanded immediate reinforcement. Nelson despatched ten ships of the line to Minorca but declined to leave Palermo himself, arguing his presence would deter a French naval thrust towards Naples and Egypt. He thereupon collected the forces available to him, which constituted by the end of May sixteen ships of the line, abandoning the blockade of Malta in the process.

Meanwhile in Naples, with the help of local jacobins, the French land forces established the Parthenopean Republic. In June a Neapolitan priest, Cardinal Ruffo, raised a counter-revolution against the French occupation and defeated their forces near Naples. Nelson was begged to reinforce the insurgents and returned, with the Hamiltons on board, to the bay of Naples on 24 June 1799. There, he found Ruffo had imposed terms on the French garrison, by which its members, chiefly Neapolitan jacobins, could evacuate the three forts around the city with full honours of war and sail for Toulon on board a cartel should they wish to do so. Though the Hamiltons and Ruffo maintained the terms of the treaty were sacrosanct, Nelson rejected it as having no legitimacy without the sanction of Ferdinand of the Two Sicilies. Though all other terms of the treaty had been honoured, French garrisons from two of the forts were thus detained in their cartel ships. Furthermore on 30 June Prince

Francesco Caracciolo of the Neapolitan navy was tried by a court martial set up by Nelson and condemned to be hung for his collaboration with the Parthenopean Republic – though he maintained this had been under duress. The arrival of King Ferdinand precipitated similar slaughter on board the cartel ships. These signals of refusal to treat with revolutionaries immediately raised further resistance on their part. In Naples fighting broke out again, to which Nelson contributed with a supply of arms to royalists and by sending marines on shore to assist them.

One garrison of French troops still held out in Naples within the castle of St Elmo. On 29 June it refused to surrender. Batteries of guns were accordingly established under Captain Troubridge which opened fire on 3 July. However, return fire proved equally destructive and it was not until the middle of the month that the garrison surrendered, this time under terms of repatriation that were honoured. Forts at Capua and Gaeta were thereafter similarly reduced, the French to be repatriated, their Neapolitan allies to be executed.

The surrender of these forts coincided with a general French weakening in Italy where in the north Austrian and Russian land forces were active. They evacuated Leghorn on 17 July and thereafter the remainder of Tuscany. In August a small Neapolitan and British force was landed at Civita Vecchia where the surrender of the local French commandant permitted a British flag to be rowed up the Tiber and hoisted over Rome.

Further east, the far greater French force in Egypt was proving more difficult to remove. Even after the destruction of their battlefleet in Aboukir Bay, the French possessed a squadron of smaller warships comprising two 64s, eight frigates, four brigs and nine gunboats. Following the battle, these were blockaded in the harbour at Alexandria by Captain Samuel Hood, relieved on 2 February 1799 by Thomas Troubridge who in the next week mounted six bombardments of the city with mortars. These achieved little, for the French forces already fully occupied most of Upper Egypt.

His military successes, indeed, encouraged Bonaparte not to abandon his objectives for his Egyptian expedition. Deprived of conveyance by sea, he marched overland. Drawn east early in 1799 in pursuit of the former Mameluke ruler of Ottoman Egypt, Ibrahim Bey, in a night attack he took the Ottoman border fortress of El Arish. Turning north along the sandy coastal strip, Gaza surrendered without resistance on 24 February. He reached Jaffa on 4 March and slaughtered 4441 Turks, Egyptians and Moroccans; over half were prisoners bayoneted to death on the beach to save shot. He reached Haifa on 15 March, to lay seige to Acre next day.

The crumbling fortifications of Acre should not have presented a serious obstacle for Bonaparte. However, shortly after his army arrived, the town was reinforced and its fortifications improved through the landing of the crews and marines from two ships of the line under Sir Sidney Smith. He had relieved Troubridge off Alexandria, also having been invested with the responsibility of acting jointly with his brother, John Spencer Smith, as minister plenipotentiary to the Sublime Porte, which ruled the Ottoman empire from Constantinople. Suspecting an expedition towards the east, Sidney Smith had pursued this intuition. Moreover, as soon as he realised the French were without siege cannon, and suspecting they were coming by sea, on 18 March he intercepted and captured seven gun-vessels carrying most of the army's battering train. Over the next seven weeks the town of Acre underwent twelve assaults. However, all were repulsed, with the help in May of reinforcements from Constantinople.

With a sickening and fatigued army, unable to advance and leave Acre in his rear, on 20 May Bonaparte decided to retreat to Egypt. There he must have realised that allied forces were by degrees closing on him. In April British ships had ventured as far north as Suez at the head of the Red Sea, where they chased French gunboats, gave refuge to Maltese troops in reluctant French service who swam off to the ships, and attacked a fort at Kosseir.

More threatening were large-scale Turkish landings at Aboukir on 11 July. The Ottoman army had been assembled at Rhodes and 18,000 men were landed from over a hundred vessels including thirteen 74s. The Turks stormed the French defences and slaughtered the defenders. But on 23 July, with 11,000 infantry and cavalry from Cairo, Bonaparte retaliated, swept over their entrenchments and retook the defensive fortifications with even greater slaughter.

Sidney Smith had accompanied the Turkish army and it was he who, during negotiations aboard the *Tigre*, passed on to the French newspapers reporting defeats of French armies in Italy and Germany. Bonaparte reacted promptly. Leaving Kléber in command in Egypt, he sailed for France on 23 August, to land at Fréjus, between Toulon and Nice, on 9 October 1799.

Here in the western Mediterranean, the British navy had been cooperating with the Austrians in their efforts to expel the French from Piedmont and Tuscany. In the absence of a French fleet to blockade in Toulon, Lord Keith on 16 March 1800 landed from the *Queen Charlotte* at Leghorn and directed his flag captain to reconnoitre the island of Capraia, 36 miles offshore and still held by the French. Next morning, still close to Leghorn, the *Queen Charlotte* was found to be on fire. Boats went off to her but the overheating and firing of her shotted guns deterred most from approaching close: 673 men perished.

Cut off from supplies from France by an Austrian army, and blockaded by sea by the Royal Navy, the French army in Italy was reduced to little more than 25,000 men. In April 1800 it retreated on Genoa where Keith himself supervised the blockade and bombardment by gunboats and mortars. Determined to retaliate, the French themselves equipped a flotilla of gunboats and galleys, which occasioned small boat fighting and the seizure by boarding of a galley. Starved to terms, the French evacuated 8000 men to Nice on 4 June, permitting the British to occupy the harbour on the 5th.

On 4 June, however, Napoleon, now First Consul of France, had entered the city of Milan, capital of Lombardy, to preserve what he termed the Cisalpine Republic. Abandoning Piedmont, the Austrians concentrated their forces at the Italian town of Alessandria. On 14 June Napoleon defeated the Austrians at Marengo, the subsequent convention ceding Genoa as well as Milan, Turin, Savona and Tortona. The Royal Navy was consequently obliged to withdraw from Genoa harbour on 22 June.

Meanwhile the seige of Malta was gradually drawing to a close. In February 1800 the French attempted to push through the blockade a small squadron bearing 3000 troops and provisions. The squadron included the 74-gun *Généreux*, which would have escaped if she had

not been cut off by the British frigate *Success* and delayed until the 80-gun *Foudroyant* and the *Northumberland*, 74 could come up. The *Généreux* surrendered without further action.

Food supplies on the island by this time made relief from France imperative to the survival of the garrison. The French governor attempted to get information of this to France, but on 30 March the French 80-gun *Guillaume Tell* was caught, reduced to a mastless hulk and taken. By August all animals and most potable water had been consumed and troops were dying at the rate of between 100 and 130 a day. Such was their state a frigate was dismantled for fuel. On 24 August the last two frigates made their escape from Valletta. The *Diane* was promptly captured; but the *Justice* got into Toulon. Without succour, the garrison could no longer survive and surrendered on 5 September.

Although some single ships got through, attempts to send larger relief forces to Egypt suffered a similar fate as those vessels that set out from Malta. By the autumn of 1800 the French force in Egypt was fruit ripe for picking. The British government accordingly planned an expedition under Sir Ralph Abercromby, to be reinforced through the Red Sea by troops from India and the Cape of Good Hope. For this purpose, 14,000 British troops were landed for training at Marmaris on the southern coast of Turkey, near Rhodes, late in December 1800.

Hearing of the expedition, Napoleon determined on immediate relief to his forces in Egypt. Rear-Admiral Ganteaume was instructed to sail from Brest with three 80-gun ships, three 74s, and two frigates carrying 5000 troops for Alexandria. He put to sea on 23 January 1801, passed Cape Finisterre on the 27th, and through the Gut of Gibraltar on 7 February. North of Cape de Gata, however, the squadron took the frigate *Success*, from which Ganteaume was informed of the likelihood by that time of British landings in Egypt and, rather than continue towards that destination, he turned north and entered Toulon on 19 February. A month later, urged to sea by Napoleon, on 19 March he sailed again for Alexandria. However, suffering damage from a gale, he once more put back, only to be ordered to sea for a third time, a departure he made on 27 April. Shedding under-manned ships at Leghorn, Ganteaume proceeded with four ships of the line, a frigate, a corvette and four storeships, to approach the coast of Egypt on 7 June. Despatching the corvette, *Heliopolis*, to reconnoitre Alexandria, her failure to reappear was taken as an indication of her capture and that the port was well guarded. Ganteaume therefore sailed west along the north African coast and began to land his reinforcements and supplies at Bengazi.

Throughout these voyages, Ganteaume had not gone undetected. From off Cadiz on the 8 February Sir John Warren had followed the French squadron as far as Minorca. Having sailed east to Sicily to ensure British interests were safe there, he had missed Ganteaume's first voyage from Toulon. Returning reinforced to Minorca, on 25 March Warren had sighted Ganteaume southwest of the island of Toro on his second outing. And then, on his third and final voyage, having been warned of Ganteaume's probable appearance, Lord Keith was waiting for him off Alexandria and, on the run of the *Heliopolis* into harbour, had searched along the coast for the rest of the squadron. Discovered off Bengazi, Ganteaume had no alternative but to abandon two storeships to capture and run once more for Toulon, which he made on 22 July.

For Ganteaume, the main military achievement of this voyage was the capture on 24 June of the British 74-gun ship, *Swiftsure*, commanded by Sir Benjamin Hallowell off Cape Derna on the North African coast. Hallowell was steering for Malta to reinforce Sir John Warren, recognised Ganteaume's force, and attempted to make his escape. However, the faster sailing of the French ships ensured he was overhauled, when, after an action of an hour, he was virtually surrounded by three 74s and an 80.

On 13 June 1801 another squadron of three of the line and a frigate under Rear-Admiral Linois escaped from Toulon, destined for Cadiz. Learning in the Straits of Gibraltar of the superior force blockading Cadiz, on 4 July Linois put into Algeciras, in full view of the British at Gibraltar. Sir James Saumarez with his squadron off Cadiz was notified and, passing through the Straits, attacked Linois' squadron where it was moored in a defensive line, reinforced by gunboats and land batteries, within Algeciras Bay. Though possessed of five 74s and his 80-gun flagship *Caesar*, Saumarez's force was frustrated by baffling winds and difficult cur-

rents. In the confusion and a rising breeze, the British 74 *Hannibal* went aground and the French deliberately grounded themselves in shallows. Realising his losses were likely to exceed the *Hannibal*, Saumarez directed his remaining ships to withdraw.

However, on 9 July, summoned by Linois from Cadiz, a Franco-Spanish squadron of five ships of the line and three frigates entered Algeciras bay, to emerge on 12 July, together with Linois' ships, and head back through the Straits for Cadiz. Saumarez's squadron of five of the line got under way and chased them through the night. About midnight, after receiving only three broadsides, the 120-gun *Real Carlos* took fire, which, from a collision in the dark with another Spanish 120, the *San Hermenegildo*, spread to her—an irony as by mistake in the dark the latter had been firing into the *Real Carlos*. Shortly afterwards, within a quarter of an hour of one another, both ships blew up with the loss of 1700 men.

Meanwhile the British campaign in the east had been proceeding by studied stages. Landings in Egypt had begun at 2am on 8 March. Over sixty warships under Lord Keith had escorted transports from Marmaris to arrive in Aboukir Bay on 2 March. Gales and a heavy swell had delayed the disembarkation, giving the French time to arrange 7000 men to oppose the landings. However, practice landings at Marmaris and the strategic positioning of bomb and gun-vessels on the flanks of the landing craft, ensured the whole army was landed before the evening of 9 March. The French forces on the coast proved not the obstacle expected, in spite of defensive positions behind a low hill. Turning east along the coastal strip between the sea and the dry Lake Mareotis a battle was fought on 13 March which forced the French army of 7000 back towards Alexandria. With reinforcements from Cairo, the French counter-attacked at 3am on 21 March. However their plan of attack produced confusion in their own forces and they were repulsed.

In the battle, Sir Ralph Abercromby was fatally wounded and succeeded by Sir John Hely-Hutchinson. He did not immediately press forward on Alexandria but, keeping the forces in that city under observation under Sir Eyre Coote, turned his attention to reducing the other French forces in Lower Egypt. On 9

May Turkish and British forces drove the French south from Rahmanieh, and reached Cairo by 20 June. Also approaching were British troops landed at Suez on 21 April; native troops from Bombay landed at Kosseir on the Red Sea for a march to the Nile, down which they intended to take boats; and a Turkish army advancing from El Arish. The latter had been met on 16 May, but the French had been able only to withdraw from the overwhelming horde of irregular, swirling Turkish horsemen. The great dread of the French was to fall victim to the atrocities practiced by the Turks, and those at Cairo, seeing themselves caught in a pincer movement, surrendered to the British army on 27 June.

Returning to Alexandria, Hely-Hutchinson proceeded to reduce this final pocket of French resistance by approaching along the coastal strip towards the city from both sides. While an amphibious operation on 18 August took the fortified island of Marabout which protected the entrance to the harbour of Alexandria, the French forces were pushed back into the town, upon which guns were opened on 26 August. That was enough. An armistice was followed by surrender on 2 September. Both the garrisons at Cairo and Alexandria were conveyed by cartel to France.

While Egypt was being rid of French forces, there was less success on the island of Elba. By his treaty with the Two Sicilies of 8 March 1801, Napoleon was ceded the whole of the Neapolitan half of the island, including Porto Longone. In May, French forces landed at that port with the object of seizing the western Tuscan half of the island, including Porto Ferrajo. There the French lay siege to the Tuscan garrison and blockaded the harbour. The blockade was only raised on the appearance of Sir John Warren's squadron on 1 August. On the 4th the *Carrère*, attempting to deliver 300 barrels of powder to the French batteries, was taken by the *Pomone*, and the batteries themselves were attacked on 13 September, by a landing force of half Tuscans and peasants, and half British marines and seamen. Casualties were severe and the French army was not driven off. Moreover, the British military force was deprived of Warren's squadron on 22 September. The landing force nevertheless remained to reinforce the Tuscan garrison in Porto Ferrajo until the Peace of Amiens.

1

The *élite* of the navy of England

AT the beginning of 1798 not a British battleship was to be found east of Gibraltar. The Earl of St Vincent's 'Mediterranean' command was based in the Tagus at Lisbon, and despite a close blockade of the Spanish fleet in Cadiz, the French had a free hand in the Middle Sea. Some members of the British government were pressing for the re-establishment of a British naval presence, if only to ease the diplomatic task of coaxing Austria back into the war, but action was finally precipitated by rumours of a massive armament being prepared at Toulon and the northern Italian ports under French control. Its destination was variously reported as Naples, Portugal, or, after a conjunction with the Brest fleet, southern Ireland – there was even a wild suggestion in some quarters that it was intended for Egypt to threaten British communications with India.

It was essential to discover what was happening and on 29 April Spencer, the First Lord of the Admiralty, instructed St Vincent to reconnoitre either with his whole fleet or a detached squadron. He added, 'If you determine to send a detachment into the Mediterranean, I think it almost unnecessary to suggest to you the propriety of putting it under the command of Sir H Nelson, whose acquaintance with that part of the world, as well as his activity and disposition, seem to qualify him in a peculiar manner for that service.'

Nelson, a newly created rear-admiral and now recovered from the loss of his right arm at Tenerife the previ-

2

ous year (1), arrived in the fleet on 30 April, flying his flag in the *Vanguard*, 74 guns, with Edward Berry (2) as his flag captain. Spencer's instructions did not arrive until the 10th, but with remarkable prescience St Vincent had already sent Nelson (by orders of 2 May) on just such a mission, with three 74s (*Vanguard, Orion, Alexander*), the frigates *Caroline, Flora, Terpsichore* and the sloop *Bonne Citoyenne.*

On the 17th Nelson captured a French corvette, from which he gleaned some news, including Bonaparte's arrival at Toulon, but only contradictory accounts of when it would sail and no notion at all of where it was bound. Three days later the squadron ran into a storm and the flagship was virtually dismasted and almost lost. *Vanguard* was saved by the seamanship and perseverance of Captain Ball, whose *Alexander* was able to get a line aboard the stricken ship (3) and tow her to safety in a Sardinian bay. It was touch-and-go at times and Ball had to disobey a direct order from Nelson to cast off the tow when the combination of a calm and a heavy swell threatened to carry both ships down on to a rocky headland. One bravura display of skill succeeded another. As Berry exulted:

> The ready assistance of our friends Sir James Saumarez, Captain of the *Orion*, 74, and Captain Alexander John Ball of the *Alexander*, 74, by their united efforts, and the greatest exertion we all used, the *Vanguard* was equipped in four days, and actually at sea, not bound (I would have you observe) to Gibraltar or any English port to be refitted, but again cruizing after the enemy on their own coast!

With understandable exaggeration, Nelson told his wife that at a dockyard 'months would have been taken to send her to sea'. But if his flagship was again battleworthy, he had lost his frigates, which were dispersed and never regained contact, a loss that was to hamper his efforts during the crucial stages of the coming campaign.

In the meantime, St Vincent had received Spencer's orders, which made it clear that the Admiralty intended not just a reconnaissance in force in the Mediterranean, but a fleet strong enough to thwart French plans, whatever they might be. So that the blockade need not be lifted, eight ships under Sir Roger Curtis were sent from the Channel Fleet, allowing St Vincent to promise Nelson, 'You shall also have some choice fellows of the Inshore Squadron' (4). When the reinforcement arrived, to avoid alerting the Spaniards, they changed places with the Inshore Squadron overnight (and were even painted to resemble them). Ten crack 74s and the 50-gun *Leander* under Troubridge's command sailed immediately.

On 5 June the brig *Mutine*, Captain Hardy, met Nelson's squadron with the welcome news of the reinforcement, and on the 7th Berry sighted 'ten ships of war standing upon a wind in a close line of battle'. They were described by St Vincent to Sir William Hamilton, Ambassador at Naples, as 'the *élite* of the navy of England', but to Nelson their captains would become his 'Band of Brothers'—men like Berry, Ball, Saumarez, Troubridge, Sam Hood, Miller, Louis, Hallowell, T B Thompson, Foley and Hardy—who made up a squadron whose fighting efficiency was probably unmatched in the entire age of sail.

1. 'Earl Nelson. From a sketch taken from life, by C. Grignon, at Naples', brown etching after an original by C Grignon, no date.
NMM ref PAD4155

2. Captain Sir Edward Berry (1768-1831), oil painting by John Singleton Copley (1737-1815).
NMM ref BHC2554

3. 'The Vanguard disabled and in tow by the Alexander 22 May 1798', watercolour by Nicholas Pocock (1740-1821), no date.
NMM ref PAF5877

4. 'The Inshore Squadron off Cadiz', watercolour by Thomas Buttersworth (1768-1842), 1800.
NMM neg 3833

3

4

Bonaparte's oriental adventure

1

2

THE fleet so fervently sought by Nelson sailed on 19 May 1798, the day before the *Vanguard* was dismasted. It comprised thirteen ships of the line under Vice-Admiral Brueys, in the 120-gun *L'Orient*, escorting some 400 transports with 35,000 troops embarked – and contrary to most intelligence estimates, it was bound for Egypt.

After his stunning successes in Italy in 1797, General Bonaparte (1) was the man of the moment. Only Britain remained in arms and the republican Directory appointed their dangerously ambitious protégé to the head of an army of invasion. However, one look at his new command persuaded Bonaparte that the venture was impossible without control of the sea, and as early as February he told one confidant that 'the Army of England shall become the Army of the East and I go to Egypt.' It is not entirely clear when Bonaparte first dreamed up the scheme, but he is known to have carried away all the books on the area from Milan's famous Ambrosian Library the previous year.

Another prize of the 1797 campaign was the whole Venetian navy, along with the naval stores in the Arsenale, once the largest and most efficient military-industrial complex in Europe (2). Although the Venetians were best known for their oared fleets, of which small numbers survived (3), they also had a relatively modern battlefleet of eight 64-gun ships. All of these were taken to Toulon, after a brief refit at Corfu, and incorporated into the French navy, being earmarked for the Egyptian expedition. In the event only two were fit to sail, and then only armed *en flûte* as troopships. Their condition was an open secret and Nelson reported to St Vincent, 'The Venetian ships are considered as very bad in every respect . . .' Nevertheless, ex-Venetian resources served to expedite preparations.

When the fleet finally sailed, its first target was the island of Malta, which possessed superb and well defended harbours (4) which could protect communications between Egypt and mainland France. Although one of the most heavily fortified places in Europe, Malta under the moribund rule of the Knights of St John was ripe for the plucking. It was strong in the depth and sophistication of its defences and well armed, but the garrison was too small for the miles of walls, poorly trained and even

more poorly motivated. Of the once-formidable Knights there were but 332 and 200 of these were Frenchmen, who proved reluctant to oppose their countrymen.

The armada of transports from the Italian ports arrived off the island on 6 June, providing an intimidating show of strength before the main fleet from Toulon hove into sight on the 9th. Bonaparte went through the formality of requesting permission for his immense fleet to water, and when the Grand Master agreed to only four ships at a time (as laid down by the Order's laws), massive landings were carried out on both Gozo and the main island. When in exile on St Helena Napoleon dictated his memoirs of the campaign to General Bertrand and the published work included some exquisite cartography, one map being devoted to the Malta invasion (5).

It is widely believed that Bonaparte had suborned the garrison and was somewhat surprised to find there was any resistance at all, but in any event it was short-lived and ineffective – the Knights surrendered on the 11th after barely 24 hours of conflict. Going ashore on the following day (6), Bonaparte showed little interest in sightseeing, but set about the establishment of a French colony. As J C Herold summarised it:

> In the six days he spent in Malta, he dictated no less than 168 reports, despatches and orders. In a single day – June 15 – he liquidated a centuries-old state, established the basis of a new government, and confiscated close to 7,000,000 francs' worth of treasures belonging to the Order, not to mention 35,000 mus-

3

kets, two battleships, one frigate and four galleys. The administration of the island was set down in an order containing sixteen terse paragraphs.

The warships comprised the whole remaining navy of the order, the battleships being renamed *Athénien, ex-San Giovanni,* 70 and *Dégo, ex-San Zacharia,* 64 . The former was not complete, and it was intended to fit her for sea, but both were still in Grand Harbour when Malta fell to the British in 1800, although Bonaparte took one of the galleys to Egypt when he sailed on 19 June. Most of the sequestered treasure went to the bottom of Aboukir Bay when *L'Orient* blew up during the Battle of the Nile.

4

5

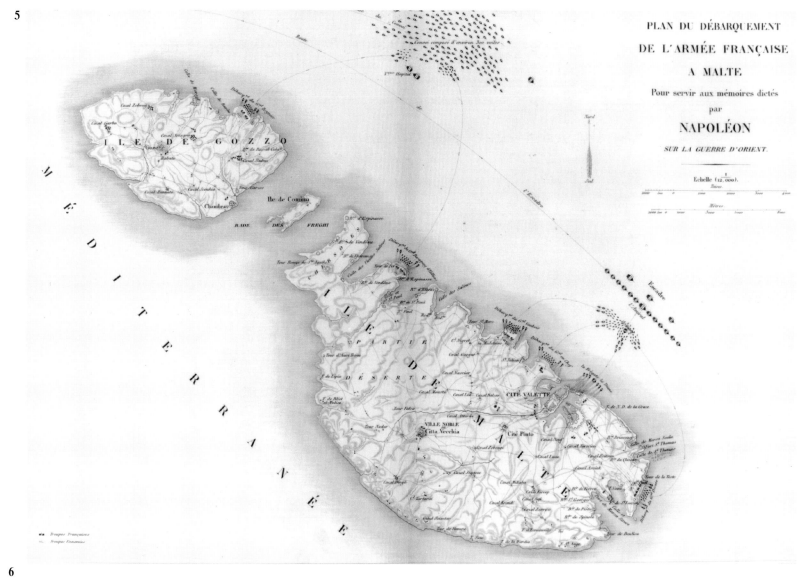

PLAN DU DÉBARQUEMENT
DE L'ARMÉE FRANÇAISE
A MALTE

Pour servir aux mémoires dictés
par

NAPOLÉON

SUR LA GUERRE D'ORIENT.

6

1. The young Bonaparte, lithograph engraved by Delpech, no date. Memorably described by J C Herold as having 'the face of an eagle and the hairdo of a spaniel'.
NMM ref PAD8209

2. 'A View of the Great Arsenal at Venice, which has two Gates, one for the Workmen to enter at, the other for the Ships', coloured engraving and etching by Bowles after an original by Michele Marieschi, published by Laurie and Whittle, 12 May 1794.
NMM ref PAH2316

3. 'Galeotta Veneta stretta al Vento', anonymous watercolour, 1780.
NMM ref PAF8255

4. 'A View of the City of Malta, on the side of the Jesuits Garden, or of the Island of Marsa', engraving and etching by Benoist after an original by Joseph Goupy, no date. In the left foreground are the Floriana Lines, protecting the open ground before the main defences of the city; Grand Harbour is to the right, with the prominent defended peninsulas of Senglea, Birgu and Fort Ricasoli jutting in sequence into the harbour. To the left of Valletta is the harbour of Marsamuscetta, protected by a fort on Manoel Island and the small tower of Fort Tigné at the entrance.
NMM neg A1427

5. The French landings in Malta, plate from Napoleon Bonaparte, *Campagnes d'Égypte et de Syrie 1798-1799: Mémoires . . . Napoleon dictés par lui-même . . . et publiés par le Général Bertrand* (Paris 1847).
Chatham collection

6. 'Debarquement à l'Isle de Malta', coloured lithograph engraved by C Motte and Grenier after an original by Gudin, no date.
NMM ref PAH7932

1

Malta and the Knights

WHEN on 13 June 1798 Napoleon Bonaparte ordered the expulsion of the Knights of St John he effectively destroyed the last of the Crusading Orders. Established in the twelfth century as the Knights Hospitaller of St John of Jerusalem, it was an Order of military monks devoted to the holy war against the Infidel. After the collapse of the Christian states of

Outremer in 1291, the Knights emigrated first to Cyprus and then in 1308 to Rhodes, which for two centuries acted as a centre of resistance to the growing power of the Ottoman Empire. Despite having made their crusading reputation as cavalry, they were forced by their island base to become seamen, and the galleys of the Order became one of the foremost naval powers of the

1. 'Isola de Malta Vendata dell Ingresso ne Porto Grande', aquatint and etching published by Bardi, no date. Two Maltese ships approaching Grand Harbour; Fort St Elmo at the seaward end of Valletta is to the right, with Fort Ricasoli opposite. *NMM neg A4903*

2. The main gateway of Valletta, defended by what is regarded as the deepest man-made ditch in Europe. Anonymous lithograph, no date, but before 1798. *NMM ref PAD1717*

2

3

medieval Mediterranean. Indeed, it was the Order's proud boast that not one of its vessels ever struck her colours to the enemy.

Ottoman patience finally ran out in 1522, and Suleiman the Magnificent besieged the island and forced the surrender of the Order. Once again homeless, the Knights were granted the perpetual and unfettered sovereignty of Malta by the Emperor Charles V, who as King of Sicily was Malta's feudal overlord. The island's greatest asset from a naval point of view was a series of superb harbours on the eastern side, the most magnificent being that which would be christened Grand Harbour (1). However, the strategic value of its central position was even greater, and Suleiman determined to evict the troublesome order from its latest base; but the so-called Great Siege between May and September 1565, although

it cost about 30,000 casualties, finally failed. The Knights had learned a hard lesson and over the next 150 years they embarked on a programme of fortification that was to make Malta one of the most heavily defended places in Europe (2). At the centre of the scheme was Valletta, the new capital built on the peninsula between Grand and Marsamuscetta Harbours and named after the victor of the Great Siege, Jean de la Valette.

By the beginning of the eighteenth century the world had changed irrevocably. The Christian states had ceased to see any value in a perpetual holy war, and the Ottoman Empire had been gradually drawn into the European balance of power. The Knights' last campaign against the Turks came in 1716; thereafter its continuing commerce warfare was confined to the Barbary States. Originally, Malta was also the centre of anti-Muslim privateering, which was a significant contributor to the economy of the island, but the realities of Great Power politics tended to reduce its scope: for example, the *corso* was banned from waters east of Crete after 1728.

The Order was still predominantly a galley power (3), but in 1700 an important decision was made to reduce the galley squadron from seven to five and to build four line of battle ships of 50-60 guns (4). They also maintained a few tartans, galleots and small craft, but thereafter the battlefleet became the Order's chief weapon (5) – between 1722 and 1741 its sailing ships captured fifteen Barbary vessels and one Turkish, whereas the galleys took only five Tripolitan galleys.

After the 1740s no more galleys were built, although the old ones were retained. Between 1764 and 1796 there were only six captures or sinkings by the galleys, but in truth the sailing fleet's successes were also declining due to lack of targets. By 1793 the whole fleet comprised the 64-gun *San Zaccaria* (which on 20 November took their first prize for many years, a pink from Tunis), two frigates (*Santa Elisabeta* and *Santa Maria*), the patronal galley, and four *sensile* galleys. The latter, however, were very old and in 1795 two were laid up and two substitutes purchased from the Papal navy.

Service in the galleys was still part of the apprenticeship of every Knight, and before he could be promoted he had to perform four 'caravans', or cruises, of at least six months. The expertise of the Knights in this area was highly regarded: for example, from 1789 they helped train the Russian Baltic galley fleet, and Count Guilio Litta distinguished himself in charge of the galleys at the Battle of Svenskund against the Swedes in 1790. Sailing ships, however, required a more intense grounding in seamanship, and in 1782 a school of mathematics and nautical sciences had to be set up.

As the century wore on, the life of the Knights seemed increasingly anamolous. The Order appeared wealthy,

4

5

with tithes from tax-exempt estates in many countries, but it had to maintain the apparatus of a nation state, a navy and the island's elaborate fortifications from declining revenues. Its warlike *raison d'etre* had virtually disappeared, opening the Order to accusations of slack, if not loose, living – in Gibbon's famous sneer, they 'neglected to live, but were prepared to die, in the service of Christ'. The Grand Master lived as a great prince, and the symbols of his power included a gilded barge (6), which was used in the lavish and meaningless ceremonies to which the Order became increasingly addicted.

Given the separate law and privileges that applied to the Knights, the Maltese could never see themselves as equals, but the resentment rarely spilled over into overt conflict. The Maltese provided seamen for the Order's fleet, and they enjoyed a good reputation – Admiral Hood sought to hire 1500 of them in 1794 when attempting to defend Toulon (in the event, he only obtained 414 and they were a motley international collection of the waterfront unemployed).

Malta survived great power politics for most of the eighteenth century under French protection, so the Revolution presented them with a real dilemma. The sequestrations of their lands in France dealt the final blow to the Order's already parlous finances, although the

establishment of a Russian 'Priory' by Tsar Paul (7) in 1797 threw them a very temporary lifeline – the Grand Master was so grateful he sent the Tsar two of the Order's greatest treasures, the crosses of de l'Isle Adam and la Valette. After the French expelled the Knights, the Tsar had himself elected Grand Master, which gave the Russians a future interest in Malta and added an element of diplomatic complexity to the Mediterranean situation.

Considering its long-standing reliance on France, it is ironic that French ambitions should prove the nemesis of the Order. As Bonaparte saw it, 'Malta could not withstand a bombardment of 24 hours; the place certainly possessed immense physical means of resistance, but no moral strength whatever. The Knights did nothing shameful; nobody is obliged to perform impossibilities.' He was right about the unwillingness to fight, but his own agents had undermined their resolve; and since Nelson's fleet was within days of Malta, resistance was far from impossible. Certainly the behaviour of some Knights would have shamed Jean de la Valette, but the French attack also provided the last moment of glory for the galleys of St John – the only seaborne opposition was the galley of the Chevalier de Soubiras, with two galleots in support, which sallied out to oppose the landings in St Julian's Bay, and sank a French landing boat.

3. 'Galera di Malta in Cattivo tempo', anonymous watercolour, 1780. *NMM ref PAF8250*

4. 'Comandante Maltese pronto a far Vela', anonymous watercolour, no date. *NMM ref PAF8219*

5. 'Isola di Malta. S. veduta del Castello Ricasoli e S. Angiolo della Scaglia', coloured aquatint and etching published by Bardi, no date. It shows Grand Harbour from Valletta, with ships of the Order – a two-decker and a frigate at anchor and another two-decker being towed to sea by a galley. From left to right, the facing peninsulas are Fort Ricasoli, Bighi, Birgu (with Fort St Angelo prominent) and Senglea. *NMM neg A5907*

6. 'Barca per li sign officiali di Palazzo Gondola di S A S Gran Maestro di Malta', anonymous watercolour, 1780. *NMM ref PAF8294*

7. 'Paul 1st, Emperor of Russia', stipple engraving by John Chapman, published 1 August 1797. *NMM ref PAD4508*

6

7

The French landings in Egypt

1

THE French fleet sighted Pompey's Pillar, the most prominent landmark of Alexandria, on 1 July. Despite the deteriorating weather, an immediate attack was essential because the British fleet had been off the coast only two days previously and its present whereabouts were unknown. Aboard the flagship a heated debate ensued about the location and timing of the landings. The tricky navigation of both harbours, as well as the town's defences, rendered a direct assault on Alexandria out of the question. Aboukir was Admiral Brueys' choice but it was fifteen miles to the east, which was too far for the army to mount a rapid attack on the town. Marabout (1), a village eight miles to west, was chosen but the bad weather and lack of charts (2) appalled Brueys; so much time had been lost that any landing would go on well into the night, and he favoured postponement until the following day.

Bonaparte, who never showed much understanding for the limitations of wind and tide, told him: 'Admiral, we have no time to waste. Luck grants me three days, no more. If I don't take advantage of them, we're lost.' The landings began about noon, but it was 8 o'clock before any soldiers reached the beach. The divisions of Desaix, Menou and Reynier were on the transports about three miles offshore, with Bon and Kléber's divisions aboard the battlefleet nearly twice as far off. In distinct contrast to the neat plan in La Jonquière (3), the landings were a

1. 'The Tower of Mirabou at the entrance of Porto Vecchio or the Old Harbour of Alexandria (shows Swiftsure)', watercolour by Cooper Willyams, 9 September 1798. *NMM neg 1744*

2. A copy of a French chart of the old harbour of Alexandria, commissioned by Admiral Brueys, and captured in the frigate *Courageuse* in 1799. Brueys was dismayed by the lack of safe anchorage for ships of the line, having previously expected the old harbour to be suitable, but no local pilot would take in ships drawing over 20 feet. Captain Barré and Lt Vidal of the *Alceste* frigate therefore undertook this survey in an attempt to discover a usable channel. 'A' marks the tower of Marabout where the French landings occurred, 'I' is the Pharos fort, and 'L' Pompey's Pillar. *NMM neg A8585*

3. 'Débarquement del'Armée Français a Alexandrie', from C de la Jonquière, *L'Expedition D'Égypt 1798-1801*, Vol II (Paris 1889). It claims to be based on an original deposited in the Dépot de la Guerre around 1800. *Chatham collection*

4. 'Conquête de l'Égypte Par les Français en Messidor, an 6e', engraving by Desaulx after his own original, no date. *NMM ref PAD5598*

2

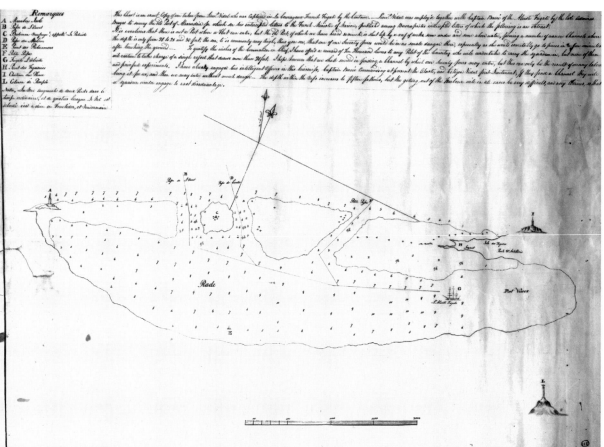

shambles – the French had very little experience of amphibious operations, and it showed. There was little prior planning, no specialist landing craft, and no practice at embarkation: the troops were expected to shin down ropes into boats crowding round the transports, and inevitably boats overturned and men were lost. Lacking any organisation or direction, some boats took eight hours to find the beaches – and Bon and Kléber had their men ashore before Reynier and Desaix (the latter had landed no men by the time Bonaparte arrived about 1am). Later, while rewriting his personal history on St Helena, Bonaparte said only nineteen men drowned, but nobody believed him.

Bonaparte set out about 4pm in a Maltese galley (seen centre in '4'), which had to anchor half a mile offshore, whereupon he transferred to a launch. As Brueys had predicted, the landings went on well into the night, and it was not until about 3am that about 5000 men of the army – cold, wet, and unfed – set off for Alexandria. One officer confided to his family, 'I can assure you that it was thirst which inspired our soldiers in the capture of Alexandria. At the point the army had reached, we had no choice between finding water and perishing.' The French army was to find itself poorly equipped for desert conditions, but whether the lack of suitable equipment was an oversight or a conscious decision to preserve secrecy about its destination, nobody knows. However, Alexandria was assaulted and terrified into submission the following morning.

Where was Nelson? He had reconnoitred the coast and sailed away a bare two days earlier. A sail had caused a few missed heart-beats during the preparations but it turned out to be the French frigate *La Justice* from Malta. It was to be four weeks before he returned, by which time Bonaparte had crushed local Mameluke power at the Battle of the Pyramids (21 July), entered Cairo and effectively secured the country.

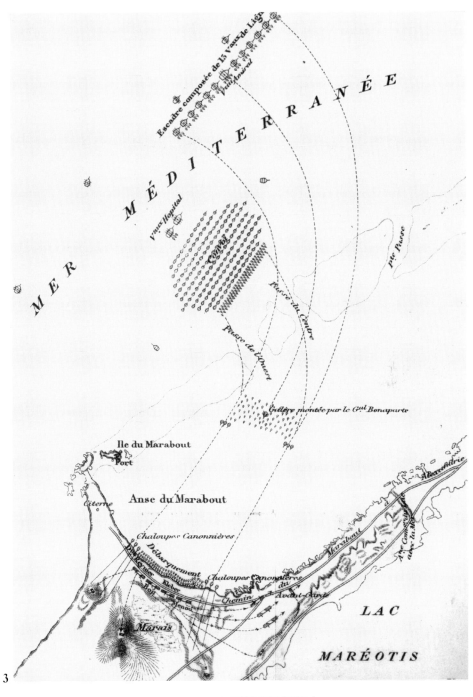

3

4

1

1. 'General Chart of the Mediterranean with the tracks of the British Fleet . . . and of the French Fleet . . . till they met in the Bay of Aboukir off the Nile on the First of August 1798', anonymous coloured aquatint, no date. *NMM neg X1950*

2. 'The British Fleet under Rear-Admiral Sir Horatio Nelson KB in the Vanguard at anchor in the Bay of Naples, June 17th 1798 waiting for the News of the French Fleet prior to the Battle of the Nile', watercolour by Giacomo Guardi, no date. *NMM neg 2374*

Nelson's pursuit of Bonaparte

WHEN Troubridge's squadron joined Nelson off Toulon on 7 June, the French fleet had been gone three weeks, nor did the admiral possess any firm information on which to proceed. The next seven weeks, with its famous wild-goose chase across the Mediterranean (1), was probably the most anxious and stressful of the great sailor's career, aware as he was that the fate of Europe might depend on his decisions.

A meeting with a ship from Tunis suggested the French had been sighted off Sicily, which ruled out any destination outside the Straits like Portugal or Ireland. His first concern was for the Kingdom of the Two Sicilies, the decadent monarchy that ruled most of southern Italy from its capital at Naples. A wavering ally of Britain for most of the war, it was currently in a state of nervous neutrality, with the forces of French republicanism

2

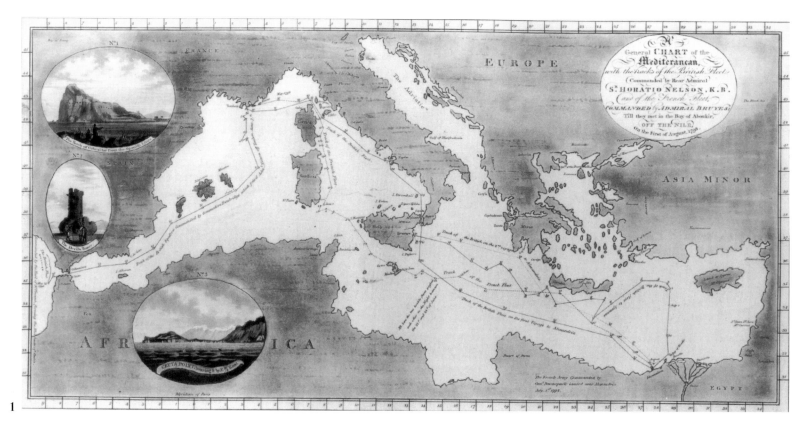

3

menacing its borders. Nelson needed supplies, if possible the co-operation of some Neapolitan frigates (its navy had half a dozen fine examples), but above all information; and he dispatched Troubridge in Hardy's brig *Mutine* to seek these concessions through the good offices of the British ambassador, Sir William Hamilton. Nelson anchored his fleet off Ischia—and not within the Bay as suggested by (2)—and he himself did not go ashore.

Troubridge negotiated some surreptious help, but no frigates, and received a report that the French were attacking Malta. Nelson had his first lead and sailed that same day, but Hamilton had failed to mention a French assurance to the Neapolitan government that their fleet was destined for Egypt—he thought it was intended to mislead. On 22 June Nelson picked up information from a Ragusan brig that having captured Malta the French had sailed on the 16th, and believing that their goal must be Egypt, he set off in rapid pursuit, recalling the ships investigating four strange sail to the southeast. In fact, the French had not left Malta until the 19th and the frigates he had just given up chasing were the outlying pickets of the main French fleet.

3. 'Alexandria', coloured lithograph engraved by Louis Haghe after an original by David Roberts, 1 December 1848.
NMM ref PAH2862

4. 'Fort and Harbour of Aboukir. Ancient Canopus', coloured aquatint and etching by T Milton after an original by L Mayer, published by R Bowyer, 1 October 1801.
NMM ref PAH2409

4

His fast-sailing squadron easily outpaced the lumbering invasion convoy, but when Hardy, who had been sent on ahead, reported no French ships, Nelson decided to retrace his steps, even though the Egyptians were clearly expecting a French attack. As we have seen, the French fleet arrived the day after he began a sweep of the Turkish coast and a slow beat back to Sicily for watering at Syracuse. From there he sailed again on 23 July to search the Greek islands, but it was not until he reached Coron in the Peloponnese on the 28th that he received firm news from the Turkish governor that the French were in Egypt.

Another rapid passage followed and as the squadron neared the coast on the 31st the *Swiftsure* and *Alexander* were sent on ahead. About noon on the following day they spotted the shipping crowding Alexandria harbour (3), mostly flying the *tricolore* — but in a final bitter blow to Nelson's hopes, signalled that the main battlefleet was not present. However, this time disappointment was short-lived, for by about 2.30pm they had been found by *Zealous* and *Goliath*, moored in a defensive line in Aboukir Bay (4), some fifteen miles to the east (5).

Luck had played a major role — and all in favour of the French - which for Nelson was epitomised by the saying, 'the devil's children have the devil's luck'. The campaign suggests some of the great '*if only*'s of naval history — if Nelson had not lost his frigates, if Hamilton had passed on his information, if the Ragusan brig had been more accurate, if the French frigates had been pursued, if Nelson had waited off Alexandria — since one or more conditions could have spelt the end of Bonaparte's career, and perhaps saved Europe another two decades of warfare.

Whatever might have happened, the reality was that by the afternoon of 1 August Nelson had at last run his prey to earth.

5. 'Chart of the coast of Egypt From the Western Mouth of the Nile to the Tower of the Arabs, Laid down from various materials and Observations, in HM Ships on that Station in 1798 and 1799'. Published 25 May 1801 by A Dalrymple, Hydrographer to the Admiralty. This was one of the first official publications of the newly established Hydrographic Office, and includes a key to the landing operations in March 1801.
NMM neg A8581

5

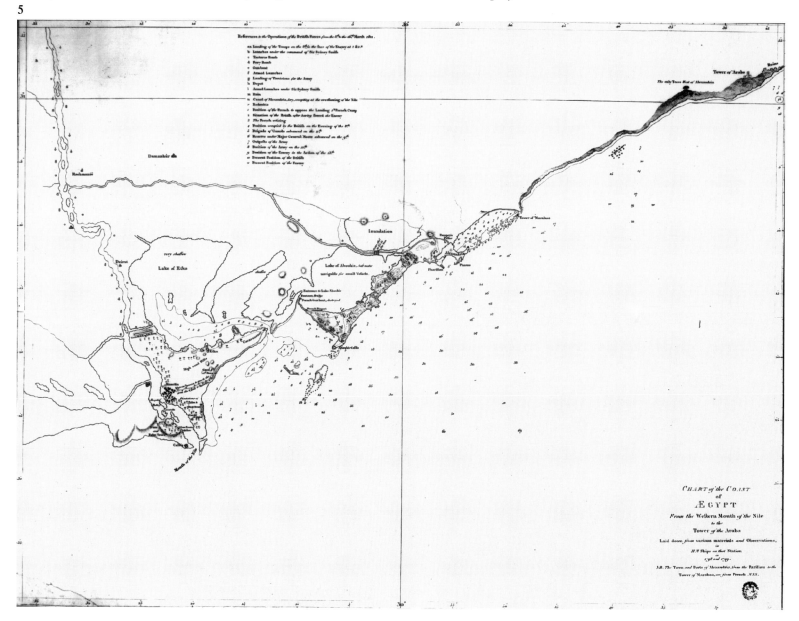

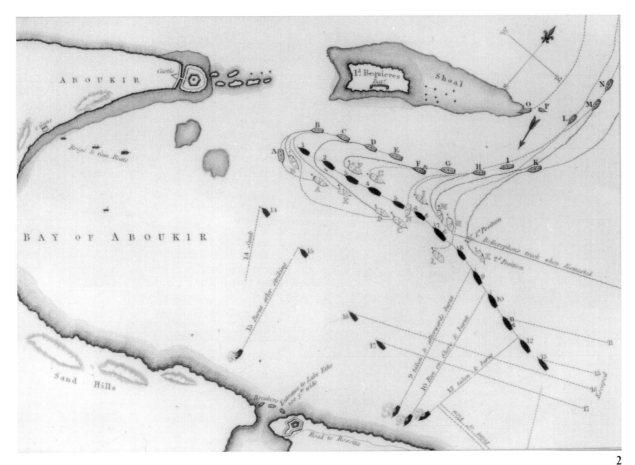

1

2

Battle of the Nile – the attack

ABOUKIR BAY was reasonably sheltered and gave Brueys (1) the chance to land the stores still aboard his ships whilst moored in a position which should have been relatively easy to defend. The western end of this semi-circular bay was marked by Aboukir Point and Aboukir Island and shoals to seaward of it, with a connecting line of rocks and shoals narrowing the mouth of the bay. The island and the point were fortified. Brueys' ships of the line were moored in a slightly bent line stretching south from the shallows just inside the Island. Four frigates were anchored at intervals inside the line, and the smaller ships in shal-

3

1. 'Francis Paul Count De Brueys', coloured lithograph engraved by Alexandre Lacauchie, published by Rigo Frères et Cie, no date.
NMM ref PAD0113

2. 'Plan of the Battle of the Nile, August 1st 1798', anonymous engraving, no date.
NMM ref PAD4026

3. 'Battle of the Nile, Augt 1st 1798', coloured aquatint engraved by Thomas Sutherland after an original by Thomas Whitecombe (born c1752), published 1 March 1816.
NMM ref PAD5565

4. The opening moments of the battle as the *Goliath* rounds the head of the French line, a watercolour illustration by the author from the Rev Cooper Willyams, *A Voyage up the Mediterranean* (London 1802). The frigates inside the battle line are apparent.
NMM neg D8619-C

5. 'Battle of the Nile, 1st August 1798', watercolour by Thomas Buttersworth (1768-1842), no date. It shows the opening salvoes and the loss of *Guerrier*'s foremast.
NMM neg A3822

6. 'To the Right Honorable Horatio Nelson . . . This Print representing the Glorious Victory over the French Fleet on the night of the 1st of August 1798, in the Bay of Bequieres', coloured aquatint and etching by Robert Pollard after an original by Nicholas Pocock (1740-1821), published by the artist 13 April 1799.
NMM ref PAH7942

4

5

6

lower water. The thirteen French ships of the line were anchored with the 120-gun flagship, *L'Orient*, by far the largest ship present, in the middle of the line and a concentration of powerful 80-gun ships at the apparently more vulnerable rear, whilst the ships at the other, windward, end would be in a good position to come down to assist. Brueys' line was, indeed, well positioned overall, but not enough care had been taken to position and link the individual ships (2).

Brueys passively awaited the British onslaught, happy in the belief he was in a nearly impregnable position, and reasonably expecting his opponent to do nothing before nightfall would put an end to any reasonable chance of battle until the next morning. Nelson, however, had no intention of allowing the long-sought enemy to have any more time than it took him to get his thirteen 74 gun ships and one 50 into position. This paid off handsomely—British eyewitnesses saw the decks of enemy ships still cluttered with crates and other stores as they opened fire, and these greatly hampered the efforts of the French gun crews.

By 5.30pm Nelson was abreast the island and instructed his ships to form line of battle ahead and astern of the flagship as convenient. He then hailed Captain Samuel Hood of the *Zealous* to ask him if he thought the ships were far enough to the eastwards to clear the shoal. No-one had a trustworthy chart of the Bay (except, perhaps, Foley of the *Goliath*) but Hood offered to go in, sounding as he went, to act as a guide to the fleet (3). As he turned his ship towards the French fleet, however, the *Goliath* on the inside had a slight lead over him. According to one story Captain Foley had a captured French chart which showed that there was water deep enough inside the *Guerrier*, the ship at the island end of the French line, for a ship of the line to squeeze past to the inside. The French were in any case riding at single anchors so would have needed water inside the line in which to swing, and any seaman would have noticed this (4). Whatever the inspiration, it is certain that Foley saw the opportunity to 'double' the French line, and he took it, just as his admiral wished him to. As Foley was moving into position Nelson hove the *Vanguard* to, to enable several ships to pass him, so that in the end he was near the middle of the British line – the most sensible position for the admiral if he wished to have some control over the battle as it developed.

As the British fleet moved into action the sun was setting. It was going to be a night action, not a common event, but something which would give the better-trained fleet an even greater edge over their unprepared opponents. They went into action flying that most distinctive of naval flags, the white ensign.

The first shots of the battle were fired at 6.20pm at the two leading British ships, *Goliath* and *Zealous* which were vying for first place. Ten minutes later *Goliath* successfully swung past the bow of *Guerrier*, letting fly with a destructive raking broadside as she did so, and passed on her inner side (5). From this moment the French line was effectively doomed to piecemeal destruction. Captain Foley had intended to anchor alongside the *Guerrier*, but there was a slight delay in letting go the anchor, and instead fetched up alongside the after part of the *Conquérant. Zealous*, following round the head of the French line, did manage to anchor abreast of the *Guerrier*, and fired with such effect that the French ship's foremast fell five minutes later, a most encouraging sight for the oncoming British line. Next round the head of the French column was the *Orion*, sinking the French frigate *Serieuse* which tried to intervene, then anchoring a little more than abreast of the *Peuple Souverain*, but slightly further away than he had intended, having been baulked by the unexpected appearance of *Theseus*. This vessel had contrived to pass between the first and second French ships, something which should not have been possible had their captains followed Bruey's instructions to take lines to the next astern. Thus far the seaward side of the French line was left unengaged – so Nelson took *Vanguard* along the outside of the French line and *Minotaur* and *Defence* followed suit. The five leading French ships were between the fires of five enemies to port and three to starboard (6).

It was getting dark and *Bellerophon* coming into action chose to tackle the enormous *L'Orient*, and was soon dismasted. Shortly afterwards *Majestic* anchored in position next to the 80-gun *Tonnant. Culloden*, unfortunately for her, had passed too close to the shoals and grounded. After hours of struggle, assisted by the brig *Mutine* she floated off, but with severe leaks and minus her rudder, so she could take no part in the battle.

At least *Culloden*'s obvious plight meant that *Alexander* and *Swiftsure* could avoid the shoal as they came up into action from their earlier reconnaisance of Alexandria (7). The latter contrived to anchor in a position just alongside the gap between the *Franklin* and *L'Orient*. The ship ahead of the *Franklin* had parted her cable a little ear-

7

lier and drifted out of the French line, creating an oportunity which was brilliantly exploited by the *Leander*, which contrived to anchor in the gap, raking two opponents which were unable to reply. *Alexander*, the last British ship to get into action, took advantage of another gap to anchor off the port quarter of *L'Orient* (8).

With the British ships all in position and engaging the enemy, the French line was being 'rolled up' with the unengaged French ships being able to do very little to help as the wind was blowing the British down their line whilst pinning them in position. The wretched *Guerrier* was rapidly dismasted, having been successively raked by four other ships as well as by the *Zealous* which remained battering her until she surrendered at 9pm. The *Conquérant* was knocked out in about 12 minutes. *Spartiate* was completely dismasted, and surrendered just after 9pm despite her noticeably effective gunfire. Her next astern, *Aquilon*, lost all her masts and suffered heavily before her surrender. *Peuple Souverain* with her cable either broken or shot away, drifted out of action. At first the *Franklin* had escaped without a direct opponent, but then became the target for several British ships.

7. 'Battle of the Nile 1st August 1798', aquatint after Thomas Whitcombe (born c1752), no date. It shows the *Culloden* aground (right), with the *Alexander* and *Swiftsure* coming up, far right.
NMM ref PAD5576

8. The height of the battle at the centre of the French line, with the *Alexander* anchored off *L'Orient*'s port quarter. A watercolour illustration by the author from the Rev Cooper Willyams, *A Voyage up the Mediterranean* (London 1802).
NMM neg D8619-D

8

1

The destruction of *L'Orient*

1. 'Battle of the Nile Representing the situation of the two Fleets previous to the blowing-up of L'Orient, on the Night of 2 August 1798', etching by Thomas Vivares after an original by Thomas Whitcombe (born *c*1752), published by Robert Bowyer, 1 January 1806.
NMM ref PAH7938

2. 'Battle of the Nile, Augt 1ˢᵗ 1798', coloured aquatint engraved by J Bailey after an original by Thomas Whitcombe (born *c*1752), published 1 April 1816. The British ships to the left are *Goliath, Zealous, Orion, Audacious* and *Theseus*, with *Leander* in the distance raking the *Franklin*.
NMM ref PAD5566

3. 'The Battle of the Nile', watercolour by Captain B W Taylor and G Turner, no date.
NMM ref PAD8564

4. 'Battle of the Nile 1ˢᵗ August 1798', aquatint after Thomas Whitcombe (born *c*1752), no date. The view point is the grounded *Culloden* (with *Mutine* in attendance).
NMM ref PAD5577

2

THE FIRST ship to engage *L'Orient* was given very short shrift: *Bellerophon* lost two masts in quick succession and then her third when she attempted to set a sail on it. It was the spritsail set on her bowsprit which got her away from her huge antagonist, though she did not escape being fired into by the *Tonnant* for a while. *L'Orient* was soon under attack again, this time from *Alexander* and *Swiftsure*. At about 9pm Captain Hallowell saw that fire had broken out aboard his huge antagonist, and he concentrated *Swiftsure*'s fire on the area round the blaze (1). Whether the fire would have spread without this is a moot point, but whatever the case, spread it did, and around 10pm it reached the magazines. Certainly the ship was already in a bad way. Admiral Brueys, already twice wounded, was almost cut in two by a cannon ball. Mortally wounded, he still refused to be taken below, saying 'A French admiral ought to die on his own quarterdeck'. He was dead before the fire broke out.

His death was rapidly followed by the mortal wounding of Captain de Casa Bianca his flag captain (the other captain of the ship, Gantheaume, was one of the less than 100 people who survived from her crew; he managed to swim to another French ship). Casa Bianca's young son was aboard, and refused to leave his father. This sad event was the inspiration of Mrs Hemans' much-parroted and much-parodied 'The boy stood on the burning deck/ whence all but he had fled'. Those who escaped did so by swimming—for example, fourteen of them swam to the *Orion*. Some of those who were picked up from the water had lost everything but their lives, the log of the *Alexander* recording the issue of clothing to naked French survivors.

As the fire gained and started to consume the rigging, nearby ships stopped firing and began to take precau-

3

tions. Those who could moved away, sails were wetted, ports and hatches closed. Cartridges were removed from upper decks and bucket brigades organised to fight any consequent fires. When *L'Orient* did finally blow up, however, it seems to have been an even greater shock than anyone had expected (2). The blast was appalling, as was the sheer volume of sound which temporarily deafened most of the spectators. Blazing bits of the ship fell all around, causing havoc. *Alexander* and *Franklin* were both set on fire by flaming debris, but fortunately both ships managed to put out the fire, the former by turning her stern into the wind so that the fire on the bow blew away from the ship and could be put out by the 'fire engine' and bucket brigades organised from the crew. *Swiftsure* was hit by a large chunk of mast, which Captain Hallowell later had made into a coffin which he presented to his friend, Nelson. Temporarily there was no firing, everyone seems to have been too shocked and stunned to do much for a little while (3, 4).

4

1

Pressing home the victory

AFTER THE destruction of the flagship, *Franklin* restarted the firing with the three guns left in action, but she soon surrendered with two-thirds of her crew dead or wounded. The battle began to pick up again, though at a lesser tempo. *Tonnant* was now

the focus of attack. Having been totally dismasted herself, she managed to withdraw from action by letting out her cable, having fought hard and long. Her crew's bravery and stubbornness owed much to the heroic example set by their captain, Dupetit-Thouars, who lost first one arm then the other shot off, and finally one of his legs, but still issued orders until he became unconscious and died (1).

Majestic, having been disabled by *Tonnant*, drifted down the French line to catch her jibboom in the rigging of *Heureux* whose fire caused more damage and loss. She finally came to anchor between *Tonnant* and *Mercure* both of which, by then, had shifted from their original positions. By now men were getting very tired indeed. One captain wrote : 'my people were also so extremely jaded, that as soon as they had hove our sheet-anchor up they dropped under the capstan-bars, and were asleep in a moment in every sort of posture, having been then working at their fullest exertion, or fighting, for near twelve hours . . .'

At this late stage of the night those ships still in French hands had all moved away downwind towards the eastern end of the bay, though being, as yet, hardly damaged apart from the shattered *Tonnant*. As dawn broke at about 4am on 2 August some of these ships engaged the two nearest British ones, the *Alexander* and the much-battered *Majestic*. The firing attracted *Theseus* and *Goliath*. The former came to anchor not far away from the French frigate *Artémise* which fired into her and then surren-

2

3

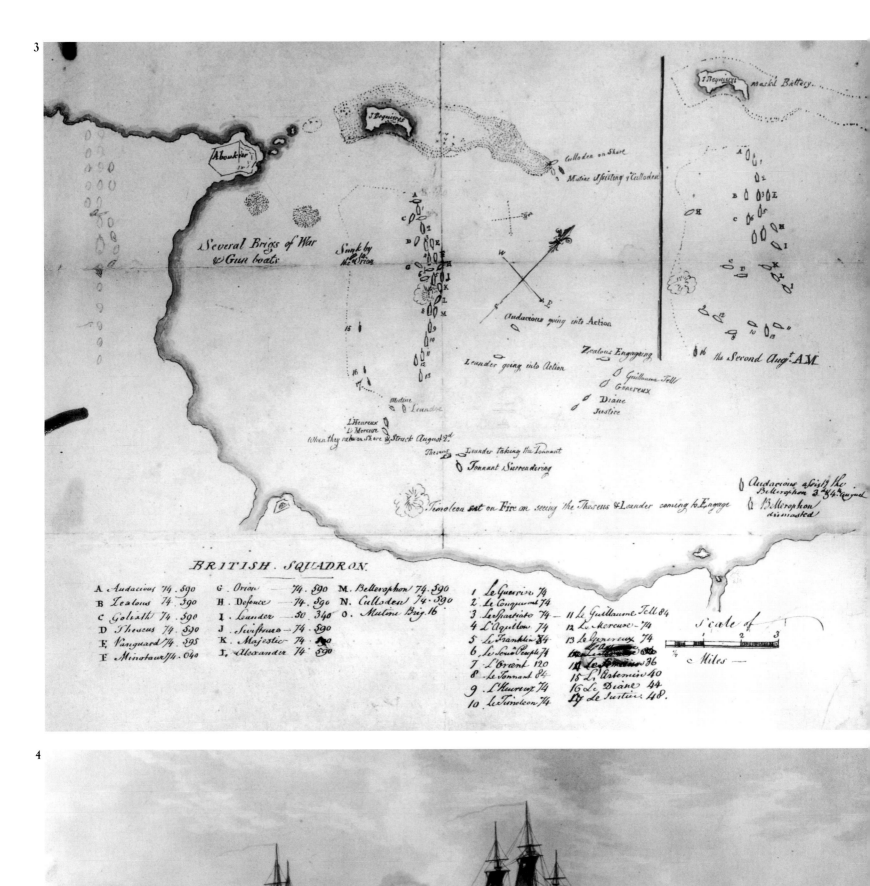

I Begniers masthd Battery

Aboukir

Culloden on Shore

Mutine Assisting ye Culloden

Several Brigs of War & Gun boats

Sunk by the Orion

Audacious going into Action

Zealous Engaging

the Second Augt. AM

Leander going into Action

Guillaume Tell

Genereux

Diane

Justice

Mutine

Leandre

L'Heureux

Le Mercure

When they run on Shore & Struck August 2d.

Theseus Leander taking the Tonnant

Tonnant Surrendering

Temoleon set on Fire on seeing the Theseus & Leander coming to Engage

Audacious assist the Bellerophon 3 & 4 Augd.

Bellerophon dismasted

BRITISH SQUADRON.

A Audacious 74.590
B Zealous 74.590
C Goliath 74.590
D Theseus 74.590
E Vanguard 74.595
F Minotaur 74.640
G Orion — 74.590
H Defence 74.590
I Leander 50.340
J Swiftsure — 74.590
K Majestic 74.
L Alexander 74.590
M Bellerophon 74.590
N Culloden 74.590
O Mutine Brig.16

1 Le Guerrier 74
2 Le Conquerant 74
3 Le Spartiate 74
4 L'Aquilon 74
5 Le Franklin 84
6 Le Sous People 74
7 L'Orient 120
8 Le Tonnant 84
9 L'Heureux 74
10 Le Temoleon 74

11 Le Guillaume Tell 84
12 Le Mercure — 74
13 Le Genereux 74
14 Le Justice 36
15 L'Artemise 40
16 Le Diane 44
17 Le Justice 48

Scale of

Miles

4

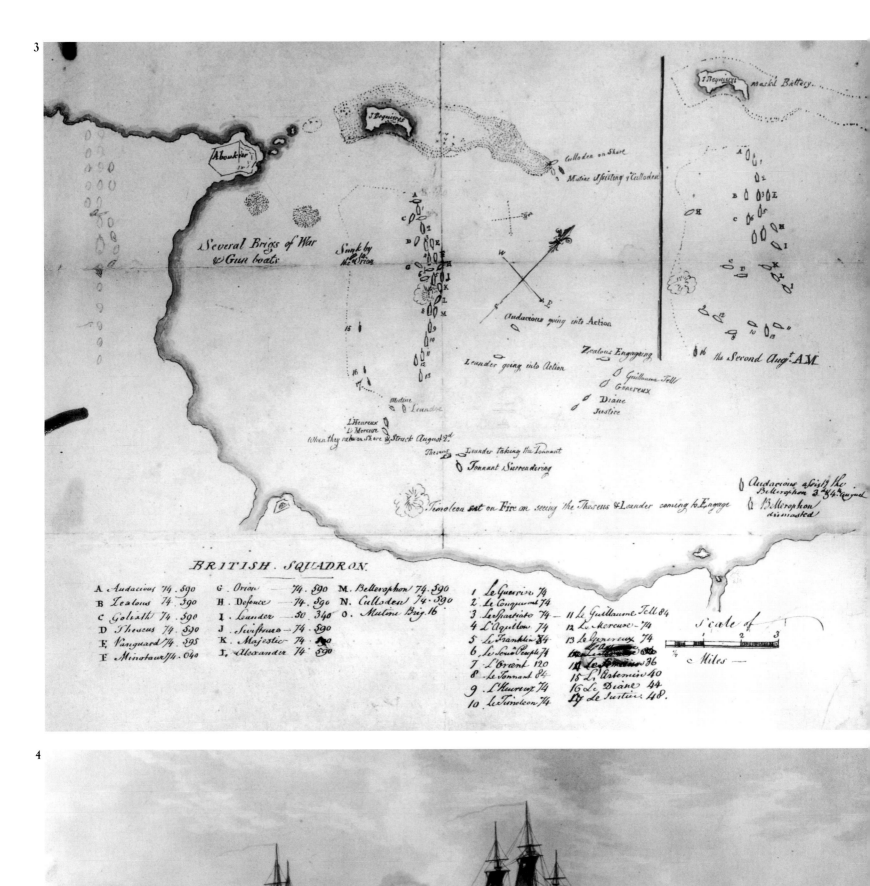

5

dered but then exploded having been abandoned by her crew (2). Meanwhile the remaining French ships moved away from their attackers into the recesses of the bay but two ran themselves aground and then surrendered after a brief exchange of shots. A French frigate briefly tried to approach the dismasted *Bellerophon,* but was soon scared off.

Whilst this was going on, at about 6 in the morning, the remaining French ships were left with no British ships in their immediate vicinity. The shattered *Tonnant* was in no condition to move, and the *Timoléon* ran herself aground whilst trying to tack (3). This left Rear-Admiral Villeneuve with his own *Guillaume Tell* and the *Généreux,* the frigates *Diane* and *Justice* and a clear escape route to the open sea, which he took (4). The *Zealous* tried to cut off the escape of the four undamaged French ships. Her fire forced the *Guillaume Tell* to turn away, but Nelson recalled her before she could lay herself alongside the *Généreux* or cut off the stern frigate. The British ships had all been damaged in their rigging though, apart from *Bellerophon* and *Majestic,* not particularly seriously, but for

the moment there was no prospect of supporting Captain Hood.

Rear-Admiral Villeneuve was much criticised for failing to support the head of the French line, and for fleeing the battlefield. It is, however, unfair to blame Villeneuve with his less well trained crews and the evidence he had of the high efficiency and fighting spirit of his enemy for saving what he could from the overwhelming disaster that had struck his fleet. Certainly Brueys was at fault in failing to check that the head of his line was close enough to the shoals to prevent the doubling of his line, but he was not really expecting the Nelsonic lightning-stroke that hit him, the pell-mell attack that pushed the French fleet off balance and kept it there. Given the initial flaw in the French position, and the quality of their opponents, there could really be little doubt of the outcome of the battle. Superb captains were matched by highly trained crews with high morale, the whole led by a man who came near to the ideal leader for such a team, someone who excelled in communicating his intentions and encouraging and enthusing his excellent subordinates. The 'Nelson touch' reached its apogee on that hot summer night off the Egyptian coast.

Nelson himself was out of action for some time. He was wounded early in the action by a splinter which hit him above his blind eye, cutting a strip of flesh which temporarily blinded him. The combination of this and shock had briefly made him think he was done for, but fortunately this was far from the case, and he could return to his quarterdeck with the wound sewn up in time to oversee the later stages of the battle, though still fairly groggy from shock and concussion (5). The British altogether lost 218 men killed and 617 wounded. It is significant that the losses of the ships which attacked the outside of the French line were much greater than those of the others which passed through that line and engaged from the inside. The French loss was, inevitably, much heavier than the British, particularly because of the destruction of their flagship. The total of dead and

6

wounded is not known for certain, but it is probable that about 1600 dead and 1500 wounded are figures that give the right idea of the scale of human suffering involved. One British seaman described the scene revealed at dawn: 'an awful sight it was, the whole bay was covered with dead bodies, mangled, wounded and scorched, not a bit of clothes on them but their trousers.'

On 2 and 3 August the British fleet cleared up after the action, seeing to wounded men and ships. *Timoléon* was set on fire by her crew and blew up on the afternoon of the 3rd when *Theseus* and *Leander* approached. *Tonnant* was finally forced to surrender to these two British ships earlier that same day. The British also landed on Aboukir Island and captured the guns and mortars of its battery.

Of the ships of the line taken in the battle (6), three were considered too damaged to save and were destroyed. Three were hulked. *Spartiate, Tonnant* and especially *Franklin* (renamed *Canopus*), had active lives in the Royal Navy, whilst all four French ships that had escaped from Aboukir Bay fell into British hands later.

The results of the battle were striking. The most obvious one was that Bonaparte was isolated in Egypt with his army. Nelson's spectacular victory established him as an international hero and heartened all opponents of Revolutionary France. Perhaps most important of all, the Battle of the Nile confirmed the moral ascendancy of the British Royal Navy over its chief rival. It also set a new standard in naval victories—of absolute victory with the loser deprived of nearly all his ships. No other battle between fleets of approximately equal size in the age of fighting sail was quite so strikingly complete. As Nelson himself observed, 'Victory is not a name strong enough for such a scene.' The performance of the British fleet was of the highest quality; the consistent impression is of smooth teamwork (7) combined with the maximum of intelligent initiative, of a powerful, well-oiled machine swinging into action. It was doing so against an enemy who did not lack gallantry, but who was nowhere near as well trained, organised or led.

1. 'Les Vaisseux Celebres. Le Tonnant, au Combat d'Aboukir (le 1er Aout 1798)', tinted lithograph engraved by Louis le Breton after his own original, printed by Bequet and published by E Morier, no date.
NMM ref PAG8975

2. 'Immediately after the destruction of L'Orient, the action recommenced', aquatint and etching by J W Edy after an original by Thomas Whitcombe (born *c*1752), published by John Harris 11 June 1799. *L'Artemise* burns far left; stern-on is *Timoleon* with *Tonnant* beyond; *Audacious* is shrouded in the smoke of her portside batteries, with *Theseus* bow-on; Villeneuve's squadron escapes in the distance, far right.
NMM ref PAH7940

3. 'Map of the Battle of the Nile 1 Aug 1798', black and watercolour pen and ink by Nicholas Pocock (1740-1821), no date.
NMM ref PAH0143

4. 'Battle of the Nile', coloured aquatint engraved by Francis Chesham and William Ellis after an original in the possession of Captain T B Thompson, published by G Riley November 1799. *Zealous* (centre) attempts to cut off the escape of *Généreux* and, astern, *Guillaume Tell* (left foreground).
NMM neg X1955

5. 'The Cockpit, Battle of the Nile', coloured aquatint engraved by M Dubourg after an original by William Heath, published by Edward Orme, 4 June 1817.
NMM ref PAD5574

6. 'Battle of the Nile 1st August 1798', aquatint after Thomas Whitcombe (born *c*1752), no date.
NMM ref PAD5579

7. 'Victors of the Nile (with 15 cameo portraits of naval officers)', engraving and etching by William Bromley and John Landseer after an original by Sir Robert Smirke, published by R Bowyer 1803.
NMM ref PAH5671

7

VICTORS OF THE NILE

The HERO   of the NILE.

1

The Hero of the Nile

I N THE months following the Battle of the Nile, as
Nelson recuperated at Naples, tokens of gratitude for
his victory arrived in a stream from celebrating
nations. The Sultan of Turkey dispatched a dress sword,
a pelisse or jacket 'of the finest scarlet cloth, lined with

most beautiful sable fur', a canteen, a scimitar with a
gold hilt, a musket mounted in silver and ivory, and a
diamond aigrette or ornament taken from one of the
Sultan's own turbans. This latter 'blaze of brilliants,
crowned with vibrating plumage and a radiant star on
the middle', turned on its centre by means of a wind-up
mechanism. Nelson was delighted with it and stuck it in
his hat (1). The Sultan even sent 2000 sequins for distribution among the wounded. From Russia came a miniature of the Tsar and a gold box set with diamonds; from
other sovereigns, silver-studded boxes. The City of
London sent swords for Nelson and his captains. The
East India Company sent £10,000 for Nelson alone.

Only the British government seemed grudging.
George III presented all the commanding officers with
medals, but these were overshadowed by the medals of
gold cast by Alexander Davison, the sole agent for the
French prizes taken at the Nile (2). His medals together
cost over £2000, and were supplemented by copper gilt
and copper bronzed medals for warrant and inferior officers. Nelson wanted to be made an earl like St Vincent or
a viscount like Duncan but, when he did receive his title,
it was only that of a baron, supplemented by £2000 a year
for three lives. Nelson was deeply disappointed, though
no doubt momentarily comforted by Lady Hamilton's
indignant claim that 'if I was King of England, I would
make you the most noble puissant DUKE NELSON
MARQUIS NILE EARL ALEXANDER VISCOUNT
PYRAMID BARON CROCADILE, and PRINCE
VICTORY, that posterity might have you in all forms'. It
was perhaps to compensate for this disappointment that
Nelson included Emma Hamilton's words in his baronial
coat of arms (3), for – as Emma perceptively assured him
– she, with Queen Maria Carolina of Naples, 'onely
wanted Lady Nelson to be the female *tria juncta in uno* for
we all love you & yet all three differently & yet all equally if you can make that out'. Later the latin phrase was
mistakenly thought to apply to Lord and Lady Hamilton
with Nelson.

While Nelson waited for this disappointing response to
his victory from his own government, Emma
Hamilton's generous and theatrical idolisation – with
the more calculating admiration of the Queen – made a
deep impression upon him. Still ill and frail from his Nile
wound (4), the festivities in Naples would have turned
the head of any successful officer far less susceptible to
honours and flattery than him. *Viva Nelson* was written
up at every street corner. The celebration of his birthday
on 29 September was marked by a dinner for 80 people, a
ball for 1740, followed by supper for 800, of which the
high point was the singing by Lady Hamilton of a newly
devised verse to the British national anthem lauding the
Hero of the Nile.

2

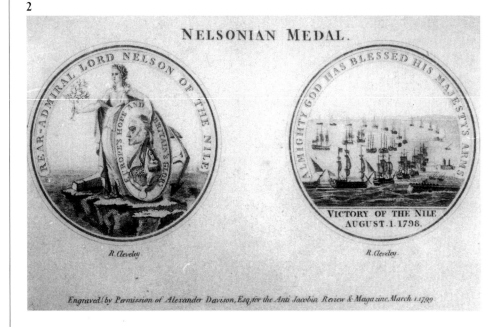

NELSONIAN MEDAL.

REAR-ADMIRAL LORD NELSON OF THE NILE

EUROPE'S HOPE AND BRITAIN'S GLORY

ALMIGHTY GOD HAS BLESSED HIS MAJESTY'S ARMS

VICTORY OF THE NILE
AUGUST.1.1798.

R. Cleveley   R. Cleveley

Engraved (by Permission of Alexander Davison, Esq, for the Anti Jacobin Review & Magazine, March 1.1799

Deep sexual infatuation with Emma Hamilton increased Nelson's vulnerability to the flatteries heaped upon him. Under these influences, the fate of the state of Naples and the Two Sicilies came to mean more to him than the calls of naval duty. In mid-December 1798 the French invaded Neapolitan territory and Nelson evacuated the royal family with the Hamiltons to Sicily; and in June, following their request, he used his naval force to restore King Ferdinand to his throne in Naples. It was a service for which he gained his most cherished reward: the Dukedom of Bronte, with the Castello di Maniace and an estate of 30,000 acres (5).

However, these were rewards gained at a cost to his reputation as an active officer. Lord Keith, when he succeeded as commander-in-chief in the Mediterranean was appalled at the 'scene of fulsome vanity and absurdity' in Naples; while Lord Spencer, First Lord of the Admiralty, on hearing of Nelson's inability on health grounds to abandon his 'friends at Palermo', advised him to come home rather than remain inactive at a foreign court. It was a loss of reputation that was not fully regained until Nelson's victory at Copenhagen.

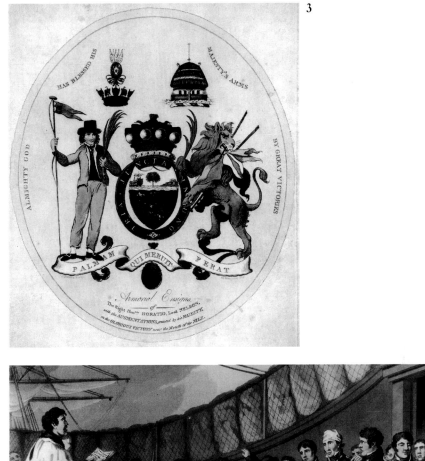

3

1. 'The Hero of the Nile', by James Gillray, published by Gillray and H Humphrey, 1 December 1798. It is significant that a bare three months after his great victory, Nelson's vanity could be seen as the legitimate subject of caricature – the aigrette, pelisse, sword, medal and star all feature in this telling portrayal of a small man weighed down by honours.
NMM neg A240

2. Davidson's Nile Medal, engraved by R Cleveley, published in the *Anti Jacobin Review & Magazine*, 1 March 1799.
NMM ref PAD3960

3. 'Armorial Ensigns of The Right Honble Horatio, Lord Nelson with the Augmentations granted by his Majesty on the Glorious Victory near the mouth of the Nile', coloured engraving by John Swaine, no date.
NMM ref PAD4003

4. 'Sailors at Prayer on board Lord Nelson's ship after the Battle of the Nile', coloured aquatint engraved by Clark and M Dubourg after an original by John Augustus Atkinson, published by Edward Orme, 1 April 1816.
NMM ref PAD5581

5. 'Lord Nelson's house, called Maniaci, near Bronte', anonymous wash over graphite drawing, no date.
NMM ref PAD3983

4

5

Leander **and** *Généreux*

1

NELSON entrusted to Edward Berry the despatches announcing his victory, but in the absence of a suitable frigate, he was forced to send them in the 50-gun *Leander*. In the first of a number of postscripts to the Nile battle, on 18 August the ship was overtaken off Crete by *Le Généreux*, a powerful 74 and one of only two ships of the line to escape from the debacle in Aboukir Bay. She came down under first Neapolitan and then Turkish colours, but fooled nobody aboard the *Leander*, according to one eyewitness not least because of 'the white patches over the shot-holes in her bows'.

Given the disparity in firepower – a broadside of over 1000lbs to his ship's 432 – Captain Thomas Boulden Thompson (1) felt justified in avoiding action, but 50-gun ships were notoriously poor sailers, and in any case the French 74 was bringing up the breeze, so escape was impossible (2). What followed was an epic, if one-sided, contest sustained for nearly six hours, and when the almost dismasted hulk of the *Leander* finally surrendered she had been reduced to firing crowbars, nails and other langrage (3).

Le Généreux was not well handled, and Tim Stewart, one of *Leander*'s lower deck gunners, remembered her coming up 'blazing away, right and left, long before she was in gun-shot, and wasting powder and shot which we wanted [*ie* were in need of].' He continued contemptuously;

We fought six hours; just think of that. Why, if she had handled her guns in a seamanlike manner, she ought to have sunk us in little more than six minutes. We had to cut through the main topsail, lying over our larboard side to make room for the muzzles of the guns, for our ship was quite a wreck – not a stick standing – but still the brave hearts would not give in.

Their captain, however, could see the folly of further resistance, despite having respulsed many attempts to board, and after consulting Berry the four-times wounded Thompson 'ordered our colours to be hauled down; and the old English Ensign, all in strips, was struck . . .'

2

3

Casualties were high on both sides: with 35 killed and 57 wounded the British ship lost a third of her total crew of 282, while the French ship with a complement reinforced to over 900 lost about 100 dead and more than 150 wounded. Neither ship had an intact boat, and the midshipman who took possession of the *Leander* had to swim to his prize. When a boat was finally patched up, the victors swarmed aboard, stealing everything in sight—even the surgeon's instruments as he was operating, thus endangering the life of Captain Thompson. When Berry remonstrated with the French captain, Lejoille, he was told with a gallic shrug, 'I'm sorry, but the fact is, the French are very good at pillaging.'

Public admiration for the heroic defence combined with outrage at the treatment of the prisoners made a heady cocktail, and Thompson was more honoured for

his defeat than many captains for their victories. Nor did *Leander* serve the French for long, being towed to Corfu where she was recaptured by the Russians in March of the following year and handed back to the Royal Navy.

_____

1. 'Sir Thomas B Thompson Kt', stipple engraving by William Ridley after an original by George Engleheart, published by Joyce Gold, 1 August 1805. *NMM ref PAD3399*

2. 'Action between Leander and French two-decker Genereux 18 Aug 1798. 1. Genereux chasing Leander. 2. Alongside', watercolours by William Guido Anderson, in a letter to his father, the marine artist William Anderson. William junior, serving in the Royal Navy, seems to have been an eyewitness; he was to be killed at Copenhagen in 1801. *NMM ref PAF5593*

3. 'Action between H.M.S. Leander of 50 guns & 282 Men and the French National Ship Le Genereux 74 Guns 936 Men August 18 1798', chalk lithograph engraved by C H Seaforth (1801-c1853) after his own original and printed by Charles Joseph Hullmandel, no date. *NMM ref PAF4706*

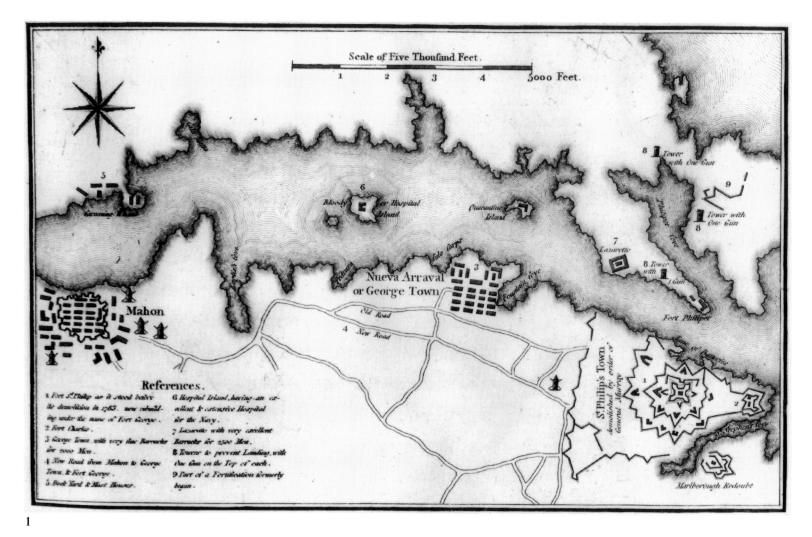

1

The capture of Minorca

WITH Nelson having disposed of the Toulon fleet, St Vincent felt it was safe to detach a squadron under Commodore Duckworth from the Cadiz blockade for the occupation of Minorca. Flying his flag in the *Leviathan*, with a second 74, two 44s, three smaller cruisers, plus several transports carrying troops under General the Hon Charles Stuart, Duckworth put the small army ashore at Addaya Creek against minimal opposition on 7 November. The first objective was Port Mahon, which was not well defended,

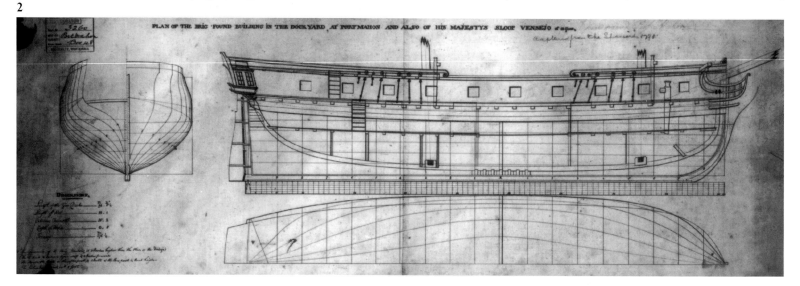

2

the Spanish having dismantled its principal fortifications when recaptured in 1781. After a rapid advance over two days, 300 men under Colonel Paget took Fort Charles at the entrance to the harbour [fig 2 in (1)], removing the boom and opening the harbour to the *Aurora*, 28 and *Cormorant*, 20.

There was only one alarm, when a Spanish relieving force was reported, and on the 11th Duckworth took his squadron to sea to intercept it. He chased what turned out to be four Spanish frigates, but was only able to recapture the British sloop *Peterel*, taken by the Spaniards the previous day. By the time he returned Stuart had forced the surrender of Cuidadella, the only remaining centre of Spanish resistance, and with it the whole island capitulated on the 15th. The British took 4000-5000 prisoners, and besides artillery and military equipment, an abundance of naval stores was discovered in the arsenal at Port Mahon. There were no Spanish warships in the harbour, but a naval brig found under construction was completed as the *Port Mahon* (2).

The strategic value of Minorca, of course, lay in the superb harbour of Port Mahon (3). As a base for a main fleet, Gibraltar was compromised by lack of shelter, and

was not self-sufficient in either food or water, and a major naval presence in the Mediterranean could not be sustained with no secure naval facilities nearer than Lisbon. Port Mahon, on the other hand, was ideally situated for the Toulon blockade and could shelter the whole Mediterranean fleet. Admittedly, its entrance was narrow (4) and difficult to get out of quickly, but that very reason made it almost impossible to attack from seaward. However, the whole island was also regarded as a potentially secure garrison for the land forces Britain was considering sending to co-operate in the campaigns on the Italian mainland.

When retaken in 1798 the British found an ideal base; indeed they had built most of the naval facilities on the island themselves during the previous occupations between 1708 and 1756 and again from 1763 to 1781. The dockyard (5), built opposite the town of Mahon itself, included storehouses and an eight-sided careening wharf on Saffron Island built between 1765 and 1774 ['5' in (1)]. The other notable structure was the naval hospital on Bloody Island in the middle of the harbour ['6' in (1)]. Originally built in 1711-12, it was the Royal Navy's first purpose-built medical facility, predating the more

5

famous Haslar at Gosport by thirty years. It was reconstructed in 1772-4 with two storeys, as seen in (6).

Since the island had a long exposed coastline, and a relatively small garrison, a high priority was some form of cheap and quickly constructed fortification. The answer was a coastal gun tower, modelled after the infamous example that had caused the Navy so much trouble at Cape Mortella in 1794 (see pages 100-101 of *Fleet Battle and Blockade* in this series). Stuart was a veteran of the Corsica campaign and considered them ideal to protect every beach and creek around the island where a landing might be attempted. Designed by the engineer C W Pasley, they were prototypes for the later British Martello towers, and thirteen were completed before the British returned the island in 1802 under the Treaty of Amiens. Examples are numbered '8' in (1).

---

1. 'Harbour of Mahon', plate 6 of Thomas Walsh, *Journal of the Late Campaign in Egypt* (London 1803).
Chatham collection

2. 'Plan of the brig found building in the Dockyard at Port Mahon and also of His Majesty's sloop Vensejo of 18 guns'. Unusually for a brig, these vessels had a quarterdeck.
NMM neg DR3260/48

3. 'A View of the Harbour of St Philips Castle for the Entrance to the Town of Mahon in the Island of Minorca with all the Different Coves and Islands &c', engraving by William Darling from an original 'drawn on the spot' by Francis Egideus Assiotti, 17 February 1766. The view is from the north side of the harbour.
NMM ref PAH2395

4. 'The Entrance to Port Mahon', anonymous black and watercolour pen and ink, no date.
NMM ref PAG9690

5. 'Mahon and the Arsenal (with Spanish man-of-war on right)', anonymous black and watercolour pen and ink, no date.
NMM ref PAG9692

6. 'Mahon, with a view of the hospital island, on the Isla del Rey', anonymous black and watercolour pen and ink, no date. The dating of these and other watercolours in this series is problematical: the Martello towers around Philippet Cove in PAG9690 suggest a period after the British capture in 1798; in this ilustration the three-decker with a White Ensign and a full admiral's flag at the main truck may indicate St Vincent's visit in 1799; but the presence of a Spanish two-decker in PAG9692 should make the date prior to 1798 or after 1801. Perhaps the series was done over a long period.
NMM ref PAG9693

6

Nelson and Naples

THE battered *Vanguard*, bearing her equally battered admiral, dropped anchor off Naples on 22
September 1798 (1) to face a rapturous welcome
from 500 small craft, led by the Hamiltons in Sir
William's barge, just ahead of King Ferdinand himself.
The highly theatrical waterfront of the city (2) was
thronged with well-wishers, and for Nelson began the
most concentrated period of adulation he ever experienced. The year and a half he spent in close contact with
the Neapolitan court has always embarrassed his admir-
ers, since it encouraged the vanity, petulance and ego-
tism that cast such a shadow over his reputation as the

1. 'The Arrival of the Vanguard Rear-Admiral Sir Horatio Nelson, September 22nd 1798 after the scene of his glory in the Bay of Aboukir', watercolour by Giacomo Guardi, no date. The ship was actually jury rigged and had been towed into the bay by the frigate *Thalia*, so this may not be an eyewitness view.
NMM ref PAG9746

2. 'Panorama di Napoli. Preso della Villa di Moma a S. Lucia', pen and ink drawing by Antonio Senape, no date.
NMM ref PAD1704

3. 'Monte Pelegrino, Palermo', lithograph engraved by H M Whichelo after an original by H Stretton, printed by Charles Joseph Hullmandel, no date.
NMM ref PAH2464

4. 'Veduta del Isola di Procida', black and watercolour pen and ink by John Thomas Serres (1759-1825), 1791.
NMM neg D2573

5. Map of central Italy to illustrate the campaigns of 1798 and 1799, from Napoleon Bonaparte, *Campagnes d'Égypte et de Syrie 1798-1799: Mémoires . . . Napoleon dictés par lui-même . . . et publiés par le Général Bertrand* (Paris 1847).
Chatham collection

6. 'Panorama di Napoli preso da S. Martino', pen and ink drawing by Antonio Senape, no date.
NMM ref PAD1705

7. 'North East side of the town of Corfu', watercolour by Lieutenant William Innes Pocock (1783-1863), no date. Shows a typical Mediterranean rowing and sailing gunboat, this one flying a French ensign.
NMM ref PAF0044

8. 'Veduta Di Napoli Della Parte Di Chiaia', engraving and etching by Gius Aloja, published by Giovanni Gravier 1759. Fort St Elmo is numbered '10', top left.
NMM ref PAI0071

9. 'Sailors from HMS Vanguard on shore', watercolour by François Louis Thomas Francia, no date.
NMM ref PAD8890

10. 'Lord Nelson Landing at Leghorn on his return to England after the capture of Malta 5th Sep 1800', engraving and etching by Carlo Lasinio after an original by Roselli, published by Lanfranchi, no date. Nelson arrived at Leghorn in the *Foudroyant* with the Queen of Naples and the Hamiltons on board on 14 June — probably the incident depicted here — and struck his flag on 13 July, finally leaving for England on the 17th, well before Malta surrendered.
NMM ref PAH7974

5

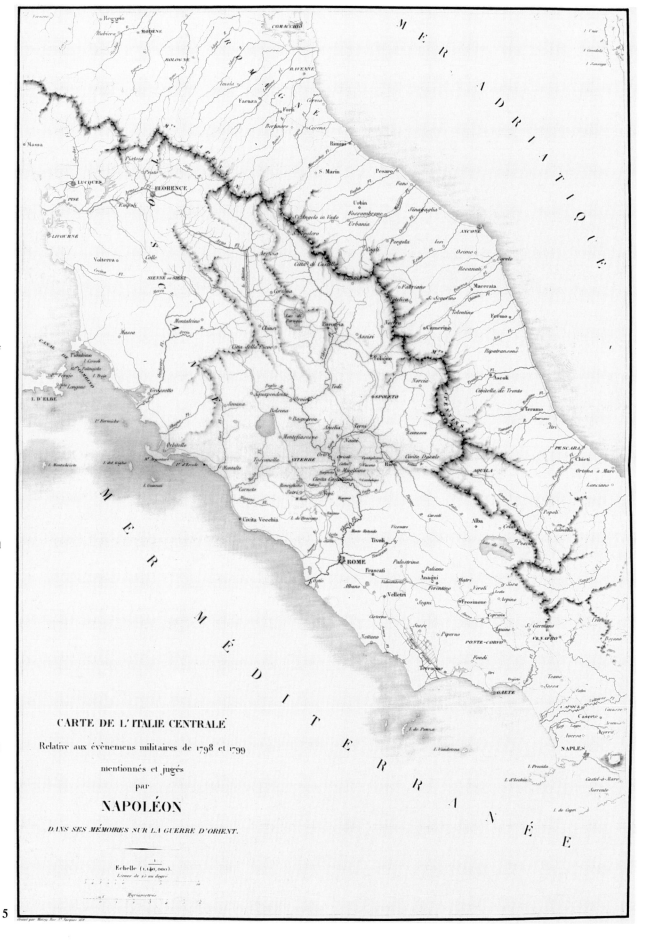

CARTE DE L'ITALIE CENTRALE

Relative aux évènemens militaires de 1798 et 1799

mentionnés et jugés

par

NAPOLÉON

DANS SES MÉMOIRES SUR LA GUERRE D'ORIENT.

Echelle (1,140,000).

selfless servant of his country. Earlier generations were scandalised by his affair with Lady Hamilton, which was one reason for his idle time at Naples and Palermo, but today his espousal of the sordid ethos of the court, and the injustice of his dealings with the Neapolitan jacobins seems a worse sin. However, for those who since Mahan have wanted to present him as the example of the perfect naval officer, his rank dereliction of duty during this phase of his career is a greater problem by far. Nelson, in retrospect, recognised the pernicious influence and referred to his 'Sicilification' in 'a country of fiddlers and poets, whores and scoundrels'.

The euphoric atmosphere of the Neapolitan court after the Nile quickly evaporated. King Ferdinand, unwisely encouraged by Nelson, decided to expel the French from Rome and engaged the Austrian General Mack—surely one of the most unfortunate soldiers in history—to lead his ill-disciplined army. Nelson supported the advance with the capture of Leghorn to the rear of the French territory, but no sooner had Ferdinand entered Rome than the French counter-attacked and drove his poorly trained troops over their own borders and advanced on Naples itself. The jacobins rose in anticipation of French 'liberation' and Nelson was forced to evacuate the court to their Sicilian capital Palermo (3). In their precipitate retreat, much of the Neapolitan navy was lost.

A counter-revolution soon sprang up in Calabria, led by Cardinal Ruffo, and as these forces closed in on Naples, Nelson sent Troubridge with a squadron to co-operate. There were no French troops on the outlying islands and Troubridge was able to take unopposed possession of Procida (4), Ischia, Capri and all the Ponza islands on 2-3 April 1799. The war in Italy was going well for the allies, with Austrian and Russian armies under Suvarov regaining most of the territory lost to the French the previous year (5).

On receiving news of the irruption of Bruix's fleet into the Mediterranean in May, Nelson roused himself from his dalliance at Palermo to concentrate his battlefleet off Marittimo, and the naval command in Naples bay devolved onto Captain Foote of the frigate *Seahorse*. By this stage resistance around Naples was largely confined to the French garrisons of the forts, especially the Castel Nuovo (right foreground in '6'), and Castel del'Uovo on the end of the breakwater, supported by gunboats (7) and small craft. These were induced to surrender to Ruffo's forces on 22 June, being promised repatriation in cartels to Toulon or freedom to remain in their home city for the Neapolitan jacobins. With the very real prospect of the intervention of a French fleet, Captain Foote was happy to sign the capitulation for Britain.

At this point it was Nelson's fleet that came into the

4

6

7

bay, and the admiral instantly annulled the truce and abrogated the agreement, arguing that it was beyond the authority of the signatories. His subsequent treatment of the local revolutionaries, and especially his summary execution of Prince Caraccioli, did not inspire artists and printmakers, so mercifully these events can be passed over without further comment. The one remaining French garrison, in Fort St Elmo (8), dominated the city, and Troubridge led the seamen and marines of the fleet in its elimination; with Russian and Neapolitan aid, the fort was besieged on 3 July and surrendered on the 11th. Much to Lord Keith's disapproval, the fleet's seamen spent more time ashore than at sea at this time (9), and Troubridge's military career continued with successful attacks on Capua, Gaeta and Civita Vecchia, following which Captain Louis of the *Minotaur* was rowed up the Tiber in his barge and planted the Union flag above the Capitol in Rome.

Nelson was superseded by Lord Keith as commander-in-chief in the Mediterranean in January 1800. Keith ordered him away from Palermo, and Nelson's skill—and luck—reasserted itself when his squadron captured the *Généreux* off Malta in February. However, by this time Nelson was chafing to return to England, and his request to be relieved was finally accepted. In one final display of contrariness, he decided (against the Admiralty's wishes) to go home overland with the Hamiltons in attendance. His final mission was to convey the Queen of Naples to Leghorn on the first stage of her journey to seek the support of the Austrian court at Vienna, his fleet arriving on 14 June (10). When he finally struck his flag on 17 July, he left Malta and Egypt still unsubdued, and many felt that the near two years since the Nile had been the most unproductive and personally damaging of his career.

1

The Neapolitan navy

THE navy that Nelson encountered at Naples was a very recent creation. Indeed, it was almost entirely an expression of Queen Maria Carolina's ambition to make the Kingdom of the Two Sicilies a power broker in the central Mediterranean. It can trace its origin to the employment in 1778 of John Acton, a Frenchman of English descent, who had served with distinction in the navies of France and Tuscany. He rose to become the kingdom's chief minister, but his first success was the establishment of a modern naval force (1).

Either economically or politically, it is arguable whether Naples could justify a great-power style battle-fleet, but that is what she set out to acquire. As a stop-gap measure two 64-gun ships were purchased from the Knights of Malta in 1783, but thereafter only the latest technology would do—74-gun line of battle ships (2) and 18pdr-armed frigates (3), the benchmark types in the most up-to-date navies. Six of the latter were laid down between 1783 and 1789 (along with six 24-gun corvettes), while three 74s were launched in 1786-89, and three more followed in 1793-95. At the outbreak of war there were five 74s in service, and *Guiscardo, St Joachim, Tancredi, Partenope* and *Samnita* formed a powerful and homogeneous squadron. That the navy was intended for more than a defensive role is proved by the addition of bomb vessels (4), of the usual Mediterranean *galiote* or ketch rig.

One notable Neapolitan contribution to warship design was the gunboat. During the American Revolutionary War the Spanish had fitted out a number of lateen rigged launches with one or two large guns (and a few with mortars), but they were of decidedly restricted seaworthiness. The Neapolitan innovation was to employ the hull form of local coasting types called the *leuto* and *paranzello*, which like the launches were handy under sail and oar but with a more robust and seaworthy hull. Large numbers of the *lance cannoniere* were built after 1785 and 122 were in service in 1799, along with 14 of a mortar-armed version called a *lance bombardiere* and despite wartime losses in 1814 there were 47 and 10 respectively, plus 9 *leuti* and 23 *paranzelli cannon-ieri* of the local variant.

2

3

A dockyard was also developed across the Bay of Naples from the city at Castellamare, but Nelson was decided unimpressed by its efficiency. Indeed, he told Lord Spencer that graft and corruption was such that fitting out one Neapolitan ship of the line cost as much as ten in an English yard: fitting out five would ruin the kingdom. Operationally, the navy inspired no more respect, although it was more efficient than the comic-opera Neapolitan army (during one argument about their uniform King Ferdinand remarked that whatever its colour, they would still run away). Neapolitan ships supported Hood's occupation of Toulon in 1793 and co-operated with the Mediterranean Fleet in succeeding years, the 74-gun *Tancredi* even suffering minor casualties during Hotham's action of March 1795. After being worked up by St Vincent, however, the crack Mediterranean squadrons looked down on their allies: 'I have nominally a great force,' wrote Nelson to General Stuart, 'but anyone is heartily welcome to both the Neapolitan and Portuguese ships.' They were poorly drilled and since all their commanding officers claimed to be commodores, they would not serve under British captains, however much greater the seniority and experience of the latter.

Like many a present-day Third World country buying the latest military hardware, for Naples the investment was neither appropriate nor sustainable once war broke out. There was virtually no new construction of large ships between 1795 and 1805, and the French invasion of Naples in the winter of 1798-99 dealt a blow to the navy from which it never recovered. Of the gunboats 80 were lost (including 8 mortar boats) and against Nelson's express orders the 74s *Guiscardo, St Joachim, Tancredi,* a

4

frigate and two corvettes were set on fire by Captain Campbell of the Portuguese squadron. Even after the French were driven out, Ferdinand and Maria Carolina never again felt safe on the mainland and spent much of the rest of the war in the Sicilian half of their dual kingdom, protected by the Royal Navy, whereupon interest in their own expensive but impotent naval force melted away. After the Peace of Amiens, the French again occupied the south of Italy, and during the attempted invasion of Sicily in 1806 the Neapolitan navy's sole contribution to the defence was the frigate *Minerva* and about a dozen gunboats.

5

1. 'The Arrival of their Sicilian Majesties at Naples, 1785', oil painting by Dominic Serres the Elder (1722-1793), signed and dated 1787. The painting shows the new navy on one of its first missions – appropriately, a ceremonial occasion. Despite the presence of ships from many nations, including a galley of the Knights of Malta, the Neapolitan two-decker is the largest vessel present, which may indicate the prestige value of the navy to the ambitious court.
NMM ref BHC0458

2. 'V[aisse]au Napolitain de 74 Canons en Galla', coloured engraving by Gio Maria Merlo after an original by Emeric, 1794.
NMM ref PAH9401

3. 'Neapolitan Frigate', anonymous watercolour, 1780.
NMM ref PAF8224

4. 'Bombarda Napolitana', anonymous watercolour, 1780.
NMM ref PAF8240

5. 'Chaloupe canonière ou Lanzone', etching produced and published by Henri Bayard, 1832.
NMM ref PAD7359

The Cadiz station 1798-1799

EVEN after the dispatch of Nelson's squadron into the Mediterranean, St Vincent's main force remained based at Lisbon, and the famous landmark of Belem Castle (1) downriver from the Portuguese capital became familiar to the men of the fleet.

Although there was no longer a permanent battlefleet presence inside the Straits, individual vessels were sent on particular missions into what was now a hostile sea. The 64-gun *Lion*, for example, encountered four Spanish frigates while reconnoitring Cartagena on 15 July 1798, and managed to cut off one, the 34-gun *Santa Dorothea*, which was hampered by the loss of her fore topmast. Her three consorts, *Pomona*, *Proserpine* and *Santa Cazilda*, tacked and bravely came down on *Lion*. For any chance of success the 12pdr-armed frigates needed to concentrate their attack, but could only manage a strung-out line of battle — the moment depicted in (2); each received a broadside in reply and after one further attempt, broke off the action. The *Santa Dorothea* surrendered and was added to the Royal Navy as a 12pdr-armed 36-gun frigate.

The Canary Islands formed a highly important nodal point in the trade routes to both the East and West Indies, so were closely watched by the cruisers of St Vincent's command. On one routine patrol the 28-gun *Brilliant* spotted the French frigates *Vertu*, 40 and *Régénérée*, 36 - six months out of the Isle de France (Mauritius) - in the harbour of Santa Cruz, Tenerife, on 26 July 1798. The puny British Sixth Rate was at that time on her own, although the 18pdr-armed *Flora* was in the vicinity, and was lucky to escape when chased, audaciously tacking across the bows of the *Régénérée* (3). After falling in with one another, the two British frigates returned to Santa Cruz, but the French were well on their way — and, to add insult to injury, escorting two extremely valuable Spanish 'galleons'.

One action which inspired many artists was the defence of her convoy by the 16-gun brig sloop *Espoir* off Gibraltar on 7 August 1798. She was set upon by a large frigate-built ship called the *Liguria*, armed with 26 guns of various calibres but amounting to about four times the brig's firepower. After a four-hour combat, the *Liguria* surrendered and proved to be a Genoese vessel (4). The ship had no privateering commission and was little better than a pirate, but provides an example of the way unscrupulous individuals sought to exploit the political turmoil in the Italian states occasioned by the French invasions.

1

2

Whatever the value of cruiser activity, the station's principal role was the continuing blockade of Cadiz. As St Vincent's health deteriorated an increasing load fell on Lord Keith (5), who was eventually to succeed him as commander-in-chief in 1800. Keith's abilities were put to the test by the concentration of Bruix's fleet with the Spanish in the summer of 1799 in an attempt to relieve the French forces in Corfu, Malta and Egypt. Hampered by the need to defend Minorca, and facing a nearly point-blank refusal from Nelson to follow orders, Keith was much criticised for not bringing Bruix to action. The blockade of Cadiz was abandoned and although closely pursued, the enemy squadrons were never encountered. Keith's sole positive success was the capture of the whole

3

4

of Rear-Admiral Perrée's squadron—the frigates *Junon* (6), *Alceste* and *Courageuse* and brigs *Salamine* and *Alerte*— fugitives from the Levant blockade. However, the allies lost their nerve and retreated from the Mediterranean before even attempting any of their aims, so Keith's dispositions prevented a serious strategic reverse.

By 12 July the combined fleet was at anchor in Cadiz harbour. If the weather had been fair as they sailed out of the Mediterranean they must have passed within sight of St Vincent, whose ship was at anchor off Gibraltar. Sick

and weary, the old admiral had chosen to return home in the *Argo*, an obsolescent 44-gun two-decker, probably because she was the most easily spared by the fleet. The ship was portrayed at this time by Thomas Buttersworth who was serving in the *Caroline*, and is shown with a small schooner (probably the tender *Earl of St Vincent*) and one of three Russian line of battle ships lying there; the admiral's flag flies from the mainmast head (7).

Buttersworth was shortly to be presented with a more dramatic subject for his brush when a week later his ship

5

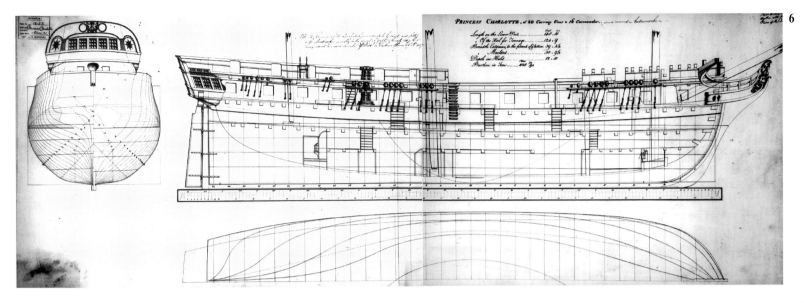

was sent to reconnoitre Cadiz. In company with *Triton*, *Caroline* chanced upon the whole combined fleet on 21 July as it was getting under way, and counted seventeen sail at anchor and twenty-two under sail, before two frigates and a line of battle ship set off in pursuit. Buttersworth chose as his subject (8) the moment when his captain decided discretion was the better part of valour: as described in the log, 'came to on the larboard tack and made all sail'. The frigates are shown maintaining their course, while the battleship is tacking; although being both to leeward and astern she has already lost the race, the pursuit was kept up for an hour and a half.

1. 'A View of the Castle of Belem at the Entrance of the Port of Lisbon', brown aquatint engraved by Wells after an original by Jean Alexandre Noel, 29 May 1793.
NMM neg A3713

2. 'Representation of the Lion Man of war of 64 guns . . . attacking four Spanish Frigates of which she captured one in the Gut of Gibraltar', etching by Thomas Vivares after an original by Thomas Whitcombe (born c1752), published by Francis Jukes, 1 November 1800.
NMM neg A5071

3. 'Engagement between His Majesty's Ship Brilliant . . . & the L'Vertu & Regeneree French Frigates . . . off Santa Cruz, on the Coast of Barbary, the 26th of July 1798', coloured engraving published by Laurie and Whittle, 21 October 1799.
NMM ref PAG7116

4. 'Capture of the Liguria Augt 7th 1798', coloured aquatint engraved by Thomas Sutherland after an original by Thomas Whitcombe (born c1752), published 1 July 1816.
NMM ref PAD5604

5. 'Vice-Admiral Lord Keith off Cadiz in 1799, in command of the blockade', grey wash by Thomas Buttersworth (1768-1842), no date.
NMM neg C861

6. Lines and profile of *Princess Charlotte* ex *Junon*.
NMM neg 1653

7. '*Argo*, 44, flying the flag of Admiral the Earl of St Vincent, Gibraltar, July 1799', watercolour by Thomas Buttersworth (1768-1842).
NMM neg 7071

8. '*Caroline*, 36 guns, being chased by French ships', watercolour by Thomas Buttersworth (1768-1842), 1799. The log confirms the actual date as 21 July.
NMM neg A1903

7

8

1

Russo-Turkish operations 1798-1800

1. Russian fireship towing the felucca employed in action to take off the crew, anonymous watercolour from an album dated about 1780. This is probably part of the fleet sent to the Mediterranean in 1770.
NMM ref PAF8230

2. 'Panorama con specie di Batimenti . . . Batimens de Guerre et Marchands', coloured engraving after an original by Vincenzo Scotti, 1790. The two frames from this large print show a Russian 74 (top) and an Ottoman 80-gun ship.
NMM ref PA12717

3. 'Vu de l'Arsenal de Constantinople', engraving and etching by Schroeder and Coiny after an original by Melling, no date. Most of the Ottoman navy is laid up opposite.
NMM ref PA10175

4. 'Town, Citadel and Harbour of Corfu, from the Island of Vido', coloured aquatint engraved by H Havell & Son after an original by Joseph Cartwright, *c*1820.
NMM ref PA10150

5. 'Ancona attacked 2 November 1799 by Russians and Turks', etching by Arcangelo Magini after an original by Giuseppe Fabbri, published by Arcangelo Sartori, no date. The Russo-Turkish bombardment was in May, and the date probably refers to the surrender of the city.
NMM neg X1942

D ESPITE the best diplomatic efforts of the Directory, the French occupation of Egypt dragged the Ottoman Empire into the war and produced one of the most unlikely operational alliances

2

of the period—between Russia and Turkey, states whose relations had barely recovered after two fiercely fought levantine wars. In the conflicts of 1768-1774 and 1787-1789, Russia had revealed an ambition to become a Black Sea naval power, having seized the Crimea and built a dockyard and base at Sebastopol. At Chesme in 1770 a squadron from the Baltic fleet had destroyed a larger Turkish force of some twenty sail of the line and a dozen supporting craft, and many saw this as a prelude to the establishment of a Russian fleet in the Mediterranean (1).

Both powers boasted substantial navies, but the levels of training and their *esprit de corps* left much to be desired. In 1795 the Russian Black Sea fleet comprised eleven sail of the line and thirteen frigates (compared with fifty and twenty-seven respectively in the Baltic). British experience refitting Baltic fleet ships sent to the North Sea suggested that they were not well built, with too much short-lived softwood in their construction, but the Black Sea vessels may have employed superior timber. Design-wise, the usual Russian battleship of this period was a relatively small two-decker, although there were a few 80-gun ships for flag roles (2).

The Ottoman navy is still something of a mystery to western historians, but there are some indications of its general size and composition. In 1788, for example, its nineteen battleships were mostly small ships of 50-60 guns, with three of 64 guns, and four larger two-deckers of 72-80 guns; there were also ten frigates and about a hundred oared gunboats, plus a handful of galleys. A significant building programme was in hand, however, and in 1796 the French ambassador at Constantinople reported that the Ottoman navy of twenty-seven of the line and twenty frigates was 'the most beautiful fleet in the world' (3). The ships were generally similar to western models, although they were reputed to have more room between decks—according to Christian propaganda to allow the wearing of turbans—which led to stability problems.

What brought Turkish and Russian interests into alignment was the French occupation of the Ionian islands and the associated mainland fortresses that had been Venetian dependencies. The Tsar regarded himself as protector of the local Christians, while for the Turks the area was a traditional sphere of influence, and neither wished to allow the other freedom of action.

The Russian contribution, under Vice-Admiral Ushakov (somewhat optimistically dubbed 'the Suvarov of the navy'), comprised ten sail of the line, four frigates and some small craft, while the Turks supplied about thirty assorted vessels and a landing force of about 8000 men. They sailed from the Dardanelles in September 1798 and quickly overcame resistance in all the islands,

3

with the exception of Corfu, where the French garrison put up a skilled and tenacious defence (4). The island eventually surrendered in March 1799, but not before the most important ships—including the *Généreux* that had been sheltering there since escaping after the Nile—managed to push past the slack allied blockade. However, her prize, the damaged *Leander*, was still in the harbour and was magnanimously restored to Britain by the Russians.

Despite British requests to lend some positive assistance in the reduction of Malta and the blockade of Egypt, the Russo-Turkish squadrons remained in the Adriatic, making minor contributions to the land war in Italy. In May the allies bombarded Ancona, whose port was defended by three ex-Venetian 64s, but without any real effect. Tensions between the unnatural allies were already manifest, and, if William James is correct, cannot have been improved by the performance of the Turks on

4

this occasion: 'Preferring a safe to an effective position, the Turks had stationed their ships outside those of their allies, and began their part in the engagement by shooting away the colours and a great portion of the rigging of the Russian admiral's ship.' The siege dragged on, and in August the Turkish force, its seamen unpaid and mutinous, was sent home. The Russians were left in rather grudging co-operation with Austrian army, which was finally rewarded by the surrender of Ancona in November (5).

Ushakov was at the mercy of the wavering policy of his Tsar, and after wintering in Trieste he was ordered to land troops in Malta, but was finally recalled to Sebastopol early in 1800 before this could be accomplished, his squadron having achieved little of use to the wider struggle in his Mediterranean deployment.

5

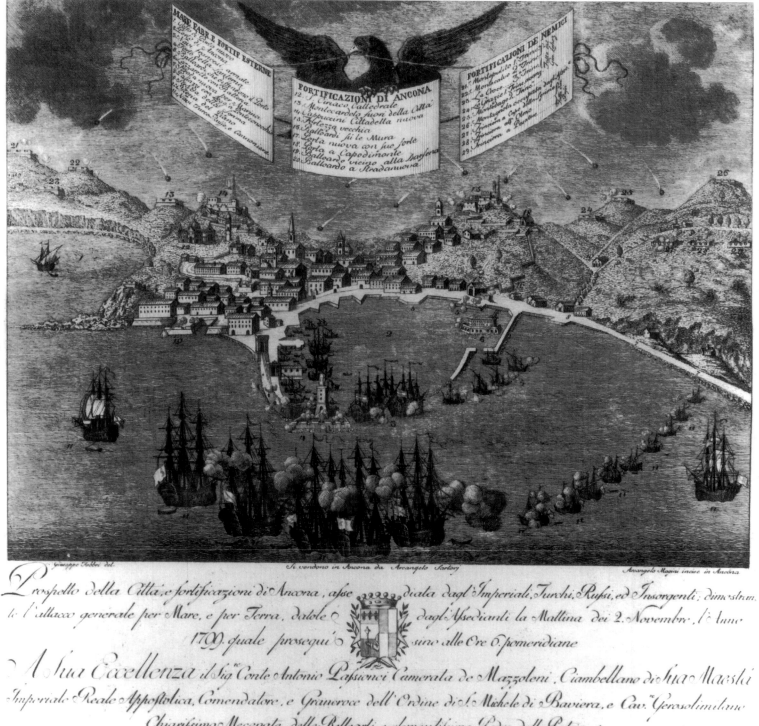

1

Defence of Acre

FOLLOWING Turkey's declaration of war on France, the Porte requested naval support and there was a general feeling in Britain that the antiquated Ottoman forces needed modern technology and training if they were to stand any chance against Bonaparte's veterans. Sir Sidney Smith was sent to Constantinople in advance of a full military mission, but the Cabinet made the unconventional decision to give him plenipotentiary powers to be shared with his brother John Spencer Smith, who was already in residence. He was ordered to take over co-operation with the Turks, and the appointment of a relatively junior naval officer ruffled the feathers of many of his superiors, not least Nelson who objected to losing control of any of his command – his sarcastic references to 'the Swedish Knight' are a sad reflection on a man who would prove all too willing to mention his Sicilian dukedom at every opportunity.

Smith's ship, the 80-gun *Tigre*, arrived in the Ottoman capital on the last day of 1798, and by 5 January guns were booming out to celebrate a new treaty of friendship. The Sultan turned over the Tophane, or arsenal, to Sidney Smith, who put in train the construction of gunboats and flatboats, which he planned to employ in the Nile delta, manned by 1000 Albanian mercenaries he had the government's agreement to hire. The sloop *Bonne Citoyenne* arrived in February with new orders, and Smith sailed to take over the Alexandria blockade (1).

Bonaparte was not content to be cooped up in Egypt and on 7 March Sidney Smith learnt that he had advanced into Syria, Jaffa had fallen and his army was advancing on Acre. Captain Miller in the *Theseus*, 74, was sent on ahead to co-ordinate the defence with the local Pasha, an Albanian soldier-of-fortune whose soubriquet Djezzar – 'slasher' or 'butcher' – summarised his path to power. Smith reasoned that the French heavy equipment would be coming by sea and on the 18th the *Tigre* located a convoy of a corvette and nine gunboats off Mount Carmel, and having chased off the escort, her boats took seven of the gunboats before fog intervened. Almost the whole of the French battering train and associated siege equipment fell into Smith's hands and were rapidly transferred to the decrepit fortifications of Acre; the gunboats themselves were also destined to play a major part in the coming struggle.

The town was still essentially the *enceinte* of the medieval St Jean d'Acre of the crusaders, built on a

2

and the shallow-draught transport *Alliance* was also committed to fire support (3).

Despite overwhelming numbers, Bonaparte's army had its problems. The lost siege train was one, but the army's morale was affected by the hardships of the desert march, the cold-blooded massacre of 3000 prisoners at Jaffa, and, more significantly, by the outbreak of bubonic plague. The attack was opened on 20 March, concentrating on the Accursed Tower, and a breach was rapidly opened (4). A major assault on the breach on the 28th was beaten off, but not before the personal intervention of both Sidney Smith and Djezzar Pasha. In as far as the stylised prints of 'The Hero of Acre' represent any particular incident, this is probably the most likely (5).

The long-expected Turkish relieving army was defeated on 16 April at the foot of Mount Tabor, but the siege dragged on, with mining and counter-mining, assault and bloody repulse. On 7 May, the 51st day of the siege, the French finally gained a footing in the tower, at exactly the moment when a large Turkish fleet hove into view. It then became a race between the French assault troops and the Turkish reinforcements: the defenders just managed to hold off the grand assault of the next day, even though they had to give ground, but the city was saved. A final despairing effort on the 10th failed and Bonaparte turned his mind to extricating his troops – and more importantly – his reputation from the wreckage. After firing off all the spare shells into the city, he broke camp and retreated on the night of 20-21 May, with losses of around 2200 dead and 2300 sick and wounded.

Bonaparte's 'triumphal' entry into Cairo fooled nobody, and reflecting in exile on Sidney Smith he admitted 'that man made me miss my destiny'.

promontary with two exposed land walls converging on the Accursed Tower (so called because supposedly built with Judas's thirty pieces of silver). Much work was needed to make any sort of a defence against a modern army, and marines and seamen laboured on improvising fortifications under the direction of Colonel Phélypeaux, a French royalist friend of Smith. The garrison, of a very mixed assortment of races, comprised about 4000 men, to oppose about three times that number of French. Smith disposed his ships to enfilade the walls, but the advantage of the British ships of the line was offset by the shoal nature of the coast which kept them at extreme range (2). The gunboats formed a closer line,

3

1. 'Constantinople, North View, taken from the Artillery Quay (called Tophana) with H.B.M.'s ships Le Tigre and La Bonne Citoyenne under the command of Sir Sidney Smith, 1799', coloured aquatint engraved by J Jeakes from an original by John Thomas Serres (1759-1825), published by Edward Orme, 1 August 1805. It depicts the time in February 1799 when the sloop had arrived with orders for Sir Sidney to sail for Alexandria.
NMM neg B7135

2. 'View of Acre & H.M. Ship Le Tigre', coloured aquatint engraved by Jeakes after an original by F B Spilsbury and D Orme, printed by Edward Orme and published by Thomas MacLean, 1 January 1819.
NMM ref PAF4679

3. 'St John of Acre Defended by the English under Sir Sidney Smith, against the French under General Buonaparte . . . from 19 March to 21 May 1799', coloured aquatint engraved by J Jeakes after an original by F B Spilsbury and Preaux, published by Edward Orme, 4 June 1803.
NMM neg 3566

4. 'Siege of St John of Acre', anonymous brown ink drawing, no date.
NMM ref PAD5623

5. 'Defence of the Breach at St Jean d'Acre by Sir Sidney Smith', aquatint engraved and published by Anthony Fogg after an original by William Hamilton, 7 April 1802.
NMM neg 3567

1

2

The French stranded in Egypt

HOWEVER conclusive Nelson's victory at the Nile appears to posterity, at the time it left many loose ends. Not only were the French transports untouched, but there remained at Alexandria a significant escort force: two ex-Venetian 64s, eight frigates, four brig sloops as well as two dozen gunboats of varying descriptions. At first Nelson left a small blockading detachment under Sam Hood with *Zealous*, Foley's *Goliath* and Hallowell's *Swiftsure*, plus three of his errant frigates which had finally turned up. In the month or so following the battle, ships of this squadron intercepted Bonaparte's dispatches, cut out a gunboat and ran ashore the advice cutter *Anémone* from Malta—some of the crew of the latter had to be rescued by *Swiftsure* and *Emerald* from the beach at Marabout, when the rest of their party was set upon and butchered by local bedouin (1).

In October the blockade was reinforced by two Russian frigates and a flotilla of Turkish small craft, including gunboats. With the latter, Hallowell made a number of assaults on Aboukir castle (2) and the French camp from the 25th onwards, but even after reinforcing each gunboat with seamen from the *Swiftsure*, he could not get the Turks to press home their attacks. Before the turn of the year the Turkish squadron left the coast, their pin-prick raids being replaced during February 1799 by bombardments of Alexandria by two British bomb vessels, but again without significant results.

After his great success in stopping Bonaparte's advance at Acre, Sir Sidney Smith returned to Constantinople in June 1799 to discharge the second half of his dual commission, as joint plenipotentiary (with his brother Spencer Smith) to the Ottoman Porte. His principal aim was to encourage a large-scale Turkish response, and whatever his personal contribution, by 11

3

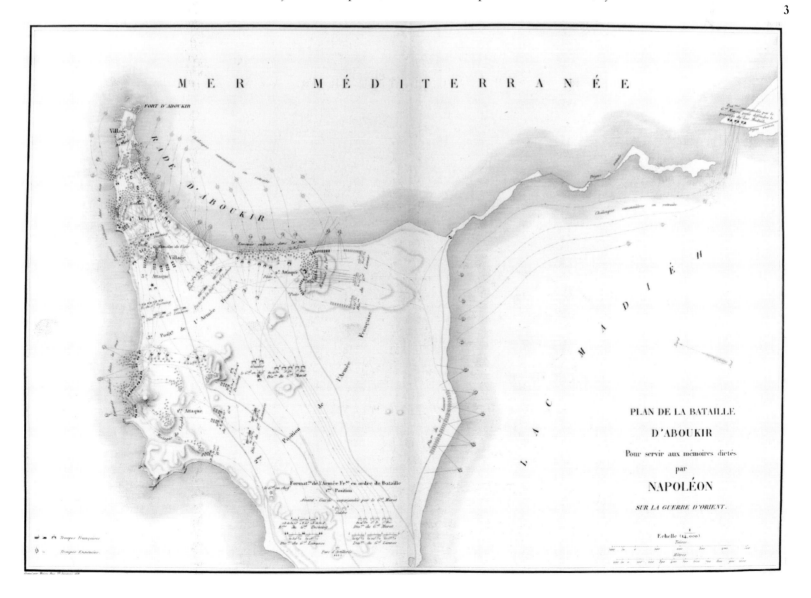

PLAN DE LA BATAILLE

D'ABOUKIR

Pour servir aux mémoires dictés

par

NAPOLÉON

SUR LA GUERRE D'ORIENT.

4

July a fleet of around twenty warships and some sixty transports was anchored off Aboukir. On the 15th the Turks landed, drove in the French defenders and laid siege to the castle on the point. When this surrendered two days later, the Turkish army—variously estimated as between 7000 and 9000 men—instead of marching on Alexandria, dug itself in on the peninsula. Bonaparte moved quickly and on the 25th he launched a precipitate attack on the Turkish lines with around 10,000 men. Turkish resistance folded, and amid great carnage, the survivors retreated into the castle or attempted to swim off to the supporting gunboats (3). A week later the remaining 2500 men surrendered, and on the first anniversary of Nelson's victory, Bonaparte was able to add the second battle of Aboukir to what would become the Napoleonic legend.

During the ensuing negotiations about prisoners, Sidney Smith let the French officers have a number of recent newspapers reporting defeats of their armies in Europe. This was just the excuse Bonaparte needed, and coupled with his latest victory, he judged the time ripe for a return to France. Waiting until Smith withdrew his squadron to Cyprus to provision, Bonaparte with a coterie of favourites set sail on 23 August in the frigates *Muiron* and *Carrère*; eluding all British cruisers he again set foot in mainland France on 9 October. Deserting the army in Egypt was a great propaganda opportunity, which British cartoonists were quick to exploit— Gillray's cartoon of March 1800 (4) depicts a vision in the sky of a sceptre and imperial crown, demonstrating that Bonaparte's ambitions were clear enough to his enemies.

The British were handed another propaganda coup, when the Navy intercepted dispatches from General Kléber (5), who had been left in command. Published by order of the British government, they revealed a profound sense of betrayal: '. . . Bonaparte quitted this country for France . . . without saying a word of his intention to any person whatever. He appointed me to meet him at Rosetta on the subsequent day!' However, there was a potentially serious sting in the tail: for political reasons of his own, Kléber understated the size and efficiency of his army, and his statements were taken at face value by the British when they came to plan the expeditionary force of 1801.

1. 'Swiftsure, Emerald off Alexandria 5 April 1800', aquatint engraved by T Hall after an original by John Theophilus Lee, published by Joyce Gold, 31 August 1807.
NMM ref PAD5640

2. 'The Attack of the Turkish Gun-boats on the Castle of Aboukir 23 October 1798', coloured aquatint engraved by Joseph Constantine Stadler after an original by Cooper Willyams, published by I White, 1801.
NMM ref PAD5641

3. Plan of Turkish landings at Aboukir and Damietta, plate from Napoleon Bonaparte, *Campagnes d'Égypte et de Syrie 1798-1799: Mémoires . . . Napoleon dictés par lui-mÍme . . . et publiés par le Général Bertrand* (Paris 1847).
Chatham collection

4. 'Buonaparte leaving Egypt', coloured etching by James Gillray, published by H Humphrey, 8 May 1800.
NMM ref PAF3965

5. 'Jean-Baptiste Kléber', lithograph engraved by Ducarne, published by Blaisot, no date.
NMM ref PAD8262

5

2

1

The siege of Malta

WHEN Bonaparte sailed for Egypt he left behind a garrison of 3000 under General Vaubois, who set about the secularisation of Malta with the usual republican vigour. Since the Maltese had refused to fight for the Knights, the French did not anticipate opposition, but they made themselves very unpopular very quickly—principally by offending the islanders' religious susceptibilities. The French were very short of hard cash and attempted to sell off the sequested property of churches and convents. On 2 September 1798 a riot occasioned by one such auction escalated into an island-wide insurrection led by Emmanuel Vitale and Canon Saverio Caruana.

The French were rapidly driven into the fortified area around Valletta, but the Maltese lacked the weapons to carry out either an assault or a formal siege. On the 19th a Portuguese squadron of four 74s (1) under the Marques de Niza arrived off Malta with orders from Nelson to blockade the island. They were joined by Saumarez in the *Orion* on the 23rd, and when the Maltese petitioned for help some arms were landed, but Saumarez's summons to surrender was curtly rebuffed by Vaubois. Nelson had considerable difficulty getting the Portuguese to obey orders and when they left their station,

Admiral Villeneuve's flagship the *Guillaume Tell* and the frigates *Justice* and *Diane*, refugees from the debacle at Aboukir, managed to slip into Grand Harbour with news of the defeat.

Nelson could not get the Neapolitans, the nominal suzerains of Malta, to shoulder responsibility, so on 25 October he sent Captain Ball of the *Alexander*, 74, to take command of the blockading forces. Ball (2) soon endeared himself to the Maltese, and scored an early success with the capture of Gozo, but again Vaubois and Villeneuve refused his generous offer of repatriation. Although the French controlled Valletta and its adjacent harbours, the British were able to mount the sea blockade from St Paul's Bay and Marsa Scirocco—modern Marsaxlokk—even if it did mean that the occasional vessel slipped through the cordon.

Ball's main problem was that Malta was not self-sufficient in food, being traditionally dependent on Sicily, which had declared an embargo since the French occupation. However, heroic exertions by Ball—and indeed other officers of the British fleet—kept the ragged and hungry insurgents in the field. With the major campaign in Italy diverting attention, and the status of Malta being a matter of Great Power dispute, Nelson could

3

4

never get sufficient resources to prosecute the siege with any hope of quick success. Although hopes were raised by the arrival of a Russian fleet under Ushakov, it was ordered to join the Turks beseiging Corfu.

In May 1799 Ball had to lift the blockade for two months because Bruix's fleet was at large in the Mediterranean and he was ordered to join his chief; the French were able to bring in some supplies as a result. At this time 3000 professional soldiers behind the strongest walls in Europe were blockaded by 500 English and Portuguese marines and what Ball termed 'about 1500 armed peasants', so no very speedy conclusion could be expected. General Erskine, the British army commander in the Mediterranean, had refused to transfer troops from the local garrisons, but the new C-in-C, General

Fox, agreed to Nelson's urgent request for troops to replace the Portuguese who had orders from home to return to Lisbon. Some 800 British troops under Brigadier-General Graham were sent from Messina to Malta in December 1799. Although blockaded, the fortifications of Valletta were too strong to be assaulted, or even damaged (3, 4).

Graham reported that he needed a larger force, and eventually in February 1800 some 1200 Neapolitan troops were embarked in the combined squadron of Nelson and the new Commander of the Mediterranean Fleet, Lord Keith. After landing the army at Marsa Scirocco Keith cruised off Valletta (5), but Nelson's luck was again apparent when his squadron intercepted a French relieving force on the 16th. Thanks to the audac-

5

ity of the little frigate *Success*, which threw herself into the track of the French flagship, Nelson's ships were able to overtake and disperse the force, capturing a transport and the 74-gun *Généreux*, one of the two battleships that had escaped him at the Nile.

If he had been able to tear himself away from the Neapolitan court for longer, Nelson might have had the other refugee as well, for the damaged *Guillaume Tell* had been refitted (6) and was preparing to make a break for France freighted with some of the garrison's sick and wounded. She sailed on the night of 30 March and might have escaped but for the vigilance of Captain Blackwood's *Penelope*, which fought a skilful extended version of *Success*'s 16 February delaying action (7). At dawn the frigate was joined by the 64-gun *Lion* and the two ships harried their prey until the *Foudroyant* – a match in firepower for the French 80 – could come up (8). Berry, Nelson's flag captain, had recently arrived back on station after delivering his admiral to Palermo, and was slow to believe the reports of *Guillaume Tell*'s sortie, but once *Foudroyant* was in action there was no hope for the French ship, which when totally dismasted was forced to surrender with casualties of 200 from her crowded complement of 1200 (9). If Nelson himself was not present, at least his flagship was instrumental in the capture of the last Nile battleship.

For the French garrison the final blow was the decision by the new commander of British land forces in the area, General Abercromby, to press home the siege, and for that purpose he ordered 1500 troops under Major-General Pigot to the island in July 1800. The French were reduced to breaking up one of their frigates for fuel, and on 24 August the remaining two were ordered to make a

dash for it – *La Justice* escaped, but *La Diane* was captured and papers aboard the ship revealed how close the garrison was to capitulation. Negotiations were soon opened and on 5 September the stubborn resistance ended on terms. Of the three major warships still in Grand Harbour (10), only the 64-gun *Athénien* (11) was of any value, and both the *Dégo* and the frigate *La Cartaginoise* never again went to sea.

Vaubois had refused to surrender to anyone except the British – not even Ball as Maltese Governor was allowed to sign the capitulation – which only exacerbated the

6

7

1. 'Vascello di Secondo Rango Portoghese', anonymous watercolour, 1780. *NMM ref PAF8221*

2. 'Rear-Admiral Sir Alexander John Ball', oil painting by Henry William Pickersgill (1782-1875). *NMM ref BHC2528*

3. 'This view of La Valletta, taken from the Marsa Battery during the Siege in 1800', coloured aquatint and etching by Francis Chesham after an original by Major J Weir, published by the artist 25 January 1803. *NMM ref PAG9002*

4. 'This view of La Valletta, taken from the Gargur Battery during the Siege in 1800', coloured aquatint and etching by Francis Chesham after an original by Major J Weir, published by the artist 25 January 1803. *NMM ref PAG9003*

5. 'Blockade of Malta', watercolour illustration by the author from the Rev Cooper Willyams, *A Voyage up the Mediterranean* (London 1802). Lord Keith off Malta in February 1800. The ships are (right to left), the cutter *Flora*, Keith's flagship *Queen Charlotte*, Nelson's flagship *Foudroyant*, the 74-gun *Audacious* and 64-gun *Lion*; the frigate *Caroline* is inshore. *NMM neg D8619B*

already controversial nature of the island's status. During the siege the Maltese had offered the sovereignty of the island to Britain, but it was regarded as legally Neapolitan by the Kingdom of the Two Sicilies, and was coveted by Russia which wanted to reinstall the Knights of which the Tsar was now Grand Master. For its part, France preferred anyone but Britain in possession and insisted upon its evacuation under the Treaty of Amiens. The British ultimately refused to comply, which was a major contributor to the drift back to war in 1803, and the island remained British until independence in 1964.

8

9

10

11

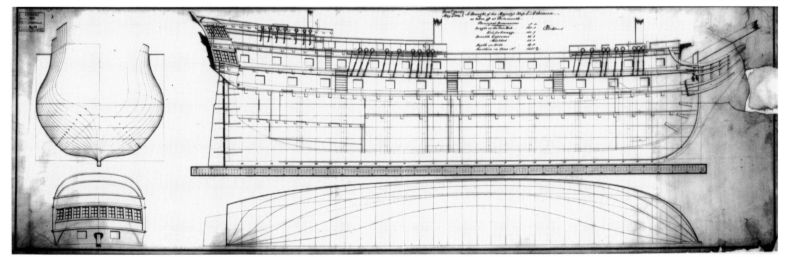

6. 'French two-decker fitting out', anonymous brown pen and ink, from a signal book, no date.
NMM ref PAH5078

7. 'The Disabled situation of the Guillaume Tell of 84 Guns . . . as she appeared at daylight on the 30th March 1800, after having been engaged by His Majesty's Ship Penelope . . . the Stromboli brig, Lion & Foudroyant coming up, by the two latter of which she was afterwards engaged', aquatint engraved by James Wells after an original by Nicholas Pocock (1740-1821), published by the artist 1 March 1805.
NMM ref PAH7973

8. 'Taking of the Guillaume Tell 31 March 1800', watercolour by Nicholas Pocock (1740-1821), 1802.
NMM ref PAF5878

9. 'Taking of the Guillaume Tell 31 March 1800', watercolour by Nicholas Pocock (1740-1821), 1802.
NMM ref PAF5879

10. 'Entrance to the Harbour of Valletta, Malta', watercolour by Percy W Justyn c1850. The blockading squadron's view from 1798 to 1800.
NMM ref PAD8961

11. Lines and profile of the *Athenienne* ex-*Athénien* as captured.
NMM ref 7260

1

The Mediterranean Fleet under Keith

1. 'Defense de Genes (25 Mai 1800) Bombardment de la ville par les Anglais', steel engraving by Skelton after an original by Bagetti, no date. *NMM ref PAD5636*

2. 'French galley at Marseilles', watercolour by Antoine Roux, 1816. Somewhat larger but generally similar to the *Prima*. *NMM ref PAG9744*

3. *Flora* and *Caroline* reconnoitring Santa Cruz, watercolour by Thomas Buttersworth (1768-1842). This is an earlier reconnaissance, the *Caroline*, interestingly, being disguised as a Spanish merchant ship to get closer to the well-defended port. According to the artist the date is 30 September 1798 but the ships' logs make it 13 or 14 October; they were searching for two reported Spanish 'galleons' but they were not present. *Peabody Essex Museum, Salem MA neg 18197*

4. 'Vista Primera de la Carraca', engraving and etching by Joachim after an original by Pedro Grollierz, no date. *NMM ref PAI0025*

ALTHOUGH he had deputised for St Vincent for some time, Lord Keith took over the formal command of the Mediterranean fleet in January 1800. Besides the continuing commitments to the blockade of Egypt and the siege of Malta, his principal strategic task was to co-operate with the Austrian armies against French possessions in northern Italy. British warships harried French communications along the length of the Riviera and Ligurian coasts, and smaller craft did their best to prevent all French coastal traffic.

2

3

Once the Austrian army had occupied Savona, driving a wedge between Nice and Genoa, a large part of the French Army of Italy was effectively isolated in the latter port. Genoa was promptly besieged by the Austrians and blockaded from the sea by Keith's fleet (1). During May the city was bombarded on a number of occasions by the fleet's cruisers and small craft, ably supported by a force of Neapolitan gunboats. The French improvised a defence flotilla, led by a large galley called the *Prima* which was armed with two long 36pdrs (2). In the confined waters of the harbour, the galley was a potent weapon to which the British could offer no counter—so a daring cutting-out expedition was launched on the

night of 20-21 May, which successfully brought off the troublesome vessel. If purchased the prize would have been the first genuine galley in the Royal Navy since Henry VIII's day, but a craft propelled by slaves was clearly out of the question and she was sold to the Sardinians.

Genoa was starved into submission on 4 June, but was no sooner occupied than news arrived of Bonaparte's lightning strike across the Alps. His crushing victory over the Austrians at Marengo on the 14th followed by an armistice put the French back in control of much of north Italy, and Genoa itself was reoccupied by a French army on the 22nd, the *Minotaur*, 74 having to be hurriedly warped out beyond the mole. Plans for landing a

4

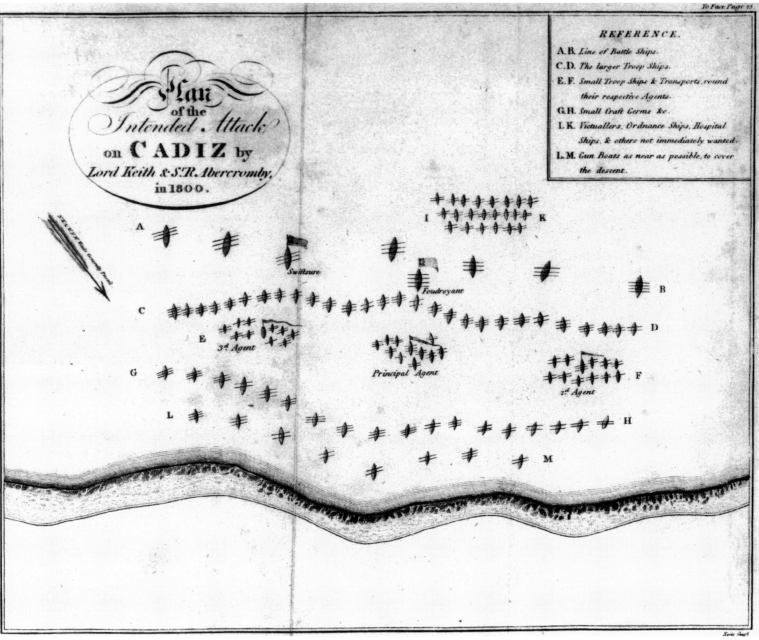

To Face Page 75

REFERENCE.

A.B. *Line of Battle Ships.*
C.D. *The larger Troop Ships.*
E.F. *Small Troop Ships & Transports, round their respective Agents.*
G.H. *Small Craft Germs &c.*
I.K. *Victuallers, Ordnance Ships, Hospital Ships, & others not immediately wanted.*
L.M. *Gun Boats as near as possible, to cover the descent.*

Plan of the Intended Attack on CADIZ *by Lord Keith & Sr R. Abercromby, in 1800.*

5

5. 'Plan of the Intended Attack on Cadiz by Lord Keith & Sr R Abercromby in 1800', etching by Samuel John Neele, published by Richard Phillips, 30 November 1805. *NMM ref PAD5633*

6. 'A view of Cadiz &c as it appeared on the 5th Oct. 1800, from HMS Hector then at anchor distant 5 miles', from Aeneas Anderson, *A journal of the Forces which sailed from the Downs in April 1800 . . .* (London 1802), p76. *Chatham collection*

7. 'View of Porto Ferrajo from the Sea', coloured aquatint engraved by Francis Jukes from an original by Captain James Weir, published by James Daniell, April 1814. *NMM ref PAH2435*

British force under the new army commander, Abercromby, were rapidly shelved, the effort being transferred to concluding the siege of Malta (duly achieved with the French surrender in September).

British army operations during 1800 followed an almost unbelievable sequence of ambiguous orders, changed priorities, hesitancy and missed opportunities. On the Biscay coast, attacks on Belleisle, Ferrol and Vigo had been brought close to execution, only to be abandoned on feeble pretexts, and Keith received a similar set of rapidly altering instructions. At one point he was told to reconnoitre Santa Cruz in preparation for a possible landing (3), and he went as far as to obtain a sketch of its defences from Nelson, who having lost an arm in one attack on the port might be expected to remember

where the opposition came from. The Ferrol and Vigo attacks had been designed to weaken the remaining units of the Spanish fleet not actually sheltering with the French at Brest, and further operation was intended against Cadiz, and in particular the facilities of La Carraca (4), the dockyard just outside the city proper.

The operation was mounted in October under the joint commands of Keith and Abercromby, but however neat the plans may have looked (5), in practice the preparations were not well executed. The ships remained at least five miles offshore—(6) is a view from one of the troopships present—and there were too few boats for the intended assault. The commanders fell out over guarantees for evacuating the troops if the bad weather then in prospect actually intervened, and to cap

6

the problems for the decision-makers, a Spanish boat came off to inform them that yellow fever raged in the city. Plague or storm, whichever weighed more heavily may never be known, but the assault was abandoned, adding another embarrassment to that year's dismal record in amphibious operations. After what one historian termed 'an ignominious Cook's tour of the western Mediterranean', the army was finally ordered to prepare for evicting the French from Egypt, a task ably discharged during 1801.

The activities of the Mediterranean fleet were still inextricably linked to the land campaigns in Italy, and in March 1801 the French, having been ceded the Neapolitan part of Elba, decided to take over the Tuscan portion, including the well-fortified harbour of Porto Ferrajo (7). They were opposed by small British squadrons, and the French blockading forces lost the frigates *Carrère*, *Succès* and *Bravoure* in fighting around the island; it had still not fallen to the French by the time of the peace of Amiens.

7

1

The loss of the *Queen Charlotte*

THE GREATEST loss sustained by the Royal Navy throughout the French Revolutionary War was occasioned not by enemy action but through an accident. In March the flagship of the Mediterranean Fleet, the 100-gun *Queen Charlotte*, at that time the second largest ship in the Navy, was stationed off Leghorn (1). Lord Keith and some of his staff were ashore liaising with the Austrian army, and the ship was dispatched to reconnoitre the island of Capraia, a possible future tar-

get of allied interest. On the morning of the 17th, while still in sight of the shore, the ship caught fire and eventually blew up.

According to one survivor, the carpenter John Baird, the fire was discovered about 6.20 in the morning, and before he could get on deck the flames had engulfed the half deck, the covers of the boats on the booms and the coat of the main mast. The main course could not be clewed up in time and soon caught fire as well, begin-

2

ning the spread of the fire through the rigging. Because of the smoke Baird could not see what if any action was being taken on the quarterdeck, and spent the next few hours on the lower deck with Lieutenant Dundas fighting a valiant battle to keep the fire from penetrating to the bowels of the ship. By plugging the scuppers and securing the hatches they were able to open the stopcocks of the ship's inlet pipes to flood the deck. They only abandoned their station when guns began falling through from the fire-damaged middle deck above. From the forecastle it was clear that the efforts of the firefighters were having no real effect, and after helping in the bucket chain for about an hour Baird decided to swim to a merchantman standing off the bow.

The fire raged for over four hours (2) before it reached the after magazine, when there was a huge explosion and the ship sank rapidly. Despite the proximity of the ship to the shore, and the long period during which the crew could have been taken off, the losses were very heavy—according to Lord Keith himself, 37 officers and 599 seamen were lost. That only 11 and 143 respectively were saved he blamed on the unwillingness of the local boats to get too close (the guns may have been loaded, as certainly was the case with the *Boyne* in 1795). In a macabre coda to the whole episode, a few days later the brig *Speedy* ran into wreckage from the ship, and for some unknown reason an artist decided to record the event (3).

Even the court martial seems to have accepted the thesis that the fire was started by a match from the signal-gun tub on the quarterdeck lighting bales of hay kept under the half deck. However, it did not address, let alone answer, the question of why a fire in so obvious a place could take such a hold before it was noticed. Although no overt allegations were made, there was a widespread feeling in the fleet that neither the ship's discipline nor its morale were of the highest state. The ship had been deeply implicated in the Spithead mutiny, and many echoed St Vincent's view that the ship was still a source of disaffection. Seamen, it is true, had a particular horror of fire—in the days of fireships crews of target vessels often abandoned ship long before the fire took an irrevocable hold—but there must remain the suspicion that a more disciplined crew might have saved the ship.

1. 'This View Representing the City and Port of Leghorn in Tuscany, H.M. Ship Queen Charlotte, and one of H.R.H. The Grand Duke's Galleys, is humbly dedicated to Rt Honble George Lord Keith, KB, by John Chessell, Royal Navy', coloured aquatint engraved by J B Harraden after an original by John Chessell, published by the artist, 20 April 1803. *NMM neg B256*

2. 'The Burning of the Queen Charlotte of 110 guns Lord Keith's flagship off the harbour of Leghorn, March 17 1800', anonymous coloured aquatint, no date. *NMM ref PAD6035*

3. 'HM Sloop Speedy falling in with the wreck of Queen Charlotte March 21 1800 at Leghorn', anonymous watercolour, no date. *NMM ref PAF7970*

3

The invasion of Egypt – an opposed landing

1

IN STARK contrast to its sister service, the British Army had known little but defeat and failure since the beginning of the war. Where the Navy had won victories over every enemy pitted against it, the Army had gone from bad to worse, reaching a depth by the end of 1800 after the fiascos of Holland, Belleisle, Ferrol and Cadiz where Lord Cornwallis could describe it as 'the scorn and laughing stock of friends and foes'. Nor was the Navy sympathetic: St Vincent was known to look forward to the abolition of the whole army, except the Guards and the Artillery, and its replacement by an expanded corps of Marines.

To be fair, much of its recent failure was the product of Cabinet-level dithering and rapidly altered priorities – and hot on the heels of the Cadiz embarrassment, another set of orders arrived, instructing this demoralised and inexperienced force to prepare itself for an invasion of Egypt, where it would face the veterans of Bonaparte's old Army of Italy. The government was worried that with France once again victorious in Europe, Bonaparte would revive his eastern schemes;

furthermore, with peace negotiations in prospect, the eviction of their army from Egypt would give the French one less bargaining counter.

Luckily for its future reputation, the British Army in the Mediterranean was commanded by Lt-General Sir Ralph Abercromby (1), who although he was no original thinker was a fine administrator who excelled in the training of men. To prepare for the invasion, the fleet of troopships, carrying some 14,000 men put into Marmaris (2) on the coast of Asia Minor where the British expected to find horses, provisions and landing craft collected from their Turkish allies. Today Marmaris is known as a holiday destination for European tourists, but at that time its magnificent bay was unfamiliar to the Royal Navy and Commander Charles Inglis of the sloop *Peterel* has left a lively description of how it was only his local knowledge that allowed the fleet to be brought in safely: it was blowing hard and visibility was poor, and when land loomed through the mist the ships were apparently steering a course directly towards the wave-lashed cliffs, but the *Peterel* altered course sharply

2

3

at the last moment when a huge and sheltered natural harbour was revealed.

To Abercromby's dismay, there were none of the anticipated supplies, and it was to be seven weeks before an adequate stockpile could be assembled. However, the army set about solving its problems with great energy, and began to collect the horses and hire the local small craft needed as landing craft (3). The unavoidable delay was also well spent in detailed planning, preparing specialist equipment, like gabions and fascines, and in training the troops in the techniques of amphibious assault. The close co-operation with the Navy was fruitful and some innovative solutions were found – like the use of lines of concave mast-fishes as tracks over soft sand for the wheels of gun carriages. By the time the expedition left Marmaris at the end of February 1801, it was probably the best-prepared British amphibious force since the Seven Years War.

It would need to be. Its biggest shortcoming was in accurate intelligence, both at the strategic level where the numbers of French troops were wildly underestimated (there were 30,000 rather than the calculated 13,000) and at the tactical level since the staff lacked detailed maps of Egypt or any local knowledge. Admittedly, the morale of the French army was low. At the beginning of 1800 they had agreed under the Convention of El Arish to evacuate Egypt but the agreement worked out by Sir Sidney Smith was then repudiated by Lord Keith with the government's approval. Then in June their beloved general Kléber had been assassinated and replaced by Menou, who was not only less competent but as a Muslim convert was something of a joke among his troops.

Nevertheless, when the British fleet arrived off Aboukir on 2 March 1801 the French were ready for them. Furthermore, bad weather forced the landings to be postponed until the 8th, and for the week that the troopships rode out the storm in full view of the coast the French were able to reinforce their beach defences to about 2000 men under General Friant. Because of the

4

5

ing position, where they were directed into line by Captain Alexander Cochrane from the brig *Mondovi*.

The disposition of the assault force, some 5500 strong, is represented with reasonable accuracy by two presumably eyewitness sketches (4,5), which show the topography of the bay, with Aboukir fort to the left. The two large ships are the bombs *Fury* and *Tartarus* (this latter Abercromby's headquarters), with the *Mondovi* in attendance. The broader view also shows, inshore and on the flanks, the support flotillas made up of gunboats and small craft, while the other depicts the lines of boats led by launches carrying the camp colours of the individual battalions.

To the surprise and confusion of the French, who had opened up a seemingly impenetrable wall of roundshot, grape and small-arms fire, the assault lines came on in parade order and in about five minutes most of the first wave were ashore (6). It provoked the admiration of the French general Bertrand, who writing up the campaign, compared it to a movement on an opera stage. Fighting was fierce (see de Loutherbourg's magnificent conception of the event used as the frontispiece), but short-lived, and at the end of the morning the British were firmly lodged on the Aboukir peninsula. They had

6

shoal nature of the coast, the big ships had to moor five miles off, but the rigour of the planning at Marmaris now came into play: the problem had been anticipated, and the second wave was pre-positioned inshore in the small local craft, the initial assault being delivered direct from the transports. There were 180 boats for infantry (58 of them the specialist flatboats) and 28 for artillery, and by dawn they had advanced past the local craft to their hold-

achieved what was so rarely possible in the age of sail, a successful landing in the teeth of organised opposition.

The plan was to advance on Alexandria before Menou could bring up reinforcements from Cairo, and on the 13th the British met and defeated an inferior force under Lanusse at Mandara. The Army was elated by its successes, but it had still to meet the main French force. These arrived unexpectedly out of the dawn mist on the 21st, precipitating a hard-fought battle, in which the British eventually gained a significant defensive victory, albeit at the cost of Abercromby, whose habit of leading from the front finally cost him his life. The Navy was active in support, launches and gunboats under Captains Hillyar and Maitland being employed to protect the flanks of the British positions (7). The command devolved on to Major-General Sir John Hely-Hutchinson and the advance ground to a halt before the strongly defended Heights of Nicopolis to the east of Alexandria (8).

1. 'Sir Ralph Abercromby', anonymous crayon manner engraving, no date.
NMM ref PAD4359

2. 'View of Marmorice Bay on the Coast of Sirie from on board H M Ship Dictator the First of Jany 1801', watercolour by Francis Carpenter and J Pulley, no date. The expedition had arrived the previous day, and this is probably an eyewitness view.
NMM ref PAH2641

3. 'Sketch of various sorts of vessels in the Adriatic, including a zebek and a trabacolo, inscribed with vessel types below image', watercolour by Lieutenant William Innes Pocock (1783-1863), no date.
NMM ref PAF0048

4. 'Three fighting ships amongst a flotilla of small vessels off the coast of Egypt', coloured aquatint published by Thomas Cadell and William Davies, 2 May 1805.
NMM ref PAF4720

5. 'The landing in Egypt, 8 March 1801', anonymous black and watercolour pen and ink, no date.
NMM ref PAG9695

6. 'Aboukir 1801', halftone reproduction of an original by N Dupray, no date. This is not a contemporary picture, and can be faulted in details, but does convey the drama of the occasion.
NMM ref PAD4112

7. 'Plan of the Action of the 21st of March Fought near Alexandria by the French under General Menou and the English under Sir Ralph Abercrombie', plate from R T Wilson, *History of the British Expedition to Egypt* (London 1803).
Chatham collection

8. 'View of the French Fortified Heights to the Eastward of Alexandria', Plate 25 from Thomas Walsh, *Journal of the Late Campaign in Egypt* (London 1803). The ruins of the ancient walls of Alexandria can be seen in the foreground; the main French works are Fort Cretin (centre) and Fort Cafarelli (left).
Chatham collection

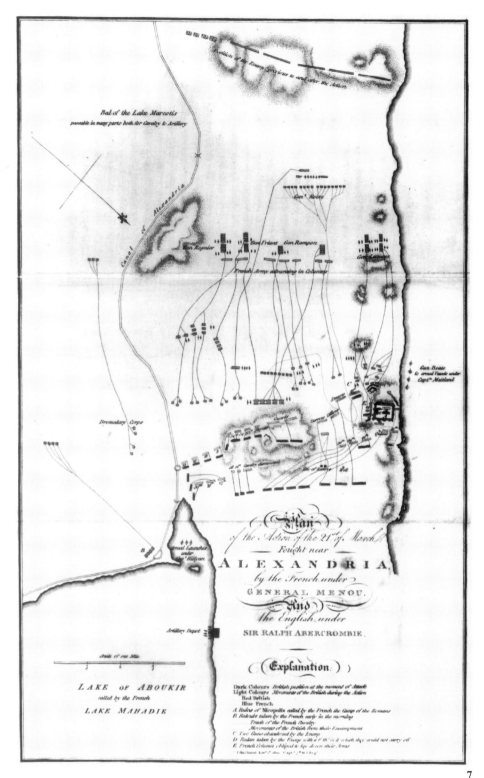

7

8

nce, N° 1 English Camp, N° 2 English advanced Camp, N° 3 On the Hill referr'd by this N° the English and French Centinals are Posted amongst the Trees, N° 4 A fortified Hill possessed by the French w

View of Alexandria w

1

Victory in Egypt

IF THEY but realised it, the British army in Egypt was heavily outnumbered, and the battles since the landing had reduced its effective numbers to about 9000. It was not strong enough to advance, and by April 1801 a stalemate had developed on the Aboukir peninsula—as sketched from on board one of Keith's squadron (1). The Navy was impatient with the lack of progress, and Keith was kept on tenterhooks by reports of relieving forces that might catch his fleet at the same disadvantage as Bruey's in 1798. Nor were these illusory, for Admiral Ganteaume made a number of attempts, which although thwarted were never conclusively defeated.

Hutchinson, in command since Abercromby's death, was unexpectedly reinforced by 4000 men of the Capitan Pacha—the commander of the Ottoman navy—some of which were Balkan troops trained in European methods. Thus strengthened, he decided to hold the Alexandria front and strike in the opposite direction, marching a force across the desert to capture Rosetta and give access to the Nile. At the same time the canal dykes were cut and the dry bed of Lake Mareotis was flooded; this cut off Alexandria from supplies, but also strengthened the British position on the peninsula. Both developments led to increased activity by the Navy's gunboats and armed launches.

Leaving General Eyre Coote to blockade Alexandria, Hutchinson transferred the bulk of his forces to the Nile and began a very successful advance on Cairo. As he

2

moved south his course converged with the advancing Turkish army of the Grand Vizier, which had reached El Arish on the Egyptian border by the time the British had won their initial victories (2). It was a large and motley assortment of units, but despite how easily the French had routed similar forces, on 16 May it actually beat a French army under Belliard. This sealed the fate of Cairo, and after enduring a short siege it surrendered on 22 June – and to the utter amazement of the British, who thought the city defended by fewer than 6000 and had agreed on this basis to ship them back to France, nearly 14,000 marched out.

This left only Alexandria to subdue, and Hutchinson was cheered by news of a 6000-strong force from India landed at the head of the Red Sea, although in the event they did not arrive in time to see action. Unfortunately, illness held up his plans, and it was not until August that active operations were recommenced. Coote's brigades, which included the Guards (3-5), were now given the chance of the action denied them all summer while tediously watching Alexandria. They were landed to the west of the city, and with their landward flanks protected by Navy gunboats, and – once the fort at Marabout had been captured – by sloops which entered the old harbour of Alexandria to seaward. Surrounded, the French asked for an armistice on 26 August and on the 30th terms of capitulation were agreed, some 11,000 including civilians being added to the numbers to be repatriated to France. Ships captured in the harbour were shared with the Turks, the most valuable British acquisitions being the huge 24pdr-armed frigate *L'Egyptienne* and the small but fast-sailing *Régénérée*, 36. On 2 September, the British occupied Alexandria (6) in fine style, their grenadiers marching to the tune 'The Downfall of Paris'.

3

4

5

It was the Army's victory, and richly deserved, but the Navy had played a significant part in terms of logistics and fire support. But, most importantly, it was sea-power that made the campaign possible at all.

1. 'View of Alexandria with the position of the English Camp, distant 6 Miles, Sketched on board HMS Renown April 12th 1801 and copied by R F Hawkins', watercolour by R F Hawkins, 12 April 1801.
NMM ref PAD8520

2.'El Arish with the Grand Vizier's camp in 1801', graphite and watercolour by Lieutenant-Colonel Charles Hamilton Smith, no date (the Turkish army arrived at El Arish on 30 March of that year, and left on 19 April). Note that in contrast to European strictures about the lack of all discipline and arrangement in the Turkish camp, the tents are pitched in an apparently orderly fashion.
NMM ref PAF6145

3. 'Guards on and off duty at Alexandria, ca. 1804', coloured aquatint and etching by J Powell and Frederick Christian Lewis after an original by Captain Walker, published by Thompson, January 1804.This series showing the siege lines before Nicopolis must date from the summer of 1801.
NMM ref PAH2863

4. 'Guards camp at Alexandria ca. 1804', coloured aquatint and etching by J Powell and Frederick Christian Lewis after an original by Captain Walker, published by Thompson, January 1804.
NMM ref PAH2864

5. 'Transporting supplies, Alexandria, ca. 1804', coloured aquatint and etching by J Powell and Frederick Christian Lewis after an original by Captain Walker, published by Thompson, January 1804.
NMM ref PAH2865

6. 'Part of the New City of Alexandria, with the Light House', coloured aquatint engraved by Thomas Milton after an original by L Mayer, published by R Bowyer, 1802.
NMM ref PAH2868

6

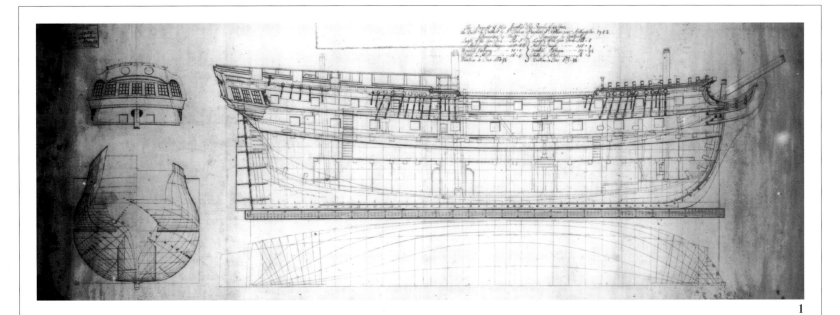

1

Ships of the Royal Navy: the 44-gun two-decker

A S A cruising class the day of the 44-gun two-decker was over by 1793; indeed, for all its effectiveness, it should have been totally extinct. To all intents and purposes the type had been replaced in the 1750s by the new 36- and 32-gun frigates, but the peculiar conditions of the war against the American colonists lead to a revival of the type in 1776. The later 44s had 18pdr lower deck guns, which gave them an advantage over existing frigates—then armed with 9pdrs or 12pdrs—and two decks gave the 44s the moral authority of miniature ships of the line (see *Navies and the American Revolution* in this series).

Like all small two-deckers, their sailing qualities could not compare with frigates and as soon as France entered the war in 1778 a new class of 18pdr single-decked cruiser was developed in 38- and 36-gun forms. Although the new frigates were superior in virtually every way, they were expensive ships and the older type, with the theoretical advantage of concentrated fire from two decks, retained powerful advocates within the Navy's establishment. As a result, twenty-seven 44s were ordered during the American Revolutionary War, leaving the Navy with a large number of relatively new ships in 1793 (1).

However, in the meantime official thinking had moved against the 44 as a cruiser, and the influential Comptroller, Sir Charles Middleton, found a more profitable use for them as fast transports. He believed that the amphibious strategy usually adopted by Britain was compromised by the length of time necessary to hire suitable merchant shipping and the subsequent slow sailing of the troop convoys, losing the element of strategic surprise. He advocated assembling a force of

coppered—and hence fast-sailing—navy-owned transports that could be instantly available. The perfect type for this task was the 44: it was obsolescent as a cruising ship, but was fast compared with most merchantmen; it had two decks and hence plenty of room for troops or stores, but could still be partially armed for self-defence so might need no convoy; it could stow the flatboats used as landing craft (2); and best of all, there were a number of relatively new hulls available. In fact, many of those ordered in the closing stages of the American War were still on the stocks in the mid-1780s and were completed as troopers or storeships during the so-called 'Dutch Armament' of 1787, a limited mobilisation in reaction to a political crisis in the Netherlands.

The majority of 44s served in these auxiliary capacities after war broke out with Revolutionary France in 1793. Few of the colonial expeditions of the war were without an ex-44: *Woolwich* acted as a storeship to the Martinique expedition of 1794; *Ulysses* and *Argo* were present at the capture of Minorca in 1798; *Regulus* carried troops on a number of West Indian operations in 1797-98 and

1. Lines and profile of *Regulus*, as built 1785
NMM neg DR1759/32

2. Contemporary mid eighteenth-century models of flatboats, the specialist landing craft developed by the Royal Navy during the Seven Years War. Troops sat in two rows along the centreline, with seamen oarsmen outboard. They sometimes carried light swivel guns in the bow and later far more powerful carronades for clearing the beach before landing. By the removal of thwarts, the boats could be carried on the decks of troopships nested inside one another.
NMM neg A1109

2

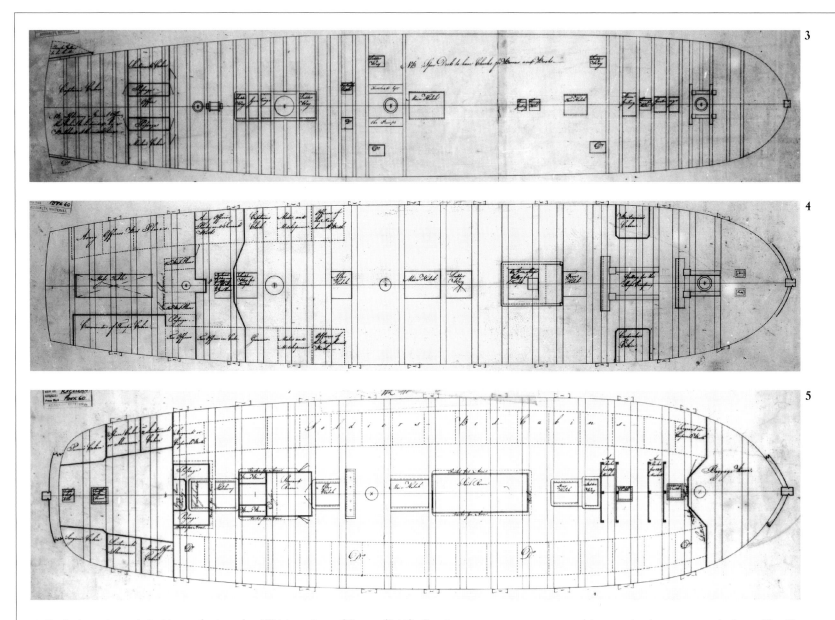

3. 'Plan for fitting the spar deck of the Regulus of 44 Guns for a Troop Ship', dated 24 April 1810. A poop was added, to be shared between the captain and, if one was embarked, a general officer. The plan notes that the spar deck is to be fitted for chocks and boats (ship's boats and flatboats). *NMM neg DR4200/60*

4. As above: upper deck. The army officers sleep and mess aft, and there are separate ladderways for troops and the ship's officers. The troops' galley is also on this deck, just forward of amidships. *NMM neg DR4199/60*

5. As above: gundeck. The troops slept and messed on this deck in what appear to be canvas-partitioned 'cabins', with the ship's officers aft. The main modifications were arms racks - two for 125 muskets each athwartship abaft the forward scuttles - and others around the centreline storerooms. *NMM neg DR4198/60*

during the 1801 invasion of Egypt (3,4,5); *Serapis* was at Surinam in 1804; and *Ulysses* at Martinique in 1808. They had some disadvantages as Captain Henry Browne found, in that they were still run as warships: 'The Officers of the Regiment also, having been used to embark on board Transports, and little accustomed to the precise arrangements, which are found necessary on board a Ship of War, were perpetually transgressing . . . and incurring the Captain's displeasure'. On the other hand, their size made them relatively popular with the soldiers: for example, Thomas Walsh, who went to Egypt in one, said '. . . men of war fitted for the accommodation of troops . . . have every advantage over common transports, being in general very roomy, and fast sailers.'

Similar criteria made them equally suitable as hospital ships, like the Channel Fleet's *Charon* (6, 7) or as transports, and *Dolphin* served successively as hospital ship (1781), trooper (1800) and storeship (1804), as probably depicted by her commander, Lt Daniel Tandy (8). As the

war progressed larger obsolescent two-deckers, like 50-gun ships, and even a few 64s, were converted for the same duties.

For these operations the ships were armed *en flûte*, a French term applied to warships not mounting their complete establishment of guns. The ex-44s usually carried twenty long 9pdrs on the upper deck and four 6pdrs on the quarterdeck and forecastle, so were not completely defenceless. As an example, in 1799 the storeship *Camel* accompanied by the sloop *Rattlesnake*, fought off the French 12pdr frigate *Preneuse* at the Cape of Good Hope. Furthermore, the conversion required little structural alteration, so it was possible to return vessels to a full cruising role if required without too much time in dockyard hands: *Regulus* was employed as a cruiser in 1798-1800 between bouts of trooping, for instance.

A few 44s remained in Sea Service – declining from five in 1797 to three in 1801 and two for most of the Napoleonic War – but usually relegated to distant and

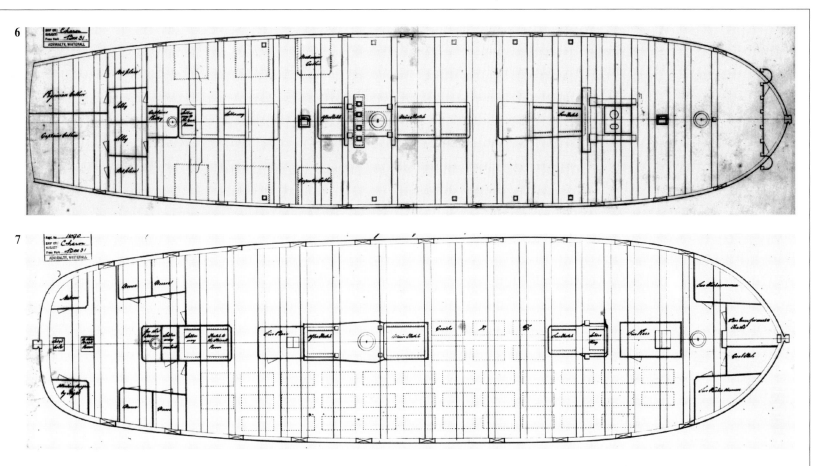

minor stations. *Diomede* and *Resistance* saw some sharp service in the Indian Ocean in the first stage of the Revolutionary War, but in the early years of the war the perceived shortage of 18pdr frigates meant that a number of 44s were pressed into service as cruisers - in 1794-95 even in the Channel. Probably the most actively employed nearer home was the *Argo*, which registered the single most impressive success of any 44 in this war when she captured the Spanish frigate *Santa Teresa* off Majorca in 1799. She was also the ship chosen to bring home the ailing St Vincent from his stint as Commander-in-Chief, Mediterranean in 1800 (see page 57).

6. 'Upper Deck of the Charon as fitted for an Hospital Ship', undated but the ship was so fitted in 1794. The captain shared his cabin area with the physician, who during the ship's first commission as a hospital ship was the famous Dr Thomas Trotter, Lord Howe's Physician of the Fleet. *NMM neg DR1691*

7. 'Gun Deck of the Charon as fitted for an Hospital Ship', undated but the ship was so fitted in 1794. This was the main hospital ward, and a large fire place was placed forward to feed the patients and keep the deck warm. *NMM neg DR1690*

8. Unidentified watercolour from the sketchbook of Lt Daniel Tandy c1798-1805. It probably depicts the *Dolphin*, a 44-gun ship converted to a storeship and commanded by Tandy in 1806. The gundeck ports have been sealed, except numbers 3, 6 and 10 from forward which were used as loading ports. *NMM ref PAF0475*

The Battle of Algesiras

1

SPAIN ALWAYS had severe problems in manning her ships and in 1801 transferred to France six ships of the line which were lying in Cadiz. These were commanded by Rear-Admiral Dumanoir Le Pelley, and at first were intended to be used in an attack on Lisbon; but the submission of Portugal made this unnecessary. The French then began a series of movements to create a force to carry reinforcements to the French army in Egypt with ships from Toulon sailing to Cadiz to collect the six newly acquired French ships, as well as six Spanish ships under Vice-Admiral Moreno.

Linois sailed from Toulon on 13 June 1801, with the *Formidable* and *Indomptable*, 80-gun ships, the 74-gun *Desaix* and frigate *Muiron*. He sighted Gibraltar on 1 July. The only British vessel at the Rock was the sloop *Calpe*, which sent a small boat to warn Rear-Admiral Saumarez (1), who was blockading Cadiz. Meanwhile, Linois learnt that Saumarez, with a superior force, was off Cadiz, and, temporarily abandoning the idea of making his port, he anchored off Algeciras in full view of Gibraltar. Saumarez had six ships of the line (one 80 and

the rest 74s) off Cadiz. Somewhat frustrated by weak and uncertain winds they proceeded slowly towards Algeciras. Because of the local knowledge of her captain, the *Venerable* led. At 7am on 6 July she came in sight of the French and saw them warping in towards the shore. Saumarez at once signalled to engage the enemy as soon as each ship came up.

Linois moored his ships with intervals of about 500 yards. The southern end of his line was covered by a battery on Isla Verde; its northern end, by the battery of Santiago. There were also guns on shore in a fort about a mile and a half south of the anchorage, and in two towers. Fourteen heavy Spanish gunboats in the shallows completed the defences.

The weak and dying breeze prevented the British ships from getting into action in the order which had been assigned to them. *Pompee*, having been distantly fired at while rounding Cabareta Point, passed close to Isla Verde, and, receiving in succession the broadsides of the *Muiron*, *Indomptable*, *Desaix*, and *Formidable*, to the two latter of which she replied, dropped her anchor at 8.45am near

2

3

the *Formidable*'s starboard bow—so near, indeed, that she brought up inside the French ship's anchor-buoy (2). About five minutes later, the *Audacious*, baffled by the wind, anchored abreast of, but not so close to, the *Indomptable*; and at 8.55am, the *Venerable*, similarly hindered, anchored still further from the *Desaix* and from the starboard quarter of the *Formidable*. As soon as these ships positioned themselves, they began a furious action, in the course of which the French ships continued to warp slowly shorewards (3). This was fortunate for the *Pompee*, which the current had swung bow-on to the French flagship's broadside and was therefore unable to use her own broadside. At that time the *Caesar*, having anchored ahead of the *Audacious*, opened her port broadside upon the *Desaix*. The *Hannibal* then also got up, and anchored on the *Caesar*'s starboard bow; but the *Spencer* fell too far to leeward and did not have much effect, though she was still near enough to suffer from the fire of the Spanish batteries. Owing to the manner in which she had swung, the *Pompee* was able to use only her foremost guns. Just after 10am, probably hoping to relieve the *Pompee*, Saumarez ordered the *Hannibal* to 'go and rake the French admiral'.

She cut her cable and made sail to the northward with such light wind as there was and then tacked so as to place herself between the *Formidable* and the shore; but at 11am grounded (4). Some of her foremost port guns bore upon the French flagship, some of her starboard foremost ones upon the Almirante Tower and the bat-

tery of Santiago, and yet others upon the Spanish gunboats; and she opened as brisk a fire as possible upon every enemy whom she could reach, while she tried to get herself off.

Worried that other British ships might be successful in getting between his line and the shore, Linois, at about 11.15am, signalled to his vessels to cut their cables and to allow themselves to run ashore. The *Formidable* actually anchored again, close inshore but the *Desaix* and *Indomptable*, however, grounded.

This left the British ships too far away to fire with full effect. Saumarez, therefore, ordered the cables to be cut, but the untrustworthiness of the breeze, the unfavourable current, and the rocks and shoals to leeward, finally foiled this. *Pompee* had got into trouble and what few boats were not already destroyed had to be sent to tow her out of danger (5). Her colours were temporarily shot away, which made the French think she had surrendered. Saumarez had too few boats left to send his marines to storm the island battery, which in any case had been reinforced by the French; and at 1.35pm he started to withdraw the five ships still afloat, leaving the *Hannibal*, partially dismasted, shattered, silent, and aground, but still with her flag flying.

Captain Ferris, when he saw that an active resistance would only be a needless sacrifice, ordered a cease fire and sent his officers and men to shelter and when all hope of rescue had gone, surrendered. A little while afterwards her flag was rehoisted upside down to indicate her cap-

4

1. 'Rear Admiral Sir James Saumarez, K.B., at the age of 45', etching by William Greatback, no date. *NMM ref PAD4291*

2. 'Battle of Algesiras. To Rear-Admiral Sir James Saumarez . . . this View of their attacking the French Squadron & Batteries in Algesiras Bay on the 6th July 1801', aquatint published by Robert Dodd, 31 December 1802. *NMM ref PAH8001*

3. 'To Sir James Saumarez . . . This Plate representing the Gallant attack of the French Squadron under the Batteries of Algesiras . . . is dedicated by . . . Edward Harding', coloured aquatint engraved by Hubert and Joseph Constantine Stadler after an original by Captain J Brenton, published by Edward Harding, 1 January 1802. *NMM ref PAH7995*

4. The battle of Algesiras, watercolour by Joseph Ange Antoine Roux (1765-1835). *Peabody Essex Museum, Salem MA neg 19806*

5. 'To Sir James Saumarez . . . This Plate representing the Ships under his command returning from the Attack of the French Squadron Warpd aground under the Batteries of Algesiras taken from a drawing . . . of the Caesar bearing the Rear-Admiral's flag', aquatint engraved by Hubert and Joseph Constantine Stadler after an original by Captain J Brenton, published by Edward Harding, 1 January 1802. *NMM neg 5310*

ture, but it was also a sign of distress and led to the confusion and capture of at least one British boat's crew.

The losses on both sides were very heavy. The British lost a total of 121 killed, and 252 wounded or missing, besides the prisoners taken with the *Hannibal* (which alone suffered 75 dead). The *Hannibal* had her fore and mainmasts shot away and many of her guns disabled; the *Pompee*'s tophamper was totally shattered. The French lost 306 killed, and 280 wounded. Their ships were much damaged in both hulls and rigging; and five of the Spanish gunboats had been driven ashore or sunk.

The well trained and led French had fought hard and skillfully and a combination of weather, luck and shore support had given them the victory against a superior force of which they had captured one. It is, however, also significant that this rare British setback occurred close inshore with all the difficulties and chanciness that implied.

5

Saumarez's revenge

AFTER THE reverse at Algesiras, Saumarez took his ships to Gibraltar, where he set to work, with almost unexampled energy, to fit them again for service (1). It was judged hopeless to attempt to repair the *Pompee* in time to make her ready for further work against Linois, so her people were turned over to help in bringing forward the rest of the squadron. Saumarez himself was inclined to despair of the *Caesar* as well, and he shifted his flag from her to the *Audacious*; but Captain Jahleel Brenton was more sanguine, and, appealing to his men not to allow the rear-admiral to go to sea in another ship, ordered them to work all day, and by watch and watch at night; the result being that the *Caesar* was ready when she was again wanted, and that Saumarez, on 12 July, rehoisted his flag in her. The business was done with an energy and rapidity that have never been exceeded.

It has already been said that Rear-Admiral Dumanoir Le Pelley was at Cadiz in charge of the six ships of the line which had been transferred by Spain to France. He had arrived there from Brest on 13 June, with the frigates *Liberté*, 40, and *Indienne*, 40, after a smart chase by the *Venerable* and *Superb*; but he still lacked many of the officers and men to enable him to take over the squadron. As soon as Linois had floated his grounded ships and his

prize at Algeciras, he sent a message to Dumanoir Le Pelley and Massaredo, at Cadiz, begging them to come or send to his assistance, before the British should be in a position to again attack him. Both flag officers were willing enough to aid him. Indeed, succour would probably have been despatched as soon as the danger to Linois became known, but for the non-arrival of the French

1

2

3

1. 'To Sir James Saumarez . . . This Plate representing the British Squadron . . . preparing to pursue the Combined Squadron of France & Spain, on the Afternoon of the 12th of July 1801 . . . is dedicated by . . . Edward Harding', coloured aquatint engraved by Hubert and Joseph Constantine Stadler after an original by Captain J Brenton, published by Edward Harding, 1802. *NMM ref PAH7992*

2. 'Gibraltar Bay. To Sir James Saumarez Bart this View of his putting to Sea on the 12th July 1801 with five sail of the line in the face of an enemy consisiting of ten sail of the line . . . each with three Frigates and several Gun Boats is . . . inscribed by . . . Robt Dodd', aquatint published by Robert Dodd, 31 December 1802. *NMM neg B7107*

4

officers and seamen, and for the impossibility of getting the Spanish authorities to move with promptitude. On 8 July, however, Vice-Admiral Don Juan Joaquin de Moreno anchored in the outer road of Cadiz with five Spanish and one Franco-Spanish sail of the line, three frigates and a lugger, in readiness to sail for Algeciras on the following morning. His proceedings were observed by the *Superb*, 74, the frigate *Thames*, and brig *Pasley*, which were by that time again off the port.

At daylight on the 9th Moreno put to sea with all his squadron except the *Saint Antoine* (ex-*San Antonio*), which was delayed, but which rejoined on the following morning; and made sail towards the Gut of Gibraltar, while the *Superb*, *Thames*, and *Pasley* kept ahead of him. That forenoon the *Pasley* pressed on and entered Gibraltar signalling the approach of an enemy; at 3pm the *Superb* and *Thames* joined Saumarez; and a little later the squadron from Cadiz joined Linois off Algeciras. On the two following days the British worked harder than ever to get

ready for sea; and when, at dawn on 12 July, the Franco-Spaniards loosed sails, the squadron of Saumarez, except the *Pompee*, was prepared to meet them. The enemy began to get under way at noon; by 1pm their headmost ships were off Cabareta Point, and the *Caesar* was warping out of Gibraltar mole, cheered on by hundreds of onlookers, her band playing 'Hearts of Oak' and the garrison band answering with 'Britons, strike home'. At 3pm Saumarez signalled for the rest of his squadron to weigh and prepare for battle.

The British force comprised *Caesar*, 80 and the 74s *Venerable*, *Superb*, *Spencer* and *Audacious*, the 32-gun *Thames* and three smaller craft. The Franco-Spanish force was considerably more powerful, including two 112-gun ships and one 94, all Spanish, one Spanish and two French 80s, one Spanish and two French 74s, one Spanish and two French frigates. The wind was from the east; and, as soon as they were clear of the shelter of the Rock, the British ships formed in line ahead on the port tack. At 7pm they wore together, and stood on the starboard tack, until a little after 8pm, when the enemy having all cleared Cabareta Point, Saumarez bore away in chase. A little previously, Don Juan Moreno, in accordance with the Spanish custom of the time, had shifted his flag from a line of battle ship to the frigate *Sabina*, and had, with considerable difficulty, persuaded Linois to leave the *Formidable* for the same vessel. At 8.40pm Saumarez hailed the *Superb*, and ordered her to make sail ahead, and attack the rearmost of the enemy's ships, none of which was visible at that time. Captain Keats, in response, quickly passed the flagship; and by 10pm, when the wind had freshened, only the *Caesar* and *Venerable*, of her own squadron, remained visible from her deck. By 11pm her next astern, the *Caesar*, was fully three miles away, and the *Venerable* could not be seen at all. Twenty minutes later, Keats distinguished the *Real Carlos*, 112, about a point before his port beam, and the *San Hermenegildo*, 112, and *St Antoine* on the three-decker's port side. He therefore shortened sail, and, quite regardless of the fact that he was alone, opened his port guns on the *Real Carlos* when he was at a distance of about a cable and a half from her. He had given the Spaniard three broadsides and had brought dowm her fore topmast, when, perceiving her to be on fire, he again made sail. In the meantime the *Real Carlos*, after having for a short time continued her course, came suddenly to the wind, dropped astern, and began, with her two nearest consorts, firing wildly. Each, in the darkness, mistook the others, it would appear, for an enemy.

Having passed on, the *Superb*, at 11.50pm, brought the *St Antoine*, to action, and, after half an hour's engagement, some of which was fought at close quarters upon a wind, the Frenchman hailed that she surrendered. She

was afterwards, owing to her broad pennant having been accidentally left flying, fired into by the *Caesar*, *Venerable*, *Spencer*, and *Thames* as they got up; but it was soon made known that she had already struck. Just before she surrendered, the *Real Carlos*, which had never succeeded in extinguishing her fire, blew up; but, before she did so, she had fouled, and also set fire to, her unfortunate consort the *San Hermenegildo* (3); the latter in her turn exploded at about half past midnight on the 13th. From these two three-deckers, 38 persons reached the *Superb*, and 262 more were taken up by other ships; but the rest of the complements, amounting to about 1700 officers and men, perished. The *Superb*, *Carlotta*, *Calpe*, and *Louisa* remained by the prize, and the rest of the squadron pressed on after the enemy.

During the night the wind temporarily increased to a gale, and by 4am the *Venerable*, Captain Hood, and *Thames* led the squadron, and were getting up with the *Formidable*; the *Caesar* was some distance astern of them, the *Spencer* was far astern of her, and the *Audacious* and *Superb* were out of sight. At about that time the wind began to drop, and even to fail; and, in spite of all that could be done, only the *Venerable* and *Thames* were able to gain materially upon the chase. At 5.15am the *Formidable* opened with her stern guns upon the *Venerable*; and, a little later, the light and baffling airs threw the two ships broadside to, within musket shot of one another. A hot action then ensued. By 5.30am the *Venerable* had lost her mizzen. topmast; at 5.45am, by order, the *Thames* hauled up and raked the *Formidable* from astern; at 6.45am the *Venerable*'s mainmast went by the board (4), and the British 74 fell alongside her opponent, who, profiting by the confusion, stood on, though slowly, and, as she went, plied the *Venerable* for some time from her sternchasers. Neither the *Caesar* nor the *Spencer* was able to get within gunshot of her. Captain Hood's ship was left unmanageable. At 7.50am, to add to her difficulties, she lost her foremast; and almost simultaneously she struck upon the shoals in front of San Pedro, about twelve miles south of Cadiz. At about 8am her mizzen mast went over the side, and Saumarez, by boat, sent to her Captain permissive directions to abandon and destroy the vessel in case the enemy should show any disposition to attack her again, while he also ordered the *Thames* to be ready to take on board her people (5). But Hood did not despair of saving his ship; and, when the *Audacious* and *Superb* at length showed in the southward, the enemy, who had previously betrayed some slight inclination to renew the engagement, hauled up for, and presently entered, Cadiz. The *Venerable* had lost 18 killed and 87 wounded, among the former being her Master, John Williams, and among the latter Lieutenant Thomas Church. The *Thames* had escaped scot free.

The total casualties suffered by the enemy cannot be ascertained; but they had lost three ships, two by fire and one by capture; and this they have never attempted to deny. The action is, nevertheless, always chronicled in French histories as a victory, and, indeed, as a most glorious victory, for France. That this is so is, no doubt, due almost entirely to the extraordinary report which, after reaching Cadiz, Commander Troude, of the *Formidable*, sent to Rear-Admiral Linois. At about midnight, so he declared, he had sustained the fire of five British ships; and at daybreak he had been attacked by three ships and a frigate, and had driven them all off, completely dismasting one of them. This exaggerated story was accepted by the French government, and was credited by the French people; and Troude, not so much on the strength of his other performances, some of which were far more worthy of applause, as on the strength of this imaginative dispatch, was then ranked among the most brilliant naval heroes of his country. That he made a good defence is true. That he disabled the *Venerable*, a ship of force inferior to his own, is true also. But that he drove off the British squadron, or that the action was, in any sense of the words, a French or a Franco-Spanish victory, is, of course, utter nonsense. Dumanoir Le Pelley, in his report to the Minister of Marine, ingenuously adopted and gave currency, nevertheless, to all Troude's self-glorification.

After the disappearance of the allies, the British, thanks mainly to the *Thames* and to the boats of the *Caesar* and *Spencer*, succeeded in hauling off the *Venerable*, which, by 8am on the 14th, owing to the energy of her own people, had got up three spars to serve as masts and had made some sail on them, though she still had to be towed. Saumarez returned to Gibraltar with her and the prize, and left the *Spencer*, *Audacious*, and *Thames* to watch the enemy in Cadiz.

3. 'Battle off Cabaretta Point – July 12th 1801', coloured aquatint engraved by Thomas Sutherland after an original by Thomas Whitcombe (born c1752), published 1 March 1816. *NMM neg B3456*

4. 'Combat entre le vaisseau le Formidable commande par le Captaine de Vaisseau Troude et les vaisseaux Anglais le Cesar, le Venerable, le Superbe et la fregate la Tamise le 23 Messidor An 9 á 2 ligues dans le Sud-Ouest de l'Ile San Pedro pres Cadix', lithograph engraved by Bernard Lemercier after an original by Ferdinand Victor Perrot, published by Victor Delane, no date. This was produced to support Troude's exaggerated account, and although it shows the *Venerable* losing her mainmast, and the *Thames* in the foreground, the presence of the *Caesar* and *Superb* is pure fiction. *NMM ref PAD5647*

5. '2eme position de fin de Combat du Vau. Français le Formidable ... contre les Vaux. Anglais le Caesar, le Venerable et le Superbe et la fregate la Tamis ... 12 Juillet 1801', grey pen and wash by Pierre Ozanne (1737-1813), no date. The *Caesar* and *Superb* did not engage the *Formidable* at this stage, but the dismasted *Venerable* receiving assistance from the boats of the *Thames* is accurate enough. *NMM ref PAG9645*

5

Cochrane and the *Speedy*

1

IN A navy which included such brilliant, eccentric and egotistical mavericks as Edward Pellew, Sidney Smith and Home Popham, perhaps the most extraordinary of all was Lord Cochrane, later 10th Earl of Dundonald (1). To his credit are some of the most amazing victories against odds in the whole history of warfare under sail; but against this must be set a vain and self-destructive career of clashes with authority, exacerbated by his short stint as a radical Member of Parliament. He had already suffered a court-martial before he was made Commander – characteristically for disrespect to a superior officer – and he was to be dismissed in ignominy from the Royal Navy for involvement in a financial scandal of which he was, perhaps, not entirely innocent. Selling his services to liberation movements in South America and Greece, he won further victories and was involved in even more controversies, largely concerning prize money. The son of a man who had dissipated the family fortune on dubious inventions, the young Cochrane inherited his father's ingenuity, playing a part in the introduction of steam into naval warfare and is even regarded by some as the father of chemical weapons.

A more senior naval nonconformist, Nelson, recognised some quality in Cochrane and gave his career a boost by ordering him to take to Port Mahon the captured *Généreux* of 74 guns, which he is credited with saving by fine seamanship when the short-handed prize crew was struck by a gale. As a result he was promoted to Commander and in May 1800 took over the sloop

Speedy, one of the first generation of naval brigs, measuring only 287 tons, and armed with fourteen 4pdrs (2). Cochrane could carry the sloop's total broadside in his coat pockets, and according to his own testimony, he could only shave with the mirror on deck and his head protruding through the open companion.

In some ways *Speedy*, like her captain, was a bit of a character, with an active and unusual history of mixed fortunes both ahead and astern of her. She had been captured in June 1794 by three French frigates off the south of France, only to be retaken by the *Inconstant* in March of the following year – and after Cochrane lost her, Napoleon presented her to the Pope as the *Saint Pierre*. She had been a very active cruiser in the Gibraltar area, her exploits including a bloody encounter with the larger privateer *Papillon* in February 1798, and the cutting out of three Spanish gunboats in August of 1799. She was responsible for the dispersal of a Spanish convoy in October 1799, but her greatest moment to date came the following month when in defence of her own small convoy she successfully fought off twelve Spanish gunboats (3). Perhaps the oddest item on her record was the gruesome task of searching the wreckage of the *Queen Charlotte* for survivors in March 1800 (see pages 76-77).

But it was Cochrane's name which would be linked with *Speedy* for posterity. His exploits against Spanish coastal traffic combined audacity with coolly thought-out stratagems: the sloop spent some time disguised as a neutral Dane, and once he talked his way out of danger by having a Danish-speaking crew member convince a

2

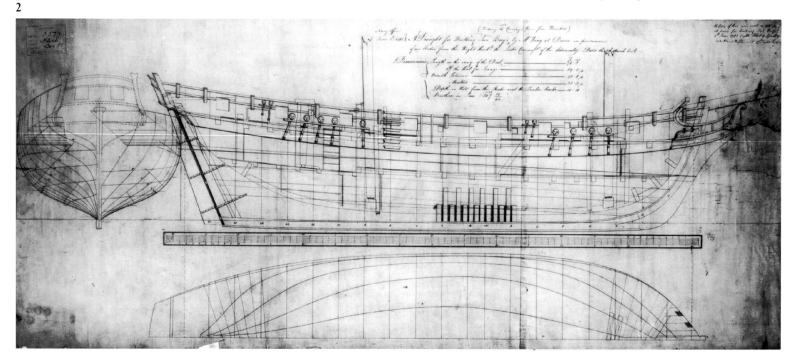

Spanish frigate's boat that the brig had just come from plague-struck North Africa, at which the nervous would-be boarders sheered off without attempting to investigate further.

Bluff was to save Cochrane on many occasions but never was it deployed for such high stakes as in *Speedy*'s epic battle with the 32-gun *Gamo*, probably the same vessel he had hoodwinked previously. This time there was no possibility of escape and after some preliminary manoeuvring, he ran the brig alongside his larger opponent. Leaving only the surgeon to man the wheel, Cochrane led his 48 remaining men in a rush up the sides of the frigate – a ship mustering over 300 men. When the outcome looked dubious, Cochrane shouted to the surgeon to send up 'fifty more men', at the same time as the Spanish colours were struck by a British seaman unnoticed in the melee. The stunned Spaniards surrendered (4).

The *Gamo* lost 13 dead and 41 wounded to the *Speedy*'s 3 and 8 respectively, like so many of the facts surrounding this action, truly amazing. The *Gamo* was armed with twenty-two 12pdrs, eight 8pdrs and two carronades, and is often described as a frigate, although in hull form she was a xebec – a Mediterranean type perhaps developed from the galley and certainly lateen rigged in its early days (5). This was not a type suitable for the Royal Navy and the ship was sold to the Algerines, provoking a bitter complaint from Cochrane of unfair treatment, since he would have earned more prize money had the vessel been taken into naval service. This was only one of many clashes between Cochrane and the authorities which cast such an unpleasant pall over his victories, but his achievement was recognised in that he was promoted to Post Captain, although he was made to wait for it.

Before he could benefit from promotion, he overstepped the mark, and was finally captured in July 1801 when *Speedy* was trapped against the North African coast by three 74s of Admiral Linois's squadron. He was soon exchanged, but his exploits as a Post Captain belong in later volumes.

4

5

1. 'The Rt Honble Captain Lord Cochrane KB', stipple engraving by William Ridley after an original by Thomson, published by James Asperne, 1 June 1809.
NMM ref PAD3651

2. 'A Draught for Building Two Brigs (To carry 14 carriage Guns four Pounders) by Mr King at Dover . . .', dated 2 June 1781. A note mentions that they were named *Flirt* and *Speedy*.
NMM neg DR3577

3. 'Speedy sloop of War attacked by Spanish Gun-Boats', coloured aquatint engraved by Wells, published by Bunny and Gold 1 July 1801. The action took place on 6 November 1799.
NMM ref PAD5631

4. The victorious *Speedy* bringing in the captured Spanish *Gamo*, graphite by Nicholas Pocock (1740-1821), no date.
NMM neg A6361

5. 'Sciabecco Spagnola essendo in calma', anonymous watercolour, 1780.
NMM ref PAF8226

Part II

THE CHANNEL AND IRELAND

IF BRITAIN between 1798 and 1801 can be said to have won the battle for command of the Mediterranean, it was achieved at the expense of only limited success on the Atlantic coast of Europe. Here the Cabinet's 'blue water policy' depended on continental alliances to contain and sap the power the military might of France while Britain blockaded the French fleet to prevent invasion attempts and to cut France off from her colonies. As part of this strategy, to relieve military pressure on her continental allies, Britain mounted a succession of amphibious operations down the Atlantic coast of France, Holland and Spain.

Unfortunately, the intensity, direction and goal of these attacks varied as government policy wavered. The most powerful voice in the Cabinet, Henry Dundas, the Secretary of State for War and the Colonies, generally favoured a go-it-alone policy exploiting British sea power for British interests; he regarded continental raids as most valuable if, like those he planned against Brest, Ferrol and Cadiz, they were intended to reduce enemy naval power. The Foreign Secretary, Lord Grenville, on the other hand, worked towards the establishment of a coalition grand strategy that would lead to the complete overthrow of revolutionary France – hence the North Holland expedition, the largest British continental commitment of the period. A third view was provided by William Windham, the Secretary at War, whose support for a royalist counter-revolution in France led to the involvement in Quiberon and Belleisle. Pitt, the Prime Minister, was an ineffectual arbiter, and policy see-sawed between one priority and another.

As a result, the threat of a French invasion of Britain or of Ireland persisted throughout the remaining years of the French Revolutionary War. It was indeed to the command of the 'Army of England' that Napoleon was appointed early in 1798 on his return from Italy in December 1797. Although he forsook this cause for the invasion of Egypt, and the army

was largely removed, sufficient forces remained at the French ports for three more expeditions to be sent to Ireland in 1798. Moreover, following the collapse of Austria late in 1800, an army of invasion was again ranged along the coasts of France around Boulogne where troop carrying craft were assembled in every port and estuary.

During these years the responsibility for Britain's defence against invasion was divided between two officers. It fell most firmly on the shoulders of the commanders-in-chief of the British fleet in the Channel: Alexander Hood, Viscount Bridport from April 1797 until April 1800; the Earl of St Vincent until he became First Lord of the Admiralty in February 1801; and then Sir William Cornwallis. But such was the threat of invasion that in 1797 a separate Downs command was formed in the narrowest part of the Channel specifically to oppose any attempted landings. This was commanded in turn by Joseph Peyton, Skeffington Lutwidge, and Lord Nelson.

The formation of the second Downs command recognised the difficulties already facing the commander-in-chief in blockading Brest, a port sufficiently capacious to accommodate great numbers of ships of the line – over forty on the return of Bruix in 1799 – yet facing west where British squadrons were liable to be driven in heavy westerly weather on to a lee shore. During such weather, Howe, then Bridport allowed his main squadron of ships of the line to take shelter in Torbay or as far east as Spithead or St Helens, in the lee of the Isle of Wight, from where they were also able to escort East and West India convoys out into the North Atlantic. A watching subdivision of the Channel fleet under Colpoys, with an inshore squadron of frigates under Pellew, facilitated such absence – except when they too were driven off station. However, the French descent on Bantry Bay in mid-December 1796, when Colpoys had been blown thirty miles into the Atlantic where Pellew was unable to find him,

the French expeditions to Ireland in 1798, and the escape of Bruix in 1799, all proved the inadequacy of these arrangements.

The difficulties of blockading Brest were enhanced by the headlands and islands surrounding the port that created dangerous channels and currents. But these did not all favour the French, as was evident in April 1798 when two 74s, the *Mars* and *Ramilles* of Bridport's squadron, forced a French 74, the *Hercule*, to anchor south of the Passage du Raz, south of Brest, on account of the current flowing too swiftly through the channel against her. The *Hercule* had just been launched at Lorient and was on her way to join the Brest fleet and the British ships had chased her from off Pointe de Penmarche. The *Ramilles* having carried away her fore topmast, the *Mars* under Alexander Hood brought the *Hercule* to action. So strong was the tide that Hood too had to anchor, upon which the anchors of the opposing ships became tangled, so that they fought for an hour grappled together: 290 of the French 74's crew were killed or wounded, 90 of the *Mars*', including Alexander Hood, nephew to Lords Hood and Bridport.

For the French, a major weakness of Brest as the principal arsenal of France on the Channel coast was the length of lines of communication to the Brittany headland and the necessity to bring all bulky naval stores by sea, which were prey to British warships. Storeships crossing the Baie de la Seine between Le Havre and Cherbourg were specially vulnerable, particularly after July 1795 when Sir Sidney Smith occupied the two small islands of St Marcouf, which were garrisoned with about 500 seamen and marines. Possession was retained of the islands, even though in the night of 6 May 1798 they were attacked by fifty-two gunbrigs and flat-bottomed boats carrying, it was reported, about 6000 men from the Boulogne marine battalions. As light dawned, the boats opened fire on the island redoubt, while the garrison replied from seventeen long guns and carronades. The boats were forced to scatter, many being shattered, with at least a thousand men drowned or wounded.

In a return attack on the French boats being assembled for an invasion across the Channel, on the night of 19 May a squadron under Home Riggs Popham disembarked 1140 troops to the east of Ostend and next morning engaged the batteries guarding the town. The landing party blew up the locks and sluice-gates of the Bruges canal by which boats could be brought from Flushing to Ostend and Dunkirk. However, a heavy sea prevented the re-embarkation of the troops, and the following day sixty-five were killed or wounded and the remainder forced to surrender.

The ports where these boats were assembled were closely watched. Off Le Havre at the end of May 1798 the 38-gun frigate *Hydra* under Sir Francis Laforey, supported by a bomb vessel and cutter, encountered the 36-gun French frigate *Confiante*, supported by a 20-gun ship rigged corvette and gun-vessel. An inshore duel developed, from which the *Confiante* extracted herself first by attempting to reach Le Havre and, when that was found too far to leeward, driving herself on shore, whereupon the French corvette did the same. Next morning, most of her crew having landed, the *Confiante* was boarded and burned. The corvette meanwhile was refloated and got into the River Dive, where guns were landed and batteries erected to protect her. She later reached Le Havre safely.

In August 1798 the French managed to get another expedition under way for Ireland, where the Catholic republicans had been promised support since the failure of the landing in Bantry Bay in December 1796; 1150 soldiers under General Humbert were taken on board three frigates at Rochefort and landed to the western end of Killala Bay, northwest Ireland, on 22 August. They were to surrender to a superior military force at Ballinamuck on 8 September.

Meanwhile a larger expedition of 3000 men had been embarked on board a squadron of eight frigates and one 74 under Commodore Jean Bompart, which slipped out of Brest on 17 September. They did not pass unnoticed, messages going immediately on their departure to Lord Bridport, north off Ushant, later to the commander-in-chief on the Irish station. The

news reached Plymouth by 23 September from where Sir John Borlase Warren was despatched to reinforce the Irish squadron with three ships of the line and a frigate. Tracked across to the Irish coast, Bompart finally lost his tail on 11 October, in time for him to attempt a landing in Lough Swilly on the northwest coast. However, at this critical moment Bompart was rediscovered by Warren's force and, after a general chase in which two French vessels were slowed by gale damage, by daybreak on the 12th his squadron was almost surrounded by British ships. In the melee that ensued, Bompart's 74, the *Hoche*, was reduced to a wreck and surrendered, along with three French frigates, to which a fourth was added on the 14th.

While these prizes were being escorted into Lough Swilly, on 15 October two fugitive French frigates from Bompart's squadron were discovered off Blacksod Bay on the northwest coast of Ireland by two British frigates and a brig sloop. The French ships separated, and in thick, squally weather the British frigates lost their prey. On the 16th, however, the French 40-gun *Loire* was rediscovered and disabled by the 32-gun *Mermaid*, to be forced to surrender after a crippling action on the 18th with the 44-gun *Anson*. Another of Bompart's frigates, the 40-gun *Immortalité*, was also intercepted and forced to surrender before she could get into Brest on 20 October by the 38-gun *Fisgard*.

All seven prizes from Bompart's force were brought into Plymouth Sound safely. On 12 October the French put a fourth expedition to sea to aid the Irish insurgents, this time from Rochefort. Four frigates reached Killala Bay; but, on learning the fate of the two earlier expeditions that year, their commander made again for Rochefort which, notwithstanding a skirmish with a British squadron off Broadhaven, northwest Ireland, they reached on 3 November.

Otherwise during 1798 the main Brest fleet remained inactive. When it eventually did put to sea on 25 April 1799, it consisted of twenty-five ship of the line under Vice-Admiral Eustache Bruix and it sailed south for the Mediterranean. Deceived into thinking the force was destined for Ireland – a deception deliberately attempted by the planting of despatches for Ireland aboard a *chasse-marée* captured in mid-Channel by the lugger *Black Joke* –

Lord Bridport took his fleet to lay guard off Cape Clear, having otherwise opportunity only to send out warnings and reinforcements to Lord St Vincent off Cadiz.

Early in June 1799, realising Bruix was not coming to Ireland, Bridport sailed with his ten remaining sail of the line for Aix Roads, off Rochefort, where a Spanish squadron of five of the line from Ferrol, failing to link up with Bruix, had taken shelter. Bridport was relieved by Sir Charles Morice Pole, who, having three bomb vessels and four frigates at his disposal, on 2 July attempted to bombard the Spanish squadron where it lay. However, mortars sited on the islands of Aix and Oléron, and floating batteries proved to have superior range and the British vessels were forced to withdraw. The Spanish later slipped out of Aix Roads and returned to Ferrol without interception.

By this time, Bruix was on his way back to Brest. He had achieved little in the Mediterranean, but he did manage to join with the Spanish fleets in Carthagena and at Cadiz which returned with Bruix into Brest on 13 August. By this time, British fleet commanders had been forced to accept that a fleet refuge further west than Spithead was necessary for the blockade of Brest, and Torbay became more frequently used. Furthermore, with a fleet under Bruix amounting to fifty-nine warships, including forty of the line, British commanders realised the necessity to keep their squadrons as far as possible together.

The blockade of Brest was thereafter maintained by a British fleet usually consisting of at least thirty of the line, which St Vincent in 1800 insisted on keeping on station, even in winter. Conscious of the wear and tear suffered by this fleet, Lord Spencer, First Lord of the Admiralty until 1801, attempted to keep a large proportion of the ships of the line in Torbay. Yet in St Vincent he met a will more determined than his own. This took its toll on men as well as ships, but had the effect of raising arrangements for victualling and refitting the blockading ships to a high state of efficiency.

Meanwhile, to take pressure from Russia and Austria in their hostilities against France in southern Europe, Britain mounted a major Anglo-Russian expedition against the French in Holland. On 13 August 1799, the very day the Franco-Spanish fleet under Bruix got into Brest, 17,000 men under General Sir Ralph

Abercromby, conveyed by 150 transports and warships, sailed for the Texel, to be disembarked on 25 August after gales and proclamations on behalf of the Prince of Orange and negotiations with the Franco-Dutch fleet commander, Admiral Story. Reinforced to 22,000 British troops and 11,000 Russians, Helder Point was occupied and a squadron of fifteen Dutch vessels taken by surrender. However, an anticipated Dutch rising against the French failed to take place, the French proved unexpectedly strong, and the Anglo-Russian force became bogged down by autumnal rains. With 4500 casualties, the expedition was withdrawn in mid-October.

In 1800 there was another smaller scale attempt to engage the French in military operations in the west. In June Sir Edward Pellew was despatched by Lord St Vincent with seven 74s, five frigates and five troopships to land 5000 men and artillery in Quiberon Bay and Morbihan to assist the royalists and *Chouan* rebels. Landings were successfully made in Quiberon Bay on 4 June and on Morbihan on 6 June. The expedition was intended next for Belle Isle, the troops therefore occupying Houat in preparation for assaulting the larger island. But the strong garrison on that island deterred the landing, and the troops were re-embarked and transferred to the Mediterranean.

That summer an attack was planned on the landward defences that protected the Spanish squadron of four of the line lying in Ferrol. The troops were disembarked on the evening of 25 August and, after a severe engagement on the 26th, took possession of the heights of Brion and Balon, overlooking the town and harbour. After some heavy fighting, the operation was successfully accomplished, but, needed further south, without pressing their advantage, the troops were re-embarked and despatched to Gibraltar where forces were being concentrated for an attack on Cadiz. There, however, the plague suspended any attempt at landings.

These amphibious operations maintained pressure on the French, Dutch and Spanish defences along the coasts of the Channel and North Atlantic. But following the defeat of the Austrians late in 1800 and their withdrawal from the war in February 1801, it was the British who were to feel a renewed threat from across the Channel. In July 1801, Bonaparte as

'*The Proserpine Frigate lost March 1799 off Newark Island in the Elbe*', coloured etching by John Thomas Serres (1759-1825) after his own original, 23 April 1799. Tom Grenville, the Foreign Secretary's brother, was sent in this ship on an urgent mission to Berlin to try to bring Prussia into the Second Coalition, but the frigate became icebound and was then wrecked in the fiercest winter weather for decades. The survivors suffered an horrific journey scrambling across swirling icefloes, and many died before reaching Cuxhaven. Despite his best efforts, Tom Grenville's mission was a failure. Diplomacy in the eighteenth century was subject to hazards and uncertainties unknown today. NMM neg X224

First Consul ordered the assembly of nine divisions of gun-vessels and nine battalions of troops at Boulogne. To counter the threat, at the end of July Nelson was given command of the squadron in the Downs. Promptly, for 4 August, he ordered a bombardment of the invasion flotilla moored in line across the harbour of Boulogne, and in the night of 15 August he launched an attack by the armed boats of his squadron. However, in the dark the divisions of the boats became separated, only three of the four divisions reached their objectives, and owing to boarding nets, chain moorings and heavy defensive fire, their attack was beaten off with heavy losses.

Thereafter the presence of Nelson himself between this flotilla and the British coast served to reassure the British public that inva-

sion was not imminent. Nevertheless, the continued existence of the flotilla was a strong reminder during that autumn's peace negotiations, that France remained undefeated and a ready threat to British security. The escape from Brest of the squadron led by Admiral Ganteaume in January 1801, though destined for the Mediterranean, was also a forceful reminder that the French fleet remained in being. The war in the Channel had demonstrated that the British fleet could, through force of ships and determination in its seamen, command the sea and land troops on enemy coasts, but that the dispersal of Britain's war effort, with the uncertainty of her allies, was inadequate to force France to relinquish that position in Europe which permitted her to intimidate all who opposed her.

1

Mars **versus** *Hercule*

ALTHOUGH THE period between 1793 and 1815 was the great age of 'single ship' actions, these were almost always between frigates or smaller vessels, and one-to-one fights involving ships of the line were very rare. However, a classic fight between two 74-gun ships took place in the late evening and early night of 21 April 1798.

The new French 74 *Hercule* on her first voyage from Lorient, where she was built, to Brest was sighted and chased by two British 74s and a frigate, detached earlier that day from Bridport's blockading fleet to investigate two smaller French ships. She fled across the Iroise (the bay formed by the approaches to Brest) with the three British ships in chase. One, the *Ramillies*, 74 lost her fore topmast and fell out of the chase. The frigate *Jason* was also lagging, and would not come up till 20 minutes after the battle was over. However, the other 74, Captain Alexander Hood's *Mars*, was gaining steadily.

At 8.30pm, the French Captain l'Héritier abandoned the effort to work up against the current to escape

2

through the Passage du Raz. He dropped anchor, furled his sails, and carried out a spring aft, so as to be able to bring as heavy a fire as possible to bear upon the *Mars*, then fast coming up. By this time the *Jason* was almost out of sight and soon the *Mars* was drawing close to her adversary. At 9.15pm the French ship opened fire, soon followed by the British. The strong tidal current, however, prevented Hood from maintaining his position easily under sail, so he drew slightly ahead, let go his starboard anchor and fell back alongside his opponent (1). As the two ships crashed into each other, broadside to broadside, his port anchor caught in the Frenchman's starboard one and the two ships then slugged it out side-by-side—so close that the lower deck guns could not be run out but had to be fired from within the hull—several of the gunports had been unhinged by the collision, (2). Shortly afterwards Hood was hit in an artery and bled slowly to death. However, this did not discourage his experienced and well-trained crew whose much higher rate of fire steadily beat down the enemy. The French unsuccessfully tried to board twice but were repulsed, and at 10.30pm they surrendered, having fought very gallantly.

It was significant that neither ship had any damage to the rigging, but the French ship had suffered dreadfully in the hull. The contrast between the yellow-painted port side and a starboard side which was burnt black where it was not beaten in by shot was startling (3). It was lucky that the weather whilst she was taken back to England for repairs was good, otherwise she might well have sunk. She lost 290 dead and wounded (40 per cent of her full complement) against the 30 killed and 60 wounded aboard the *Mars*. The *Jason*'s assistance in patching up the newly captured ship and her wounded proved very welcome.

Theoretically the two 74-gun ships were a very fair match in men, gunpower and size, but in fact a brand new French ship was up against what Lord St Vincent called 'an old-commissioned, well-practised ship', under an exceptionally competent captain. Captain l'Héritier and his crew had nothing to be ashamed of in their gallant fight against a much more skilled and experienced opponent. This was especially so since extra help was visibly on its way for the British ship, whilst the entire Channel Fleet was not far away. The *Hercule* served as a prize in the Royal Navy till broken up in 1810.

1. 'The Action between the Mars and L'Hercule on the Night of the 21st of April 1798', aquatint engraved by T Hillier after an original by Nicholas Pocock (1740-1821), published by John Brydon, 31 October 1798. *NMM neg 8502*

2. 'The Action between the Mars and L'Hercule on the Night of the 21st of April 1798', aquatint engraved by Robert Dodd (1748-1815) after his own original, no date. *NMM neg 8503*

3. 'Sequel to the Action of L'Hercule and Mars on the Night of April 21st 1798. Representing the Mars bringing her Prize out of the Passage du Raz, the Jason frigate . . . assisted in shifting the prisoners', aquatint engraved by Robert Dodd (1748-1815) after his own original, no date. *NMM neg 8504*

3

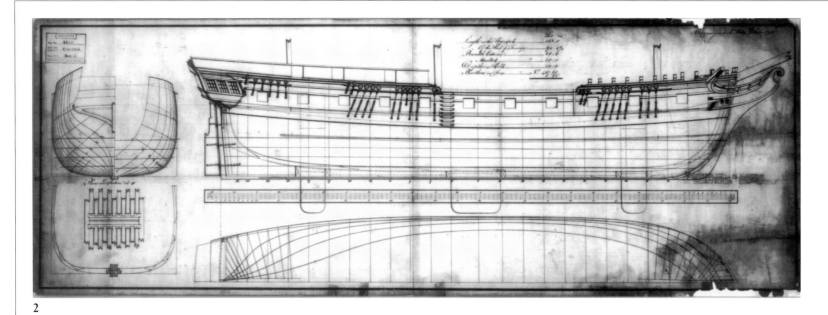

2

Ships of the Royal Navy: experimental vessels

1

IT IS often said that the eighteenth-century Royal Navy was technologically conservative, if not actually backward. Like many generalisations, it contains a modicum of truth but can be faulted on many points of detail. French shipbuilders were undoubtedly more 'scientific' than their British counterparts, but since most naval architectural theory of the period was of little practical utility—when it was not downright wrong—it is arguable how much of an advantage that was. The real 'secret' of French ship design lay in their superior dimensions for a given rating, rather than in a better designed or engineered hull form, and often the order to copy the lines of a French prize was a politically acceptable method of breaking through established norms of size.

As befits the home of the industrial revolution, in Britain improvements tended to come as a result of empirical experiment rather than theory. Certainly, the Royal Navy was never reluctant to innovate when pressed—one might cite copper sheathing and the carronade during the testing times of the American War—but in the 1790s a new openness to unconventional ideas became evident within the Navy's administration, a trend particularly marked during Lord Spencer's tenure as First Lord (1794-1801). This is most clearly manifest in funding for a series of unconventional, if not bizarre, craft, each the brainchild of an ingenious individual from outside the ship design 'establishment'.

Some of the inventors were naval officers, like Captain John Schank (1), whose development of the drop keel had been ignored during the American Revolutionary War but which received favour at last during this period.

3

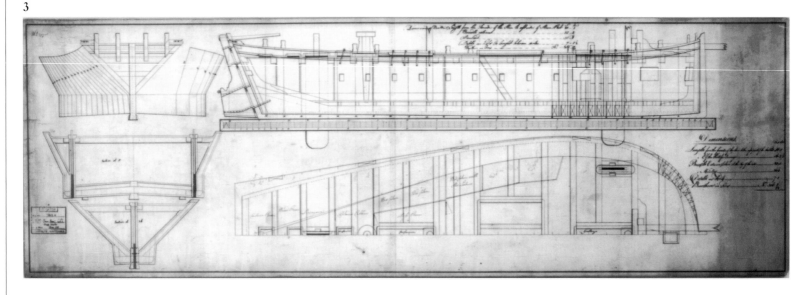

In 1795 a large 400-ton ship sloop called the *Cynthia* was ordered to his design (2); she was of notably shallow draught but compensated by three substantial dagger-boards, and although she was the largest ship to which Schank's keels were fitted, the principle was widely applied to smaller craft like gunboats. He also designed a transverse mounting which allowed guns to be run out on either broadside, which was tested on the purchased merchantman *Wolverine* (see pages 132-133).

Another ingenious naval officer was Sir Sidney Smith whose title had been gained fighting with the Swedish Inshore Fleet, a specialist army co-operation force made up of unusual sail-and-oar craft specially designed for the skerries by Frederick af Chapman, the famous Swedish naval architect. Although Chapman designed nothing remotely like them, Smith's extraordinary gunboats *Musquito* and *Sandfly* (3) must have been inspired by his experience in the Baltic. They were very powerfully armed with two long 24pdrs and two 68pdr carronades, could be rowed or sailed, and were fitted with three of Schank's drop keels, two of them abreast right forward. It is not clear whether Smith had a specific mission in mind for them, but the timing of their ordering (1794) suggests the campaign in the Netherlands. In the event, they were mainly employed as guardships in the Channel Islands and St Marcouf.

On the other side from Smith in the Baltic war was a British engineer called Samuel Bentham (4), awarded the rank of Brigadier-General by the Russians. On his return to Britain he obtained the new post of Inspector-General of Naval Works in 1796, with a wide-ranging brief to introduce the latest technology into the dockyards. But he too harboured ideas on ship design, and he was able to persuade the Admiralty to fund the construction of two so-called sloops and four schooners to be built under his supervision. All had a number of innovative features in common, including shoal draught and Schank keels, characteristic rounded hull lines, solid bulkheads and a powerful array of carronades fitted on Bentham's own non-recoil principle.

The 'sloops' were the famous *Dart* and *Arrow* (5), whose armament of twenty or more 32pdr carronades made them more powerful than many a Sixth Rate. The schooners are less well known, but the largest of the four was the 167-ton *Netley* (6) whose characteristics are well documented in the diary of Jacob Nagle, who served as her quartermaster from 1798 to 1801. By heaving up the drop keels the ship's draught was reduced from 16ft to 11ft, which not only allowed her closer inshore than the enemy would expect but also functioned like a crude depth gauge—she often followed her quarry until both were aground, bombarded them into submission, then raised the keels and sailed off. These qualities made the ship very useful for clandestine duties on the coast of France and the schooner spent the later months of 1798 landing and recovering agents.

However, it was when *Netley* was sent to protect trade on the coast of Portugal that she really made her name, becoming fondly known as the 'tres keelus' to the locals, who ascribed her near-magical sailing qualities to the three centreboards. Nagle himself says the schooner 'could lay closer to the wind than any vessel I ever saw' and she was remarkably successful in capturing small privateers and retaking their prizes. Apart from her windward qualities, as an anti-privateer the ship had two other advantages: she could be rowed in a dead calm at 3 knots and she could carry an innocent-looking Dutch galliot rig that could be converted to a schooner in twenty minutes. But the drop keels were a mixed blessing: they jammed easily and the huge cases leaked, so badly that the captain eventually had them removed. This probably explains why they were fitted only to small craft in future.

It remains only to pose the question of why the Spencer Admiralty was so friendly to technical experiment. Part of this may be Spencer's own self-confessed ignorance of naval technicalities, which led him to listen to his experts, the naval officers on his Board. Although it flattered their competence to exaggerate the power of their captured adversaries, many sea officers had an

4

1. Captain John Schank (1740-1823), anonymous oil painting of the eighteenth-century British school. *NMM ref BHC3014*

2. Lines and profile draught of *Cynthia* sloop, showing the three large drop keels and a structural plan of the centreboard casing. *NMM ref 6352*

3. Lines and profile draught for the *Musquito* class gunboat. The unusual hull form—concave floors, flared sides and tear-drop plan—and the three-cornered drop keel arrangement is apparent. The rig was a topsail schooner. *NMM ref 7012A*

4. Sir Samuel Bentham (1757-1831), anonymous oil painting of the eighteenth-century British school. *NMM ref BHC2549*

5. Lines and profile of the *Dart*. The shaded areas below the waterline are the drop keels. As built the ship had a small topgallant forecastle and poop on which further carronades were mounted. *NMM ref 6060*

5

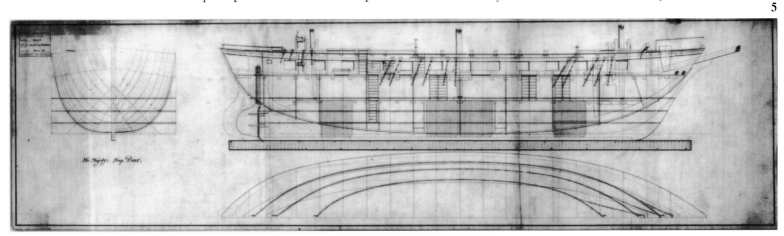

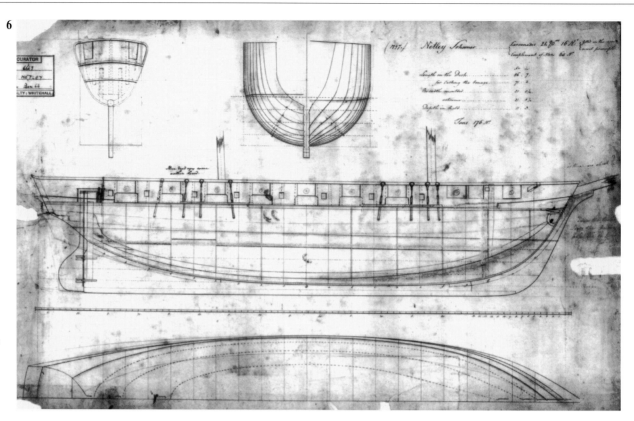

6

6. Lines and profile of the *Netley* schooner. The general resemblance to the *Dart* is obvious, although the schooner does not have the round stern of the sloop.
NMM ref 6669

7. Model of the *Triton* frigate. The main features of the design were a heavily raked and flared bow and a very flat sheer line. James Gambier was so proud of his creation that, besides this model, he also commissioned a painting of the ship by the most fashionable marine artist of the time, Nicholas Pocock; this latter is also in the National Maritime Museum (BHC3675).
NMM neg 8243

entrenched prejudice in favour of French designs, and some believed they knew better what was wanted than the hidebound British shipwrights. One of these was James Gambier, who was another officer with a penchant for amateur ship design. He was responsible for the largest entirely experimental ship built during this period, the frigate *Triton* of 32 guns (7), although he probably designed the larger *Ethalion*, 36 and had a hand in the 74-gun *Plantagenet*. He was also an influential voice in the Admiralty's policy of increasing ship size, another feature which taken along side its willingness to experiment makes the Spencer Admiralty one of the most technologically innovative of the eighteenth century.

7

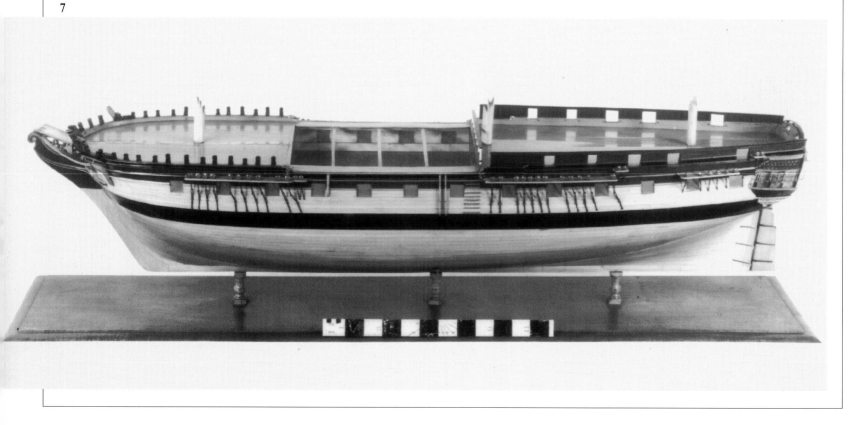

Rehearsing the invasion: attack on St Marcouf

T HE SERIOUS threat of invasion began in 1797, inspired by Napoleon Bonaparte. From the autumn of 1797, all the harbours along the coast, from Antwerp to Cherbourg, began rapidly filling with gun-vessels and flat-bottomed boats for the invasion of England. The flat-bottomed landing boats, which were built in hundreds for the Commission, were popularly known as 'Muskein boats' after the Antwerper who had produced their plans. However, it seems likely that he was inspired by, if not actually copying, the designs of that great Swedish naval architect, F H Chapman. As these boats, and the seamen and soldiers who were

intended to man them, gathered in the ports, it occurred to someone that they might be used to clear up a local annoyance, whilst obtaining experience and a small taste of action.

There was a British garrison on the two small islands of St Marcouf, which lie three kilometres off the eastern shore of the Cotentin peninsula, and near the route of coasters sailing between Le Havre and Cherbourg. As he considered they would form a good base for harassing French coastal trade, and the French had no forces on them, the enterprising Captain Sir William Sidney Smith took them over in July 1795. By 1797 they were held by a

1. 'Islands of St Marcou from E.S.E.', tinted aquatint from an original by Colonel Gosselin, engraved and published by Nicholas Pocock (1740-1821), 4 June 1798. *NMM ref PAH2288*

2. 'Isles St Marcou Lt Chas Price Commandant . . . 15 Miles from La Hogue . . . attacked by the French on the 7th May 1798 . . . but obliged them to retreat', etching published by Laurie and Whittle, 12 June 1798. *NMM ref PAH2287*

3

islands and batteries mounted (1, 2). The French decided to use part of their invasion force to attempt the recapture of these well-defended islands. On 5 April, the 38-gun frigates *Diamond* and *Hydra* found thirty-three flat-bottomed boats in Caen roads, escorted by a few gun-brigs and commanded by Muskein himself. They were on their way from Le Havre to attack St Marcouf. The British frigates attacked but *Diamond* grounded and they were unable to do anything effective that night. On the following morning the flotilla carried on westward; but, upon the appearance offshore of a British 50-gun ship, it turned back east, pursued by the frigates, and took shelter in the mouth of the river Orne. There it was later joined by about forty more landing craft and armed fishing boats and seven gunbrigs from Cherbourg. Captain Muskein, with his increased force, managed to reach La Hogue undetected, where he lay, awaiting calm weather, in order to attack Lieutenant Price.

His opportunity came on the night of 6 May. The British had warning of his approach; but, there was a dead calm and the *Adamant*, 50, *Eurydice*, 24, and the sloop *Orestes*, the only warships in the area, could not get near the islands to help in their defence. In the darkness, the French, with fifty-two craft with some eighty guns and carrying between 5000 and 6000 men, placed themselves to attack at dawn. At daybreak on the 7th the French brigs were seen at about 350 yards from the British forti-

4

force of about 500 seamen and marines, under the orders of Lieutenant Price, of the *Badger*, a 4-gun gunboat converted from a Dutch hoy which had been purchased and armed for the service. Blockhouses had been built on the

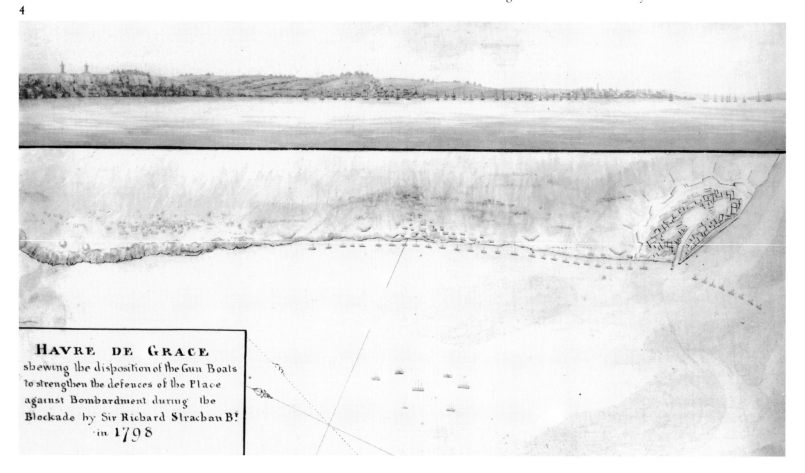

HAVRE DE GRACE
shewing the disposition of the Gun Boats
to strengthen the defences of the Place
against Bombardment during the
Blockade by Sir Richard Strachan Bt.
in 1798

5

fications. The seventeen guns which would bear on them opened fire. The French replied vigorously, and their landing craft advanced with great determination to land their men; but the effect of the sinking of six or seven of these laden boats caused the others to change their mind and withdraw. The loss of the attackers was probably upwards of 1200 killed, drowned and wounded. On the British side, only one man was killed, and only four were wounded, in spite of the powerful artillery carried in the French barges.

An opposed landing is always one of the most difficult actions of war and the combination of well-prepared defenders and strong fortifications on shore made up for the imbalance of numbers. Also the French seem to have had more enthusiasm and bravery than skill and training. As the enemy drew off, the three British warships managed to get within range, but the calm prevented them from cutting off the retreat of the flotilla. As a recent French book has stated, this gives a fair idea of the

probable result had the invasion of Britain been attempted at this time, even in the unlikely event of the mass of the flotilla evading attack from warships in mid-Channel. Contemporary British cartoonists certainly agreed (3).

The invasion menace was not ended however, and a blockading squadron under Sir Richard Strachan keeping an eye on Le Havre—whose defences could be strengthened by gunboats against possible bombardment (4)—was only one of several such forces in the Channel. As part of their blockading work on 30 May the *Hydra*, *Vesuvius* bomb, and the *Trial* cutter, 12, of that squadron were closing the port on a reconnaissance when they discovered, chased, fought and drove ashore the French frigate *Confiante*, 36, and the *Vésuve*, 20, which had sailed from Le Havre for Cherbourg (5). On the following morning the boats of the *Hydra* burnt the frigate, but the smaller vessel was refloated by the French and escaped.

3. 'Rehearsal of a French Invasion as Performed before the Invalids at the Islands of St Marcou on the Morning of ye 7 of May 1798', coloured aquatint by Thomas Rowlandson, published by Ackermann's Gallery, 18 May 1798.
NMM ref PAG8992

4. 'Havre de Grace shewing the disposition of the Gun Boats to strengthen the defences of the Place against bombardment during the blockade by Sir Richard Strachan, Bart, in 1798', anonymous black and watercolour pen and ink, dated 1798.
NMM ref PAG9687

5. 'Capture of La Confiante – May 31st 1798', coloured aquatint engraved by Thomas Sutherland after an original by Thomas Whitecombe (born c1752), published 1 August 1816.
NMM neg X2038

French naval bases: Le Havre

LE HAVRE (in full, 'Havre de Grace' or, to English speaking seamen 'Harbour of Grace' – its literal translation), was founded in the early sixteenth century on a marshy site at the mouth of the river Seine (1). It was intended to supersede the two older ports of Honfleur and Harfleur (sited on opposite sides of the Seine, slightly further upstream) and largely succeeded in doing so. It was by far the largest and most important haven between Calais and Boulogne, to the east, and Cherbourg, to the west; and far more important than these as a trading centre.

In the period preceding 1792, it played a major role in

the expansion of French Atlantic trade in slaves from Africa and tropical goods, mostly from the West Indies. Like all the major French trading ports, its prosperity was shattered by the revolt of the slaves in Saint Domingue (Haiti), which had previously been the major, and steadily expanding, source of sugar and other such products in the French empire. Le Havre's catastrophic fall in prosperity was reinforced and confirmed a year later when France declared war against Britain.

Although it did send out some privateers against enemy trade (a tempting target: in a good year, between 13,000 and 15,000 ships of all sizes passed through the

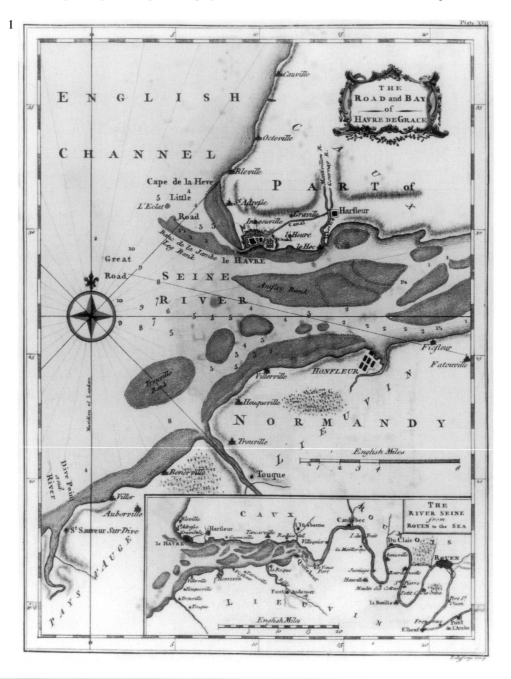

1. 'The Road and Bay of Havre de Grace. The River Seine from Rouen to the Sea', etching by T Jefferys (c1710-1771), c1761. *NMM ref PAD1522*

2. 'Le Bassin du Havre. Vu du Bureau des Constructions. Reduit de la Collection des Ports de France dessines pour le Roi en 1776. Par le Sr Ozanne Ingeneur de la Marine de sa Majeste', etching by Yves Marie Gouaz from an original by Nicolas Ozanne (1728-1811), 1776. *NMM ref PAD1521*

3. 'Havre. Vue du porte d'entree', tinted aquatint engraved by Reeve after an original by Luttringshausen, printed by Remond, no date. *NMM ref PAH2290*

2

Channel), Le Havre was never, unlike Saint Malo or Dunkirk, a major privateering port. Instead, Le Havre continued to build numbers of frigates and smaller vessels for the French navy, as it had done for many years (2). It had not the depth of water or the capacity to be a base for ships of the line (3); but it was an important base for fitting out raiding squadrons of frigates, and continued as such until the end of the Napoleonic War. The small force intercepted by the British in May 1798 in the action which resulted in the beaching and destruction of the frigate *Confiante* (see pages 105-107) is a case in point. The port was thus unusual in being both a fairly significant naval base and also an important commercial centre.

By 1798 Le Havre had become a major base for the gun-boats built in large numbers for the invasion of Britain (many were constructed at this port). It had also become, and remained, a major staging point for groups of these vessels passing along the coast towards the main invasion base at Boulogne. The abortive French attack on the Saint Marcouf islands was launched from Le Havre. A British squadron under Sir John Borlase Warren kept an eye on the gunboats and landing craft which, under the command of their designer (the Antwerp-born Muskein), lay at Sallenelle and other anchorages around Le Havre. These were deemed to be so well protected by shore batteries that it was useless to attempt to attack them except by the rather inaccurate (and usually relatively ineffective) method of bombardment by mortar shells.

3

1

Popham's attack on Ostend

THE BRITISH reaction to the threat of invasion was not confined to purely defensive measures: the government also considered active counter-strokes. One such scheme that found favour was proposed by Captain Sir Home Riggs Popham (1). Described by Arthur Bryant as 'that clever but incurably plausible naval officer', Popham's career was marked by a series of clever ideas – including his famous signal system used to send 'England expects . . .' – but attended in equal measure by controversy.

Popham's scheme involved an amphibious attack on the Saas Lock at Ostend, the seaward end of the canal to Bruges and Ghent, which connecting to the West Scheldt and the port of Flushing provided a safe inland route for invasion barges built in Belgium and Holland, and also formed an artery for naval stores. Its destruction would force these craft into the open sea where there was more chance that they might be intercepted.

The composition of Popham's force is interesting because it was the first of many such anti-invasion operations and throws light on the specialist uses of some of the Navy's smaller ship types. His flagship was an old 44 armed *en flûte* as a troopship, with three frigates similarly

2

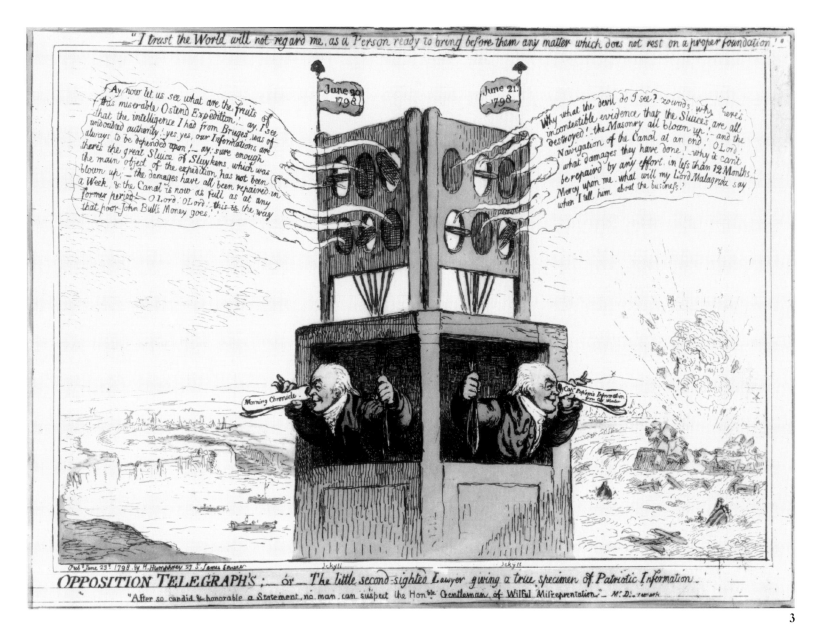

reduced, four small Sixth Rates, two bomb vessels, three brig sloops, and twelve other craft, mostly gunbrigs with sliding keels but including the 'oddities' *Dart* and *Wolverine* (2) and the ex-French gunboat *Vesuve*; a hired cutter and a lugger carried the mines or petards. Popham specified the small and shallow-draught vessel types, but in this case the Admiralty's choice was restricted by Popham's lack of seniority to junior captains below him in the Navy List.

The original intention was to launch diversionary raids against Flushing and other Channel ports but these were cancelled. The landings were eventually carried out successfully on 19 May but in deteriorating weather and against Popham's advice. The sluice gates were destroyed, but the army could not be re-embarked because of the surf on the beach and after a defensive battle some 1100 men under Major-General Eyre Coote were forced to surrender.

Although the naval part of the operation was beyond

reproach, Popham again found himself embayed in controversy when an opposition MP claimed that no damage had been done to the sluices. He was forced to retract the statement the following day, after Popham put him right, but it gave Gillray an opportunity to satirise the *volte face* using the fashionably new device of the Admiralty shutter telegraph (3).

1. 'Sir Home Riggs Popham, KM & FRS, Commander of His Majesty's Squadron at the Capture of Buenos Ayres &c', stipple engraving by Antoine Cardeau after an original by Mather Brown, published by Joyce Gold, 1 November 1806.
NMM ref PAH5888

2. 'The Wolverine Sloop of War of 12 Guns, Commanded by Captn Lewis Mortlock', aquatint by Rosenberg after an original by W T Anderson, no date.
NMM neg B9286

3. 'Opposition Telegraphs; – or – The Little Second-Sighted Lawyer giving a True Specimen of Patriotic Information', coloured engraving by James Gillray, published by H Humphrey, London 23 June 1798.
British Museum, Cat No 9232

2

1

3

The destruction of Bompart off Lough Swilly

THE SECOND French expedition of 1798 to Ireland consisted of about 3000 troops and a great deal of stores to arm Irish rebels, carried in one 74 (the *Hoche*) and nine frigates commanded by Commodore Bompart. He sailed from Brest on the evening of 16 September. At dawn he was seen by a British squadron of the frigates *Boadicea* and *Ethalion*, with the sloop *Sylph*. The first was sent to warn the Channel Fleet while the other two shadowed the French. A day later they were joined by another British frigate, the *Amelia*. Bompart's attempts to drive or shake off his pursuers failed. Instead

they were joined on the 20th by the *Anson*, and, by the 22nd, the British commander was fairly sure of his opponent's destination and sent the *Sylph* to warn the Commander-in-Chief on the Irish station.

The three British frigates kept the enemy in sight until the evening of 4 October, and then, in bad weather, parted company. On the 11th the *Ethalion* and *Anson* joined the squadron of Commodore Sir John Borlase Warren (1) off the coast of Donegal. Warren, an effective commander of detached squadrons, had been sent to deal with the French force and with this reinforcement had

4

1. 'Sir John Borlase Warren, Bart, K.B.', engraving and etching by James Fittler after an original by Mark Oates, published by J & J Boydell, 1 October 1799.
NMM ref PAG9416

2. 'To His Royal Highness . . . Attack of the French Squadron . . . by a Detachment of His Majesty's Ships . . . near the Rosses, on the coast of Ireland, October 12th 1798 . . . is respectfully dedicated', etching by James Fittler after an original by Captain Mark Oates, published by J & J Boydell, 1 October 1799.
NMM ref PAH7960

3. 'To His Royal Highness . . . the Surrender of the Hoche & Coquille, the Ethalion's Action, the Anson engaging five French frigates as they passed & the pursuit of the remainder of the French squadron . . . by a Detachment of His Majesty's Ships . . . near the Rosses on the coast of Ireland, on the evening of the 12th October 1798 . . . is respectfully dedicated', etching by James Fittler after an original by Captain Mark Oates, published by J & J Boydell, 1 October 1799.
NMM ref PAH7961

4. 'The Hoche in tow of the Doris', aquatint engraved by William Ellis after an original by Nicholas Pocock (1740-1821), published by Bunny and Gold 1 March 1800.
NMM ref PAD5607

5. 'HMS Donegal', watercolour by Lieutenant George Pechell Mends, 1840.
NMM ref PAH0760

three two-deckers (*Canada, Foudroyant* and *Robust*), two heavy frigates and three others.

On the 11th, at noon, Bompart was approaching Tory Island off northwest Ireland, when his leading ship signalled the appearance of the British. Bompart made off to the southwest, still intending to land his troops if he was granted the opportunity. Warren, on learning of the presence of the enemy, instantly ordered a general chase. That night it blew very hard; and, while the heavy frigate *Anson* carried away some of her top-hamper, the *Hoche*, still more unfortunate, lost her main topmast and her fore and mizzen topgallant masts, and the *Résolue* sprang a bad leak. At first light on the 12th, when the two squadrons were again able to see one another and the wind had moderated, the British ships were spread out on either side and astern of the French. Thus Bompart, with two crippled ships, found every avenue of escape shut against him except the direction in which he was steering.

By 7am Bompart had formed his ships in a single straggling line ahead, but minus the leaky *Résolue* which was steering inshore, and the *Biche* which had been sent after her with orders. Warren was much stronger than his enemy but instead of continuing the general chase delayed to form line of battle, directing the *Robust* to lead, 'and the rest of the ships to form in succession in the rear of the van'. This order brought the *Robust*, which was followed by the *Magnanime*, within long-range stern fire of the *Embuscade* and *Coquille*. After firing back, the *Robust*, carried on down the French line and by about 8.50am, she had closed with the *Hoche*, and began a hot

action with her, broadside to broadside, slowing to keep alongside of the enemy. The *Magnanime* engaged the *Embuscade* and *Coquille*, and, passing on to leeward of the *Robust*, had to starboard her helm to clear the latter. The *Loire*, *Immortalité*, and *Bellone* turned out of the French line to rake her as she did so; but they were soon driven to resume their southwest course, as the *Foudroyant*, *Amelia*, and *Ethalion* then coming up into action (2). These ships, as well as the *Melampus* and *Canada*, all fired into the *Hoche*,

5

6

7

struck in about an hour and a half, and that the *Bellone*, after having made a desperate resistance to the *Foudroyant* and *Melampus* in succession, surrendered to the *Ethalion* (3). The other French vessels escaped for the moment, and, as they got away, engaged the *Anson*, and inflicted considerable damage.

The British losses were only 13 killed, and 75 wounded despite the fierceness of the French resistance, which is confirmed by the *Hoche*'s 270 killed and wounded; the corresponding figure for the other prizes was 125 between them.

Warren unwisely ordered the *Robust*, which was seriously crippled aloft, to tow the still more disabled *Hoche* into Lough Swilly, and had it not been for the frigate *Doris* coming to help (4), and the hard work of the surviving crew of the *Hoche*, the largest of his prizes would probably have been lost. The *Hoche* (renamed *Donegal*), *Bellone* (renamed *Proserpine*), and *Embuscade* were added to the Royal Navy. The *Coquille* probably would have been, had she not been accidentally burnt at Plymouth. *Donegal* remained a favourite ship for a generation and was not broken up until 1845 (5).

Three of Bompart's remaining ships escaped – the *Romaine, Biche,* and *Sémillante* – but the others all ran into roaming British ships. The five French frigates which made off to leeward were chased by the *Canada, Foudroyant,* and *Melampus*. At about midnight on the 13th, the *Melampus* sighted the *Immortalité* and *Résolue*; an hour later she succeeded in bringing to action the last named (6), which was still leaking badly, and otherwise hampered so soon surrendered.

which, after a brilliant two-hour defence, struck. Aboard was the Irish patriot Wolfe Tone who would later commit suicide to escape execution.

The *Embuscade*, badly treated first by the *Magnanime* and afterwards by the *Foudroyant*, surrendered at 11.30am to the *Magnanime*, which, having herself suffered severely, remained by her prize. The other British ships, with the exception of the *Robust*, which was disabled, and the *Anson*, which was still struggling up from the southeast, chased vigorously; the results being that the *Coquille*

8

The *Sémillante* and *Loire* were sighted on the morning of 15 October by the large frigate *Révolutionnaire*, the smaller *Mermaid*, and the sloop *Kangaroo*, and soon separated. The *Révolutionnaire*, chasing the *Sémillante*, lost her in the evening. The *Mermaid* and *Kangaroo* pursued the other, and also lost her, but found her again at dawn on the 16th, and renewed the chase. In the afternoon, the *Kangaroo* caught up and attacked her much bigger opponent, until she was forced to drop out of the chase with a shattered foremast. At daybreak on the 17th, the much bigger *Loire* shortened sail to allow the persistent *Mermaid* to come up. After an engagement of two hours and a half, the *Loire*'s fire was slackening and *Mermaid* was about to cross her bow to rake when her mizzen mast came down, the falling wreckage disabling several of her after guns. Soon afterwards she also lost her main topmast, and, badly damaged, she had to discontinue the action (7). Her severely damaged enemy put before the wind and made off only to find herself, at daybreak on the 18th, to leeward of the *Anson* and the *Kangaroo*. The *Anson* was as crippled as the

Loire but the *Kangaroo* had made good her damages. An action between the two larger vessels began at 10.30am and at 11.45am, when they had almost completely disabled one another, the brig was able to throw the weight of her broadside into the scale and decide the issue (8).

The *Immortalité* had nearly reached Brest on 20 October when she was caught by the *Fisgard*, a near sister now in British hands. An action began just after noon (9) and, although the *Fisgard* had at one time to drop astern, and was, towards the conclusion, half full of water, she obliged her opponent to strike at about 3pm, after having reduced her to a sinking state and killed or wounded 115 of her crew for a loss of 36.

As a coda to the whole ill-starred operation, the Dutch contribution to the invasion force was intercepted on 24 October by the 18pdr-armed frigate *Sirius*, which captured, in rapid succession, the corvette *Waakzamheid* (10) and then her consort, the 12pdr 36-gun *Furie*. Besides troops, the Dutch ships were carrying ordnance stores and 6000 stands of arms for the planned Irish uprising.

6. 'His Majesty's Ship Melampus of 36 guns . . . in chase of Resolue & Bellone two French frigates of 40 guns each off the coast of Ireland, October 13th 1798', anonymous varnished watercolour, no date.
NMM ref PAH5223

7. 'Quatrième combat soutenu par le Loire sur la cote d'Irelande, le 26 Vendemaire an 7', coloured engraving engraved by Lambert after an original by Louis Phillipe Crepin, published by Bruce, An XII (1803-4).
NMM neg X2075

8. 'Cinquième combat soutenu par le Loire sur la cote d'Irelande, le 26 Vendemaire an 7', engraving and etching by Lambert after an original by Louis Phillipe Crepin, published by Jean, no date. Apart from making the *Loire* too small, the ships are well depicted: the *Anson*, which was a cut-down 64, is correctly shown with her great cabin above the upper deck. Note the sharpshooters, a French speciality, on the *Loire*'s roundhouse.
NMM neg B9287

9

9. 'HMS Fisgard taking the French Immortalite off Brest 20 Oct 1798', anonymous watercolour, no date. *NMM ref PAF5951*

10. 'Capture of the Furie & Waakzamheid Octr 23rd 1798', coloured aquatint engraved by Thomas Sutherland after an original by Thomas Whitcombe (born *c*1752), published 1 October 1816. *NMM ref PAD5613*

10

Ships of the Royal Navy: the Second Rate

THE SMALL three-decker of 98 guns was a characteristically British ship-type, with no exact equivalent in the navies of France or Spain. The very large two-decker of 80 or more guns favoured by those countries was the best match - and the type was actually more powerful if judged entirely by broadside weight of metal (including carronades, 1287lbs for a French 80 compared with 1012lbs for a British 98). Yet the Royal Navy exhibited so strong a preference for the three-decker that it clearly believed it had palpable advantages. These were essentially its superiority in battle: the higher command of the third deck gave it a tactical advantage, as well as a depressing effect on enemy morale (1). However small and relatively weak in firepower, the Second Rate was still a three-decker, and there were numerous incidents in which opposing fleets took to flight after over-estimating, by this criteria, the power of the three-deckers in the British fleet. In practice, this was no mean advantage.

What made this advantage particularly attractive to the British was its relative economy. The Second Rate was cheaper to build and maintain, and so could be risked in more theatres of operation, than the First Rate, but retained many of its desirable qualities in battle. It was almost as robust: for example, during the Battle of Cape St Vincent *Blenheim* was surrounded by five Spanish ships, including a three-decker and the *Santisima Trinidad*, and was reported to have received 105 hits in the hull; yet she had only 13 killed and 48 wounded.

For most of the age of sail, and well beyond, the Royal Navy had extensive commitments, which could only be covered by numbers of ships. This led to a consistent and almost unbroken policy which not only resisted growth in the individual sizes of ships but also preferred the smallest and cheapest type that could do the job. In this respect the 98, an 'economy' three-decker, is a characteristic British ship type. Unfortunately, if quantity has a

1

higher priority than quality, then economy must be bought at the expense of capability. For the Second Rate, that penalty was in sailing qualities and seakeeping. Since speed is largely a function of waterline length, short designs like the 98 tended to be slow; furthermore, because the height between decks was more or less fixed by the size of human beings, they were relatively tall for their length, which made them leewardly. In fact, the Second Rate suffered an unenviable reputation in the fleet for dismal sailing and clumsy handling. A particularly spectacular example was Lord Bridport's hurried attempt to leave Spithead in pursuit of a French squadron on Christmas day 1796. *Prince*, 98 missed stays and collided with *Sans Pareil*; *Ville de Paris* was hit and damaged by *Formidable*, 98; and *Atlas*, 98 ran aground. Admiral Jervis, not yet St Vincent, had a very low opinion of the discipline and seamanship of the Channel Fleet at this

2

3

time, but his own *St George*, 98 fouled of a Portuguese frigate and then ran hard aground not a month later in the river Tagus (2). At Trafalgar the notoriously poor sailing of the *Prince* and *Dreadnought* (and the First Rate *Britannia* for that matter), led Nelson to instruct them to make a more slanting approach, in the hope that allowing more sails to draw would help them to keep up. This is why in the more accurate depictions of the battle these ships seem to belong to neither line.

In the 1750s an attempt to improve their sailing qualities was made by reducing the quarterdeck armament to a couple of chase guns, but this was compromised in 1778 when the nominal 90s had become 98s by the addition of eight 6pdrs to the quarterdeck. Slade's mid-1750s designs, like the *London* class (3, 4), were lengthened to allow fourteen ports a side on the lower deck, but there were no further improvements until the *Dreadnought* class (5) of 1788 introduced 18pdr batteries on the upper as well as middle decks.

Numbers were always far greater than those of First

Rates, but it is noticeable that while the larger ships were kept in service almost until the end of the fighting, Second Rates began to decline in numbers after Trafalgar. This probably reflects the continuing need for prestige fleet flagships, while admirals on relatively minor stations preferred the superior sailing of large two-deckers in their choice of flagships.

Year	No in Sea Service	No in Ordinary or Repairing
1793	4	12
1796	16	0
1799	15	2
1801	14	2
1805	11	3
1808	7	4
1811	8	4
1814	5	3
1815	2	5

Since there were virtually no similar ships in enemy navies, numbers could not be augmented by capture.

Second Rates were concentrated in the Channel and Mediterranean fleets, usually carrying the flags of the subordinate divisional commanders. In this capacity they sometimes led squadrons on detached cruises, but in the context of the Channel Fleet their poor sailing made them even more vulnerable than First Rates to the perils of blockading the French coast. The close blockade was nerve-wracking enough in two-deckers, but virtually suicidal in anything larger, and some captains lobbied for the command of three-decked ships to avoid such service.

In actual combat Second Rates were in their element and many fought with distinction in all the major deep-water combats up to and including Trafalgar. Unlike the First Rates, however, some 98s were released for service further afield. From the beginning of the war important colonial expeditions were commanded from Second Rates. *Queen* (and *Duke*) were involved in the attack on Martinique in 1793, and *Boyne* carried Sir John Jervis's flag for the West Indies campaign of 1794. From then on there was often a Second Rate, or occasionally two, in these waters, while the Leeward Island station was important enough to warrant a 98 as flagship for much of the rest of the war.

One advantage of the 98 over the First Rate was a slightly reduced draught – perhaps 2ft less. As a result Second Rates were sometimes employed where their larger consorts would not float. When at the beginning of 1801 an expedition to Denmark and the Baltic was mooted – with shallow water in prospect – the proposed flagships were *St George* and *London*, 98s; Nelson eventually abandoned the former to lead the attack on Copenhagen from a 74, but there began an association between Second Rates and the Baltic that was renewed

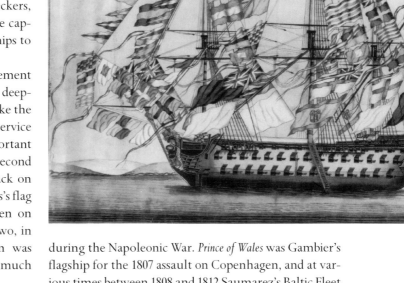

4

during the Napoleonic War. *Prince of Wales* was Gambier's flagship for the 1807 assault on Copenhagen, and at various times between 1808 and 1812 Saumarez's Baltic Fleet included the *Formidable, Dreadnought, Temeraire* and *St George*. During the war the Royal Navy became more adventurous in the use of its large ships in all weathers and all the year round, but just how great were the risks of this policy was underlined by the loss of the *St George* in a gale when returning from the Baltic in 1811; admittedly, the ship was jury rigged, but the notoriously poor handling of the 98s had some bearing on a disaster in which 850 men died.

1. 'An English three-decker fighting vessel', etching by John Thomas Serres after an original by Dominic Serres (1722-1793), 1783. *NMM neg X223*

2. 'View of HMS St George after being on shore on the bar of Lisbon', black and watercolour pen and ink by G B Lawrence, no date. *NMM ref PAH0745*

3. 'His Majesty's Ship the London a Second Rate Carrying 90 guns, and 850 men, off the Ram Head, near Plymouth', engraving and etching published by Carington Bowles, 4 June 1781. *NMM ref PAH0730*

4. 'His Majesty's Ship Impregnable on the 17th August 1789, when Their Majesties and Princesses honord her with a Visit', pen and ink and watercolour by John Burrows, no date. *NMM ref PAH0749*

5. Design draught for the *Dreadnought* class, dated July 1790. *NMM neg X163*

5

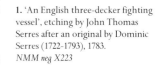

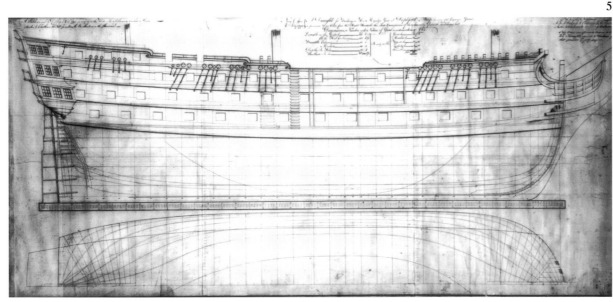

1

Anglo-Russian invasion of the Netherlands 1799

THE INVASION of the Netherlands by a British (and a British-subsidised Russian) army, was intended to be Britain's contribution to a co-ordinated attack on France by the forces of the Second Coalition. Russian and Austrian armies in northern Italy, Switzerland and southern Germany would punch through the Jura while the Anglo-Russian army advanced south through modern Belgium, to converge on Paris. It was a wildly optimistic grand strategy, given the divergent interests of the allies, but even if the Austrians had not compromised the southern offensive, the Netherland front would have stalled, destroying any chance of overthrowing the French regime. There was also belief in some quarters that the landings would inspire a rising in favour of the Prince of Orange against the pro-French Batavian republic, but this proved illusory.

Although the British had considerable experience of amphibious operations, the government perennially underestimated the time it took to assemble such expeditions. The concept had been under discussion since the previous autumn and in active planning since April, but still the fleet did not get to sea until 13 August 1799. Even at that date its destination was not fixed: it was supposedly aiming for the mouth of the Maas or Walcheren, towards the south of the country, but at sea the commander of the advance guard, Sir Ralph Abercromby, switched the landings to the Helder in the far north. It had some defensive advantages, being a narrow peninsula where the enemy could be held off until the planned army build-up could be completed, and there was shelter for the ships once the naval base of Den Helder itself was captured – but it was far further from the French border.

Tactical surprise was achieved – the defenders also expected the attack to come further south – but was promptly lost again when just as the garrison and fleet at the Helder had been summoned to surrender a gale blew the ships offshore for five days. On 26 August, with a heavy swell still running, Abercromby took the risky decision to land the troops, which were duly put ashore at first light on the following day beneath a thunderous bombardment from the supporting warships (1). The

2

beach was long and flat (2), but dominated by a ridge of high sand dunes, behind which was a tidal marsh leaving a narrow spit of firm ground. Daendals, the Batavian commander, failed to attack the invaders as they landed, preferring to attack the flanks; about 6000 men were involved on each side but after a sharp engagement the Dutch were driven off and in the night Den Helder was evacuated, the garrison escaping by marching south along the marshy edge of the Zuider Zee where the British dare not follow (3).

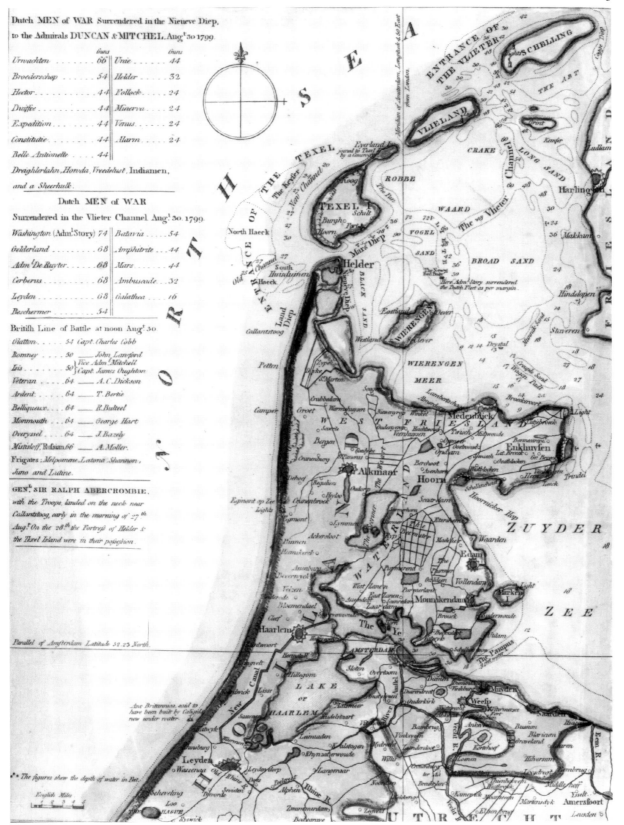

3

1. 'The British Troops Landing in Holland. View of the Second Division of the British Army commanded by Sir Ralph Abercromby, landing on the beach near Kieck Down on the 27th of August 1799, covered by the Fleet and Gun Vessels under the command of Vice Admiral Mitchell', aquatint and etching after an original by Robert Dodd (1748-1815), 1 December 1800. NMM ref PAH7966

2. 'Landing of English troops Calandsoog, North Holland, August 27th 1799', watercolour by Dirk Langendyk, no date. NMM ref PAF5561

3. 'Grand expedition. A Map of the Texel and Vlieter Roads with the Country of Holland as far South as the Hague: Intended to Illustrate the Operations of the Grand Expedition', coloured etching after an original by John Luffman, no date. NMM ref PAG8998

4. 'Sir Andrew Mitchell KB Admiral of the Blue Squadron', stipple engraving by H R Cook after an original by Robert Bowyer (1758-1834), published by Joyce Gold, 30 August 1806. NMM ref PAD3093

5. 'Surrender of the Dutch Fleet. Admiral Sir Andrew Mitchell taking possession of the whole Dutch Ships of War in the Texel on the 30th August 1799', aquatint and etching, produced and published by Robert Dodd, 31 December 1800. NMM neg 6171

6. The lines and profile draught of the *Washington*, 74 guns. This appears to be the original Dutch draught and was probably captured with the ship; original draughts of other ships taken at the time also survive at Greenwich (see, for example, page 162 of *Navies and the American Revolution*). NMM neg DR6748

7. 'Fleet of armed pinks coming to anchor at Mardyck, 5 April 1793', etching by K F Bendorp after an original by M Schouman, published by W Holtrop, no date. Although dating from the earlier campaign in the Netherlands, these are the type of vessel improvised as gunboats by both sides during the 1799 campaign. NMM ref PAF4676

8. 'Ataque van de Engelschen op de Lemmer den 19 September 1799', etching by Renier Vinkeles after an original by Dirk Langendyk, published by F Bohn, no date. NMM ref PAD5626

9. 'Evacuation de la Hollande Par les Anglo-Russes, et capitulation du Duc d'Yorck le 10 Brumaire An 8 [10 October 1799]', etching by Dupreel after an original by Duplessi Bertaux, no date. NMM ref PAD5627

With the occupation of the Helder base the British acquired some old and largely dismantled ships (one 64, a 50, six 44s and five smaller frigates, three Indiamen and a sheer hulk) lying in the Nieuve Diep, the main squadron under Admiral Story having retreated out into the Vlieter channel and removed the navigation marks. The naval commander, Vice-Admiral Mitchell (4), lost no time in pressing his advantage and even the Dutch were impressed by the speed with which buoys were laid; at dawn on 30 August Mitchell's squadron, in line of battle, entered the Mars Diep and summoned the Batavian fleet to surrender in the name of the Prince of Orange (5). Although most of the officers were nominally republicans, the crews were predominantly Orangist, and Story used the virtual state of mutiny in the fleet as his excuse for not putting up any resistance. It was the end of an independent Netherlands navy in the age of sail and a sad conclusion to the tradition of Tromp and de Ruyter.

The ships themselves, comprising a 74, five 64s, one 50 and three frigates, were ostensibly taken over in the name of the Stadtholder, but there was never an Orangist counter-revolution and the most suitable vessels were eventually bought in to the Royal Navy. They were not ships of the highest value: the only 74, the *Washington* (6), was smaller than any ship of the same rate in British service, and although the *Amfitrite* made a fine big 24pdr frigate, most of the smaller ships saw out their lives in secondary roles, as floating batteries, troopships, store carriers and the like.

On land the campaign soon ground to a halt, despite the arrival of reinforcements, including the Russian corps. The overall commander, the Duke of York, then had about 30,000 men, but the defence had been taken over by a French division under General Brune, a future Napoleonic Marshal, who thwarted the allied attempts to break out of the Helder peninsula. On 19 September, owing to a disaster to the Russian right wing before Bergen, the allied assault failed; they tried again on 2 October and reached Egmont, but the Franco-Batavian army had retired before them in good order. A tentative renewal of the advance was met by a strong counter-

attack on the 6th and finally the decision was taken to
retire to a strong defensive line on the Zijpe canal – from
where the attack had begun a month earlier.

The Navy's role in the land operations was inevitably
ancillary, but Home Popham was able to contrive a
flotilla of gunboats that saw action against similarly
improvised Dutch craft (7) and on the flanks of the
army. Seamen were also widely used to transport supplies across the difficult terrain of flooded polders and
marshy litoral that composed much of West Friesland.
Besides the main landings, the Navy had been employed
to seize a few outlying positions, including the town of
Lemmer (8), which on 11 October was attacked by a large
military force, only to be repulsed by the seamen and
marines – 157 strong – of the sloop *Espiegle,* under
Commander Boorder. Mitchell even took the 20-gun
Babet and a squadron of six smaller vessels into the
Zuyder Zee, but it was too late to turn the campaign.

Too weak to advance, but too numerous to live off the
small amount of territory occupied, under ceaseless
autumn rains, the Duke of York's army was faced with
an unpleasant alternative: surrender or evacuate under
fire. News then arrived of a disaster on the southern
front – the Austrians had withdrawn part of their forces
from Switzerland to secure their own sectarian interests
and the French had won a great victory at Zurich, forcing a retreat along the whole allied line. With the ratio-
nale for the Dutch operation removed, the Duke of York
opened negotiations with General Brune to save what
he could of the allied army. In the end he obtained better terms than a defeated commander could have
expected, and he was able to withdraw the whole army,
its artillery and most of its horses and stores (9).

Although on a tactical level the British troops had
fought well, it was a a serious and embarrassing strategic
defeat. Over the centuries it has been largely wiped from
the national memory, but although the context is now
forgotten the incident survives in the song learnt by
many children:

> The grand old Duke of York
> He had 10,000 men
> He marched them up to the top of the hill
> And he marched them down again

It is usually regarded as a nonsense rhyme, but its origin
is a satirical song of the time, which derides perfectly the
advance-retreat-advance movement of the Duke's army
and its final stranding in no man's land.

> And when they were up they were up
> And when they were down they were down
> But when they were only half way up
> They were neither up nor down

1

2

Tightening the blockade 1799-1800

Off Ushant on 27 April 1799 the cutter *Black Joke* sighted and after a four-hour chase captured the French lugger *Rebecca* (1). The previous day, in foggy weather, a French fleet of twenty-four of the line under Admiral Bruix (2) escaped from Brest and soon shook off the only watching frigate on station. News that a powerful French squadron was not only loose but also lost sent the Cabinet into panic, but the *Rebecca* was carrying dispatches that revealed Bruix's destination to be Ireland. Since this was the abiding nightmare of the British government, the intelligence was received without surprise or questioning.

But if the politicians were convinced, the Navy was not. The lugger had been three weeks off Ushant when supposedly carrying urgent dispatches and had never attempted to jettison them during a long chase. Captain Philip d'Auverne (3), who ran a very effective intelligence network in France from his headquarters in the Channel Islands, had heard nothing, and the Admiralty rapidly concluded that the *Rebecca* was a decoy. In fact, Bruix

sailed for the Mediterranean, intending to relieve Corfu, Malta and Bonaparte in Egypt, and although he achieved none of these, the incident served to underline the inadequacy of Bridport's long-distance blockade of Brest.

'The Old Lady', as Pellew derisively dubbed Lord Bridport, was finally replaced by St Vincent in April 1800. The legendary—and much-feared—discipline of the Mediterranean Fleet was slowly introduced in the Channel. Ships spent more time at sea, resupplied on station and wherever possible refitted and repaired without recourse to a dockyard. Captains were forbidden to spend nights ashore during the fleet's rare visits to Torbay, and defaulters were punished by serving a stint in the Inshore Squadron off the dreaded Black Rocks—known to naval officers as 'Siberia'. But with the hardship came a new agressiveness and *esprit de corps*. The French fleet was not to be allowed the training and experience it so desperately needed, even in the waters immediately outside Brest (4). It had the further advantage of cutting off more of the port's naval supplies, which because of the poor road system of the Brittany peninsula was mainly brought in by coastal shipping.

St Vincent's concept of close blockade, as applied off Cadiz, meant keeping big ships close in to the French coast in all weathers (5). It was immensely wearing on both ships and men, and since Bruix's abortive cruise Brest contained not only the most powerful French fleet but also that of its Spanish ally (6). This made it doubly important to keep the port well bottled up, but required the proximity of more of the Channel Fleet than had been the case earlier in the war. Its successful execution allowed the British to plan the various amphibious attacks of 1800 with less fear of interruption by powerful enemy naval forces. That the opportunities were largely squandered is not the fault of St Vincent or his block-ading squadrons.

3

1. 'British naval cutter firing on a French craft', graphite drawing by Admiral of the Fleet Sir Graham Eden Hamond, no date.
NMM ref PAG3876

2. 'Admiral Bruix', stipple engraving by Lambert, published by Ambroise Tordieu 1816.
NMM ref PAD8214

3. 'Philip d'Auverne, Prince of Bouillon', stipple engraving by William Ridley, published by Joyce Gold 30 March 1805.
NMM ref PAH5906

4. 'HMS *Montagu* forcing the enemy to move from Berthaume Bay, 22 August 1800', oil painting by Jeffrey Raegersveld (c1770-1844).
NMM ref BHC0521

5. 'A Correct Plan of the Present Position of the French & Spanish Fleets now Blockaded in the Harbour of Brest by the English Fleet Under the Command of Earl St Vincent Jan 1801', etching after an original by Lieutenant John Grey, published by John Wallis, 9 February 1801.
NMM ref PAH7991

6. 'French and Spanish fleets at anchor', anonymous watercolour, no date. The port is certainly Brest, seen through the Goulet, and is most likely to be 1800-1801.
NMM ref PAG8374

4

5

6

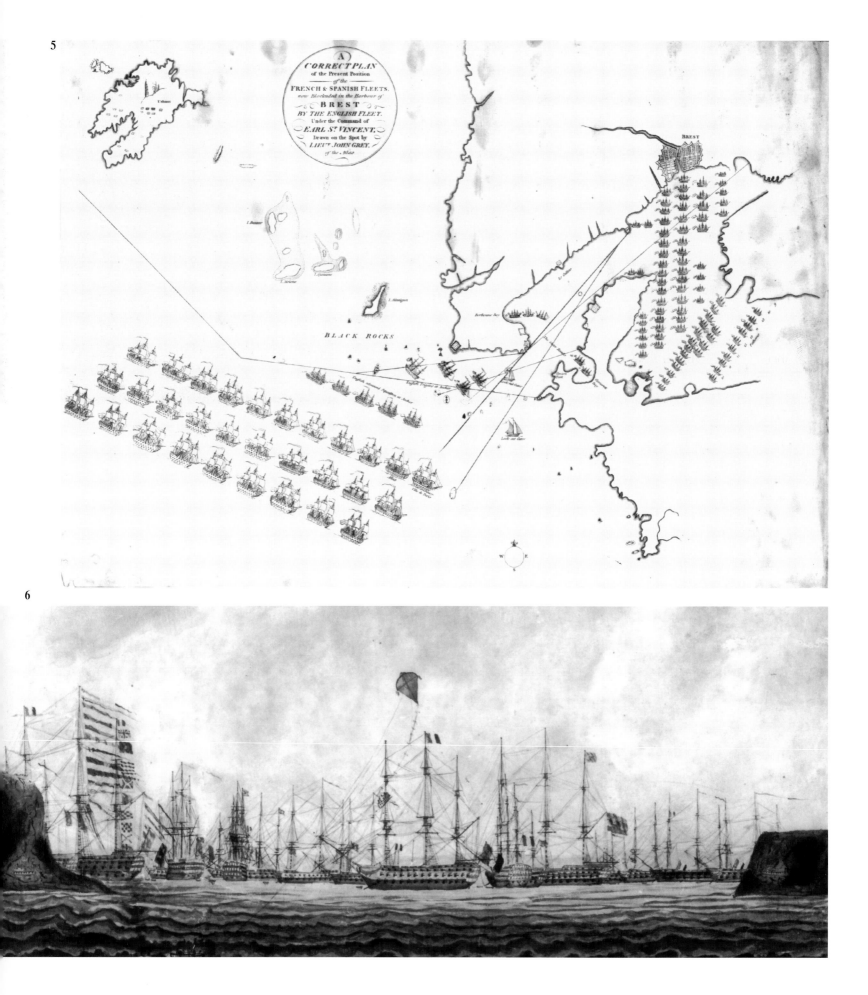

Watching the Biscay ports

WHILE THE attention of the Channel Fleet was principally concentrated on Brest, the other ports of the enemy's Atlantic coast were watched by smaller detachments, ranging from a few sail of the line down to a single frigate or sloop depending on their importance. Thus for many a French or Spanish ship the most dangerous portion of a voyage was often making a landfall on their own coast. The frigate *Seine*, for example, three months out from Mauritius and heading for Lorient after long service in the Indian Ocean, was almost in sight of the French coast when on 29 June 1798 she ran into a British squadron comprising the frigates *Jason*, 38, *Pique*, 36 and *Mermaid*, 32. In the ensuing chase, *Mermaid* soon fell behind, but while the *Jason* steered to cut off the quarry from Lorient, *Pique* brought her to action in a long running fight.

Seine was a 40-gun 18pdr-armed ship and gave her 12pdr opponent a pounding for two and a half hours before the *Jason* could close. During the battle the antagonists had been edging ever nearer to the coast, and all three took the ground – although, fortunately, on a rising tide. The *Jason* swung stern-on to the *Seine*, also masking the fire of the *Pique*, so the action was sustained for some time, despite the total dismasting of the French ship, before she surrendered (1). *Jason* was soon afloat and the next day *Seine* was also freed, but the *Pique* was so hard aground that she had to be destroyed (2). The captain and crew were turned over to the prize, which in every way was an advantageous exchange for the *Pique*.

The Royal Navy's presence on the Biscay coast was such that French ships could not feel safe even in their own inshore waters. The growing self-confidence, if not arrogance, of the British frigate captains was amply demonstrated off Lorient the year after the capture of the *Seine*. Two British ships, *San Fiorenzo* and *Amelia*, refused to be driven off their station by three French frigates and a gunboat, despite existing damage to *Amelia*'s top hamper occasioned by a squall. The action lasted two hours, before the French force retired, and was well enough regarded to inspire a representation by Nicholas Pocock in one of his typically detailed and well-researched depictions (3).

Rochefort was another port that built a number of warships and also harboured privateers and naval small craft, requiring a watch to be kept on such activity. The 38-gun *Clyde* was employed in exactly this mission when on 20 August 1799 she sighted a French frigate and a corvette, the *Vestale*, 36 and *Sagesse*, 20. The latter escaped inshore, but the two frigates fought a two-hour duel in

1

which the more powerfully armed British ship was victorious (4). The *Vestale* was so badly damaged in this and an earlier action that she was not thought fit for purchase into the Royal Navy.

While the larger harbours were usually allocated frigates to keep an eye on them, the smaller ports could be monitored by sloops, although the poor sailing qualities of the quarterdecked ships sloops made their position precarious if surprised by a faster frigate. On 6

2

3

4

February 1800 one of this class, the 16-gun *Fairy*, in company with the 18-gun brig *Harpy* was reconnoitring St Malo when they fell in with the French frigate *Pallas*, 38 guns. Despite being out-gunned, the sloops attacked without hesitation, and a two-hour battle followed (5) before three unidentified sail appeared on the horizon and *Pallas* broke off the action. The Royal Navy's domination of these waters made it a strong possibility that they were British warships, and they proved to be the *Loire*, 38, *Danae*, 20 and *Railleur*, 16. Now greatly inferior in firepower, the *Pallas* made for the land, but despite reaching the protection of a small shore battery, the French frigate was surrounded and forced to strike her colours. She was taken into British service and renamed *Pique*, to replace the ship lost in the *Seine* action the previous year.

Eventually the Royal Navy's grip on the Biscay coast was extended to include the ports of northern Spain, even if nothing larger than a brig could be spared for such a task. Brig sloops were close to ideal for this purpose, because they were usually weatherly enough to escape from more powerful opponents, and even when trapped by adverse circumstances could give a good account of themselves thanks to their powerful short-range armament of 32pdr carronades. A textbook demonstration of this was given by the brig *Sylph* in the summer of 1801 off Santander when she on two occasions encountered and fought off a French frigate (6).

5

1. 'Capture of La Seine . . . The Action commenced in a running fight, between La Pique and La Seine . . . and the Jason coming up ran between & received the fire of the Enemy', aquatint engraved by Robert Dodd (1748-1815) after his own original, no date.
NMM neg X1631

2. 'Situation of the Jason and La Pique and their prize (La Seine) on the morning after the action', aquatint published by Robert Dodd (1748-1815), April 1801.
NMM neg X1632

3. 'To Captain Sir H. B. Neale Bart, of His Majesty's Ship St Fiorenzo the Honble Captain Herbert of the Amelia . . . This Print Representing their Engagement with Three French Frigates and a Gun Vessel aided by a Battery on the Shore, close in with Bellisle April 9th 1799', coloured aquatint engraved by Robert Pollard after an original by Nicholas Pocock (1740-1821), published by the artist, 12 February 1801.
NMM ref PAH7963

4. 'Capture of La Vestale, Augt. 20th 1799', coloured aquatint engraved by Thomas Sutherland after an original by Thomas Whitcombe (born c1752), published 1 August 1816.
NMM ref PAD5625

5. 'A representation of La Pallas making Sail from His Majesty's Sloops Fairy and Harpy after an action of two hours off St Maloes, 6 Feby 1801 [sic]', aquatint engraved by Francis Chesham after an original by William Anderson, published by C Richards, 1 January 1818.
NMM neg B4494

6. 'To Charles Dashwood Esqr commander of his Majesty's Sloop of War Sylph engaging a French Frigate . . . 44 guns, on the night of July 31st 1801 . . .', aquatint and etching produced and published by Robert Dodd, no date.
NMM neg A4307

6

One against the odds

DURING THE course of the wars of 1793-1815, it has been calculated that while the British captured 229 enemy frigates, the Royal Navy lost a mere 17, of which 9 were recaptured. This lead many—including contemporary naval officers—to believe that British victories in single-ship actions, if not actually inevitable, were the natural order of things. The War of 1812 was to jolt this complacency, but there was at least one earlier salutary lesson.

On the morning of 14 December 1798, the British 12pdr-armed, 32-gun frigate *Ambuscade* (Captain Henry Jenkins) was patrolling off Bordeaux. When a vessel approached her from seaward, she assumed the new arrival to be the *Stag* (32 guns, Captain Yorke), whom she was expecting, failed to make or request the private signals, and sent her crew to breakfast as usual. When almost within gunshot, the stranger—who was the French *Bayonnaise* (28 guns, commanded by Lieutenant de vaisseau Richer) suddenly hauled her wind and made all sail to get away. Realising her mistake, the *Ambuscade* gave chase; and opened fire towards noon. The *Bayonnaise* shortened sail and accepted the challenge. After about

an hour's fight, a 12pdr gun on the main deck of the *Ambuscade* burst, wounding 11 men and stoving in the boats on the booms.

In the confusion, the *Bayonnaise* made more sail and sought to break away. The *Ambuscade* recommenced the action from leeward and, in so doing, shot ahead of the *Bayonnaise*. The French, who had suffered considerable loss in officers and men (including both the captain and first lieutenant, badly wounded) and damage to hull, rigging and spars, then boldly decided to board. Putting up the helm, the *Bayonnaise* ran foul of the *Ambuscade*, carrying away with her bowsprit the *Ambuscade*'s starboard quarterdeck bulwark, mizzen shrouds and mizzen mast, unshipping the wheel, and eventually catching the *Ambuscade*'s rudder-chain. From the bowsprit, the contingent of 30 French troops from Cayenne on board the *Bayonnaise* subjected the *Ambuscade*'s unprotected quarterdeck to sustained musket fire (1). Within a few minutes the *Ambuscade*'s captain, first lieutenant, master, third lieutenant and lieutenant of marines were all either killed or wounded. No sooner had the purser assumed command than the gunner reported the ship to be on

1. 'Combat de la fregate française La Bayonnaise contre la fregate anglais L'Embuscade 14 decembre 1798', steel engraving by the elder Chavane after an original by Phillipe Crepin, no date.
NMM ref PAD5616

2. 'Combat de la Fregate française la Bayonnaise contre la fregate anglais l'Embuscade 14 Dec 1798', engraving by Doherty after an original by Hue, no date.
NMM neg B9362

3. 'Abordage de l'Ambuscade par La Bayonnaise', engraving by Best and Letour after an original by Morel Fatio, no date.
NMM ref PAD5615

2

fire (2). Cartridges carelessly left on the rudder-head had exploded, blown out a portion of the *Ambuscade*'s stern and caused such panic amongst the crew that the majority bolted for the safety of below-decks. Meanwhile the French poured across the bridge created by their vessel's bowsprit (3), onto the *Ambuscade*'s quarter-deck and, after a short struggle, carried the ship. The *Ambuscade*'s losses were 10 killed and 36 wounded; those of the *Bayonnaise*, 30 killed and 30 badly wounded, with perhaps another 60-70 less seriously wounded.

Although the surrender of the *Ambuscade* has been described as 'one of the very few actions in this war which are disgraceful to the British arms', it is perhaps fairer – and certainly more generous – to regard it as an example of a better-trained French ship, with a more determined and resourceful captain, getting the better of a sloppy and irresolute British crew. As so often happened the other way round, each vessel got the luck that she deserved.

3

1

2

Captain Schank's Q-ship

AN EARLIER section (pages 102-104) pointed out the contribution made by Captain Schank's drop keels to the sailing qualities of the Navy's small craft, but he was also responsible for an experiment in mounting large calibre guns in a small hull. The collier *Rattler* of 286 tons was purchased in March 1798 and fitted out under his direction. She carried five small carronades on deck but the unique feature of her armament was the 'tween deck battery of six 24pdr carronades fitted on transverse tracks or grooves in the deck so that they could be run out on either broadside, which with two long 18pdrs gave the ship a surprising firepower for its size. As he had done to demonstrate his ideas on drop keels, Schank had a model made which now resides at the National Maritime Museum (1).

This might have remained an obscure and insignificant experiment if the ship had not enjoyed such an eventful career, for her collier-build and bark rig gave her the appearance of an easy victim, attracting commerce raiders to her like a First World War Q-ship. However, she was not able to use her armament to advantage in the most famous engagement of this nature, which turned into a vicious little hand-to-hand struggle with two French privateer luggers, *Furet*, 14 and *Rusé*, 8 off Boulogne on 3 January 1799 (2). Outnumbered two to one, Captain Lewis Mortlock's crew managed to fight off the attempts to board, the ship's Newfoundland dog being singled out for particular praise in many accounts. For once the print (3) depicts a precise moment: while the assault over the bow was being repulsed, three men from the *Furet* boarded over the stern and one leapt on to top of the companion, but Mortlock ran aft and as his assailant's pistol misfired he pitchforked him over the side with a half-pike. The luggers eventually threw incendiaries into the *Wolverine* and escaped while the fire was being extinguished, but a parthian shot mortally wounded Captain Mortlock.

The ship enjoyed greater success in September when with another 'oddity', the Benthamite sloop *Arrow*, they captured the Dutch *Draak*, 18 and brig *Gier*, 14 off the Dutch coast. *Wolverine* eventually perished in March 1804 in a suitably heroic mode, defending her convoy from a far more powerful privateer, the frigate-built *Blonde* of 30 guns; she was so badly damaged in the action that she sank shortly after surrendering.

3

1. Model of the *Wolverine* as converted. The quarterdeck planking is not fitted, to show the runners in the deck below to transfer the carronades from one side to the other.
NMM neg B2290

2. 'His Majesty's Sloop of War Wolverene of 12 guns and 63 men, Attacking and defeating two French luggers . . . 1799', coloured aquatint and etching by F Warburton after an original by William Anderson (1757-1837), published by the artist, 12 September 1799.
NMM ref PAG8996

3. 'Captain Lewis Matlock gallantly defending His Majesty's Sloop of War Wolverene . . . against the united attack of two French Luggers . . . near Boulogne Jany 3rd 1800 . . . attended by his favourite Newfoundland dog . . .', mezzotint engraved by Charles Turner after an original by John James Masquerier, published by the artist, 20 August 1800. Note that the action took place in 1799 and the captain's surname was Mortlock.
NMM ref PAH7962

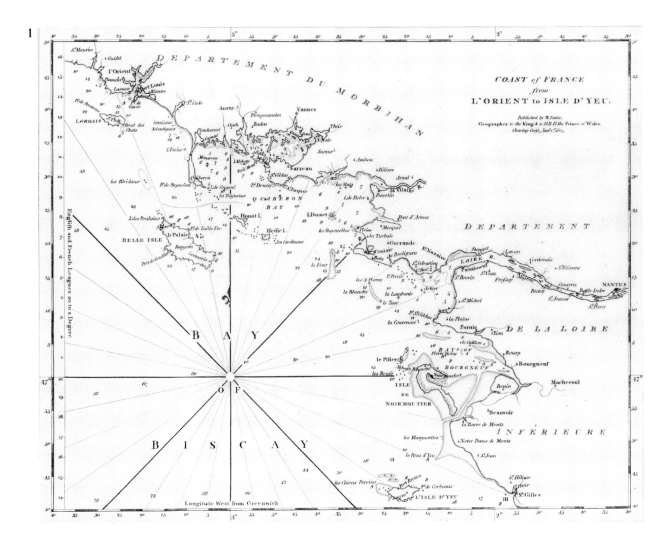

The wandering army

THE YEAR 1800 probably marked the nadir of the British Army's reputation in this war: to quote a contemporary, there were '22,000 men floating round the greater part of Europe, the scorn and laughing-stock of friends and foes alike'. Substantial British amphibious forces went from abandoned objective to half-completed landing to arrival too late to take advantage of a fleeting opportunity. Dithering politicians, half-baked plans, and the rapid flow of events all form part of the explanation for why nothing of any worth was attained.

There was controversy in the Cabinet between supporters of the opportunities offered by the renewed revolt of the *Chouans* in northwest France and those who felt that the French army was over-extended in Italy. The Mediterranean strategy was eventually pursued by a British force which sailed from Minorca to Leghorn, being diverted to Malta, and returning to Minorca, before being ordered to Gibraltar—achieving little and wasting most of the summer.

In the Channel, Sir Edward Pellew was appointed Commodore and sent to Quiberon Bay (1) with five ships of the line, six frigates and one sloop, escorting one ship of the line, one 50-gun ship and three frigates fitted as transports and carrying five regiments of foot plus artillery. They arrived at the beginning of June but too late to assist the royalist forces which had been decisively defeated. On the 4th, the frigate *Thames* and the shallow-draft sloop *Cynthia* (equipped with Schanck sliding keels) attacked some small forts, which were afterwards destroyed by a landing party; and early on the 6th, a body of troops, acting with a division of boats, burnt the *Insolente*, 18, carried off several small craft and about one hundred prisoners, destroyed some guns, and blew up a magazine. These proved to be the only achievements of this large expedition.

It had been intended to occupy Belle Isle, which had fallen to a British landing during the Seven Years War, and Pellew developed an elaborate plan for its capture. Troops were stationed on the island of Houat in prepara-

1. 'Coast of France from L'Orient to Isle D'Yeu', Plate XIX from *Le Petit Neptune*, published by William Faden, 1 January 1805.
NMM neg D8658

2. 'Ferrol Harbour', anonymous watercolour, no date.
NMM ref PAD1642

3. 'Plano del puerto del Ferrol', black and watercolour pen and ink by A Sascher, no date. The annotation lists the Spanish ships as *Real Carlos* and *San Hermenigildo*, 112s, the 80-gun *Argonauta*, the 74s *San Augusto* and *Monarca*, four frigates and some smaller craft.
NMM ref PAG9001

tion, but, much to Pellew's disgust, the scheme was abandoned on the receipt of some dubious royalist intelligence that suggested the garrison of Belle Isle was too strong.

In Cabinet, there was another change of policy, returning to Dundas's preferred strategy of amphibious raiding in support of British, rather than coalition, interests. This time the aim was to be the reduction of Spanish seapower by destroying her remaining squadrons in their ports. Pellew's force was increased, put under the command of Rear-Admiral Sir John Borlase Warren, and sent to take Ferrol (2). On 25 August, Sir John reached the bay with one 98, four 74s, five frigates and the *Cynthia*, plus some small craft and transports, carrying troops under Lieutenant-General Pulteney. That evening, after a fort had been silenced by the fire of the *Impetueux, Brilliant, Cynthia,* and the gunboat *St Vincent*, the troops, with sixteen field guns, were disembarked without loss, and aided by a detachment of seamen drove back a body of the enemy. This skirmish was followed by a somewhat more serious one at daybreak on the 26th, which resulted in the British occupying the heights overlooking the town and harbour (3). At this stage the general abandoned the attack.

Military and naval accounts diverge in their explanation of this—the former allege that the defences were impregnable, the latter that the general lost his nerve

2

and that the place was weakly manned and ready to give up. The military historians allege that prize-hungry naval officers were over-sanguine in their hopes. There are indications that both sides were right: the town could have been taken, but only by assault; and this was unacceptable to a general with ambiguous orders which seemed to exhort him not to risk his troops unduly. Whether Pulteney was pusillanimous or prudent, the Spanish were handed a cheap propaganda victory, the Navy re-embarked the Army, and amid mutual recriminations, the expedition returned to Gibraltar.

There it was reinforced in preparation for the even more farcical Cadiz operation (see pages 72-75).

3

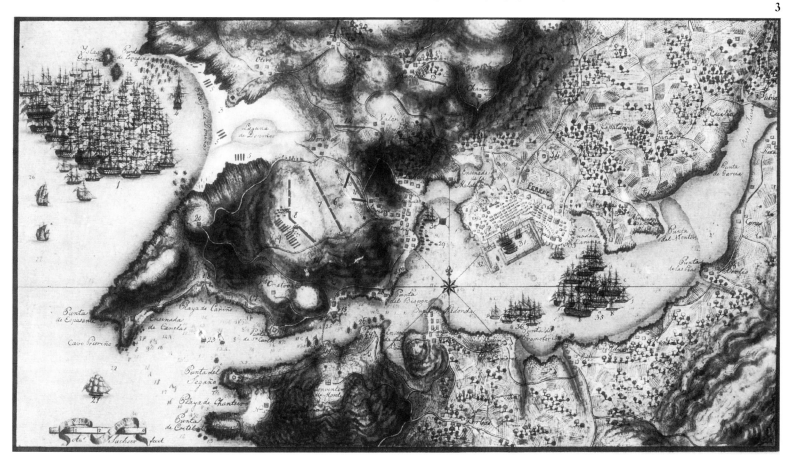

Cutting-out attacks in the Channel

AS THE Royal Navy's dominance of French waters grew, British naval officers became ever more daring in their attacks on shipping in what were supposedly protected harbours and anchorages. Using the ship's substantial complement of boats—five or six

for a frigate—enterprising captains launched numbers of 'cutting-out' raids, designed ideally to bring out valuable prizes from the ports and roadsteads of the French Channel coast. They were desperate ventures, but very spectacular when successful, and therefore popular subjects with artists and printsellers. Here are representations of three of the best known from the 1798-1801 period.

On the night of 3-4 August 1798, the British frigate *Melpomene* and brig *Childers* sent in their boats to the harbour of Corréjou, in the Ile de Bas, to cut out the French brig *Aventurier*, which was anchored there with some merchantmen. 'Heavy rain, vivid lightning and frequent squalls' covered the British approach. At three in the morning the *Aventurier* was surprised and captured after a sharp scuffle (1). In spite of the wind having moved round to blowing straight into the harbour and two hours of bombardment from the forts protecting the harbour, the *Aventurier* was eventually sailed out of the port.

Four French frigates, blockaded in Dunkirk roads, had long formed a tempting target and part of the anti-invasion forces were eventually tasked with their destruction. After waiting several days for suitable wind and tides, favourable conditions were finally found on the evening of 7 July 1800. The powerfully armed shallow-draught experimental 'sloop' *Dart*, 30 led the way (2), with two gunbrigs (*Biter* and *Boxer*), four fireships (*Wasp, Falcon, Comet* and *Rosario*), hired cutters and luggers, plus the boats from the *Andromeda* and *Nemesis*, 28. It seems that the French mistook the force for one of their own convoys. The *Dart* answered a hail in French, and arrived abreast of the innermost frigate but one without a shot being fired. The French vessel then opened on her, and she replied with her 32pdr carronades, passing on and running on board the innermost enemy. Her men dashed on to the deck of the Frenchman, and in a moment the frigate *Désirée* was carried. She was successfully taken out by her captors and was purchased for the Navy. Meantime the fireships ran up to the other three French frigates, but, though well handled, could not destroy them, and they escaped. The smaller British craft cannonaded the French gunboats. The total British loss in this dashing enterprise was only six killed or wounded.

On the night of 20-21 July 1801, the boats of the British frigates *Beaulieu*, 40, Captain Stephen Poyntz, and *Doris*, 36, Captain Charles Brisbane, made an attempt to cut out the French corvette *Chevrette*, 20, which was lying in Camaret Bay, but failed to arrive before day had dawned. They retired, but they had been seen, and the *Chevrette* prepared for another attempt by embarking a party of soldiers, which brought her crew up to 339, and by loading her guns to the muzzle with grape. On the following night, the boats of the above frigates with those of the *Uranie*, 38, Captain George Henry Gage, as well, embarked 280 men, and rowed in. Six boats, however, proceeded to chase a French guard boat, and did not return. The other boats, with 180 men, grew impatient, and dashed at the *Chevrette*. They were received with a heavy fire of great guns and small arms, both from her and from the shore, but pressed on; and the British seamen forced their way on board (3). A party of topmen, appointed for that purpose, fought their way up her rigging and spread her topsails, and presently the *Chevrette* stood out of the bay. Meantime, the party on deck carried the forecastle and quarterdeck, and drove the Frenchmen down the hatches. As soon as that had been done the other six boats rejoined. The *Chevrette* was carried off, though fired upon by the French batteries. In the affair the British loss was 12 killed or missing and 57 wounded, whilst the French lost 92 killed and 62 wounded. The gallantry of the British officers and seamen was above all praise. The *Beaulieu*'s quartermaster, Henry Wallis, who had been ordered to take the *Chevrette*'s helm, fought his way to his post, and continued at it, though badly wounded.

3

1. 'The boarding and capturing l'Avanturier near the Isle of Bas, Augt 3rd 1798', coloured aquatint engraved by Thomas Sutherland after an original by Thomas Whitcombe (born c1752), published 1 September 1816. *NMM ref PAD5603*

2. 'The Dart sloop of war, boarding La Desiree French frigate', aquatint produced by Robert Dodd (1748-1815) and published by Bunny & Gold, 1 October 1801. *NMM neg A4305*

3. 'The cutting-out of the corvette La Chevrette', engraving by J Rogers after an original by P J de Loutherbourg (1740-1812), no date. *NMM ref PAD5649*

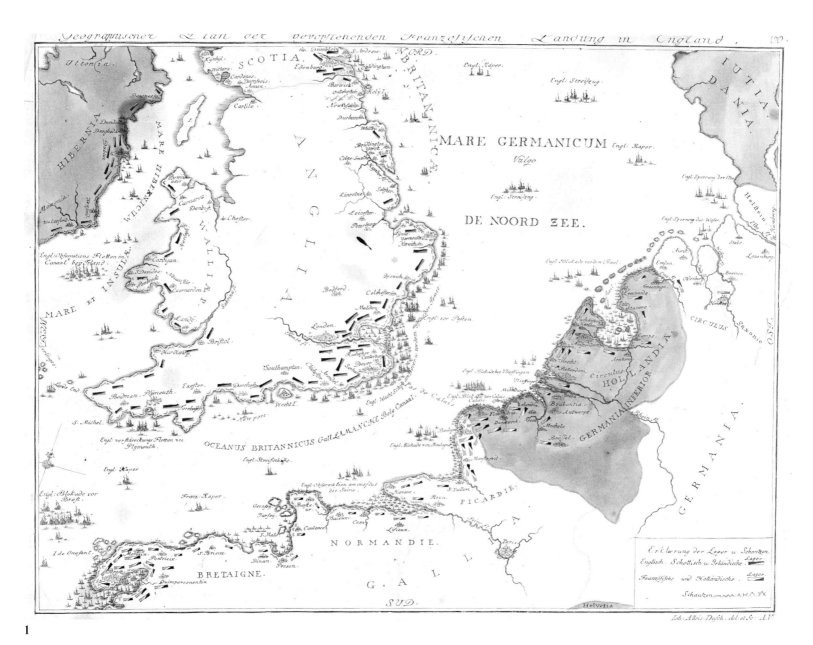

1

Invasion threat

IN 1801 Napoleon, fresh from continental victories over the Austrians, turned his attention to revitalising the invasion threat from the flotilla of assault craft gathering at Boulogne (1). This, the French port most conveniently situated to launch an invasion, was being developed to hold the maximum number of the specially designed invasion barges and gunboats. The convoys of such craft creeping round the coast from the ports where they were built were frequently attacked by the British inshore flotilla with varying success but without stopping a steady and (for Britain) worrying build up of numbers in the basin at Boulogne (2, 3).

In what nowadays would be called a 'PR move' Nelson, just returned from his victory at Copenhagen in the spring of 1801, was appointed to command the defences of the coast from Orford Ness to Beachy Head, the most threatened corner of the English coast from beyond the north side of the Thames Estuary to Brighton. He hoisted his flag in the 32-gun frigate *Medusa*, at anchor in the Downs; and on 3 August, obeying instructions from the Admiralty, crossed to Boulogne to endeavour to destroy the flotilla which was assembled under the guns of the lately strengthened fortifications of the place. He had with him thirty vessels, mostly gunbrigs (a type of light, shallow draught warship specially designed and built in numbers against the invasion threat) and bomb vessels (4). On the 4th the latter shelled the part of the French flotilla which was within range of their mortars (5). There are conflicting claims about this bombardment, but it seems that the fire was too inaccurate to do serious damage, the two gunboats which had been damaged were easily repaired and that no Frenchmen were either killed or wounded. On the British side three persons were wounded. The bombs had fired more than nine hundred shells to little effect except to their own structure. Nelson, therefore, determined to try the effect of a 'cutting-out expedition' on a large scale.

He organised the armed boats of the squadron into four divisions and, on the night of 15 August, sent them in accompanied by a division of boats armed with howitzers to provide fire support. The boats, having assembled round the *Medusa*, and started off from her at about 11.30pm. Owing to the darkness, the tide, and the currents, the divisions soon became separated, and could not co-operate as had been planned. The boats of one division, driven far to the eastward, had to split up and proceed independently. Just before dawn on the 16th, some of these succeeded in reaching and attacking a brig which lay close to the pier-head; but, though they carried her, they were forced to abandon her, as she was secured by a chain which they could not cut, and was swept by the fire of four craft moored quite close to her. As daylight broke, they retreated, with heavy losses.

The second group of boats was less affected by the current, and, at about 12.30am, some ran alongside the brig *Etna*. But boarding nets arranged to prevent easy access to the deck and a heavy fire forced the men back. Other boats captured a lugger, but were repulsed by the brig *Volcan*; and the two sub-divisions retired with a loss of 21 killed and 42 wounded. The third division was also driven back having lost 5 killed and 29 wounded. The fourth division, unable to get near the enemy before day broke, came back without loss.

The French, who had been reinforced since 4 August and who were clearly well prepared for such an attack, claimed to have run down eight British boats and to have taken four, and to have lost only 10 killed and 30 wounded. The total British loss was 44 killed and 126 wounded. Nelson never seems to have been particularly successful in attacks of this kind, and this one must count as a defeat.

2

3

1. 'Geographiscer Plan der bevorstehenden Francosischen Landung in England', coloured etching by L A Dusch after his own original, no date but about 1800.
NMM ref PAG9000

2. 'Boulogne, high water 1800. Boats preparing for invasion of England', anonymous aquatint and etching, no date.
NMM ref PAH2265

3. 'Boulogne low water, 1800, showing boats for the invasion of England', anonymous aquatint and etching, no date.
NMM ref PAH2265

4. 'A SE View of the Town and Harbour of Boulogne with the Encampments on the heights, Shewing also the situation of the French and English Squadrons as taken at anchor by E D Lewis, HMS Tartarus off Boulogne', watercolour by E D Lewis, no date.
NMM neg A929

5. 'Bombardment de Boulogne par l'Amiral Nelson', anonymous etching 'par un Elève de l'Ecole Centrale de Boulogne', no date.
NMM neg A3259

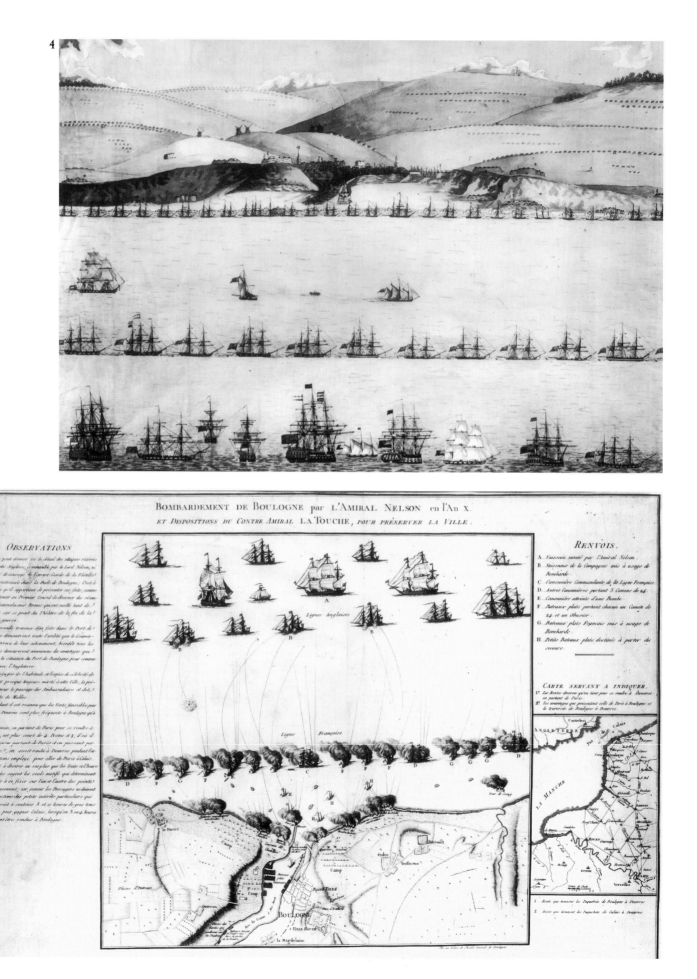

Part III

COLONIAL AND COMMERCE WARFARE

BY 1798 Britain's 'blue water' strategy had had some limited success overseas. The loose blockade of French naval bases, combined with the early weakness of the French navy, had permitted Britain in 1793-94 to capture three of France's West Indian islands – Tobago, St Lucia and Martinique, achieve a short occupation of Guadeloupe in 1794, and the maintenance of footholds on St Domingue (the French half of the island of St Domingo, later known as Haiti). In addition, with the re-entry of Spain into the war as an ally of France, Trinidad had been seized in 1797. In the east, French trading stations including Pondicherry had been taken in India and, to remove Dutch colonies and naval bases from exploitation by France, Cape Town, Trincomalee, Malacca, Amboyna and Banda had been occupied.

Nevertheless, France and her allies had been left sufficient colonial ports in Isle de France (Mauritius), Guadeloupe, Spanish Cuba and Puerto Rico to permit their privateers to wage a successful war against British merchant vessels entering the Indian Ocean and Caribbean. Moreover, within the North Sea and Channel, privateers had begun working from ports all along the coasts of France and the Netherlands, forcing up insurance rates for British merchantmen and obliging shipowners and merchants to accept the need to secure their ships and cargoes against capture. As demonstrated by heavy losses from Mediterranean and West India convoys and the Newfoundland fishing fleet, there was no complete security against marauding French naval squadrons.

In southern Europe, where normal patterns of trade were disrupted by the hostilities of warring armies, as well as in the coastal regions of France, where trade to French colonies was also checked, French naval successes against British shipping acted as incentive to businessmen contemplating investment to turn from their peacetime trades to privateering. One *armateur*, who in 1798 fitted out a privateer at Nantes, was the representative of a Swiss company which had traded in printed cotton cloth to the French West Indies. He was able to raise shares for equipping the ship from other tradesmen, but the privateer he equipped in 1798 failed to make a profit on account of his own inexperience in supervising such operations, inflation, and the expence of obtaining gunpowder, provisions and seamen. Once his privateer was at sea, prizes in the form of British trading vessels were readily available, but so also were British warships. Six prizes were taken, but three were recaptured, only three reached port, and only one was finally condemned as a prize.

This experience was perhaps typical, for at St Malo, an important French privateering base throughout the eighteenth century, the number of prizes taken by privateers during the French Revolutionary War was a severe reduction on the number taken by each privateer in previous wars. During the American War of Independence each St Malo privateer had accounted statistically for four British losses. During the French Revolutionary War, however, the number of losses for every privateer dropped to just one.

This was in part due to the fact that during the war of 1775-83 the Royal Navy had been overwhelmed by the navies of her enemies in home waters, while during the French Revolutionary War British warships predominated. But it was also due to increasing rigour in the organisation of convoys for merchantmen. This organisation was facilitated by the decline by the 1790s of the importance of the chartered companies – the Levant, Royal Africa, Hudson's Bay and East India Companies, all based in London – and rise of associations of shipowners and merchants in each port around the coast, reporting to committees in London representing the region of trade – for example, the Mediterranean, North America, or the West Indies – to where they sent cargoes. Linked with insurers at Lloyd's, now based in the Royal Exchange, these merchant committees communicated with the Admiralty, arranging the timing and rendezvous for convoys to each part of the world.

The main concentration point for convoys was the Thames estuary, but subsidiary convoys brought vessels from all the main ports around the British coast. By 1801 convoys as large as a thousand vessels were regularly assembling at the mouth of the Thames for escort to the Baltic. Among naval officers, convoy duties were notorious for their frustrating tedium. But, since the Convoys and Cruisers Act of 1708, the British public in parliament had come to expect the allocation of a requisite number of warships to convoy tasks. In addition, to deter privateers, the Royal Navy stationed warships at key landfalls: off Cape Clear, southwest Ireland; off Cape Cormoran, at the tip of the Indian sub-continent; in the Straits of Malacca; and on the Banks of Newfoundland.

These provisions did not prevent the loss of lone ships. In consequence, through pressure from Lloyd's, a Convoy Act of 1798 made convoy compulsory for all ships engaged in foreign trade, except for ships bound for Ireland, defensible East India and Hudson's Bay Company ships, and those vessels sanctioned to sail alone by licence. It seems likely that the Act subsequently reduced captures. For the whole length of the Revolutionary War, the history of Lloyd's records that less than 3.5 per cent of all sailings, including coastal voyages, resulted in captures. Moreover, some of these vessels were recaptured, reducing the net loss to 2.75 per cent for the whole war, 1793-1801. For ships on foreign voyages registered for insurance purposes with Lloyd's, the losses were greater: the gross loss was 7.72 per cent; the net loss after recaptures was 6.17 per cent.

The domination of the seas around continental Europe by British warships during the French Revolutionary War not only deterred enemy privateers but encouraged British privateers. Their success, however, very much depended on their experience, the subterfuges they adopted, and the region of the enemy's coastline they operated in. Between 1793 and 1801 the British privateers that were the most successful were those put out by Channel Islanders. Their own trade being stifled by the geographical proximity of the islands to the French coast, the islanders put much of their investment into privateers. During this period the number of Letters of Marque issued by the High Court of Admiralty was 4748 of which 454 authorised the voyages of 164 Channel Island ships. In this same period 1151 prizes were condemned, 266 to privateers, of which 181 or 68 per cent came from the Channel Islands. So successful were the islanders that they attracted investment from as far afield as merchants at

Bath and artisans working beside the River Thames.

If the balance of power at sea had a deterrent effect on French shipowners in European waters, outside those waters, especially in the West Indies, there was less deterrence and equally rich prizes. There American, as well as European, markets still provided the British, French and Spanish islands with outlets for their products. After 1795, indeed, American shipping increasingly took the place of shortages of shipping with European owners. The Jay Treaty between Britain and the United States in 1795 permitted American ships no larger than 50 tons into British West Indian ports on condition that they carried cargoes

only to ports in the United States. But large quantities of West Indian products were re-exported from the United States: 21 million pounds (weight) of sugar in 1795, rising to 50 millions pounds in 1801. In return, by the latter date, 88 per cent of the grain and 90 per cent of the dried fish entering British Caribbean islands arrived in American ships. These cargoes offered rich pickings to French and Spanish privateers, so much so that the United States and Britain operated joint convoys. It was an unoffical alliance that became known in the United States as an undeclared, or 'quasi-war', with France.

Beneath this veneer of common interest, however, the British navy also attracted the hostility of some American shipowners. American identity was often adopted by French, Spanish and Dutch vessels, so that British warships tended to stop and search all vessels, regardless of their ostensible nationali-

'South East View of Fort St George, Madras', coloured aquatint engraved and published by Thomas Daniell after his own original, September 1797. Madras on the Coromandel coast was one of the main centres of British power in southern India, acting as a check on the French at Pondicherry. It was a poor naval base, however, with no real harbour, and the surf boats in the foreground of this print graphically demonstrate the nature of the coastline. NMM neg A6278

ty. In response some Americans, almost in continuation of hostilities officially terminated in 1783, equipped and hired out privateers sailing under Swedish and Danish flags of convenience. Licensed and operating in collusion with French colonial officials, American vessels added to confusion in an area where many small predatory craft operated without licences, or with documentation of questionable authenticity, and invariably changed identity as convenience dictated.

In the West Indies the confusion of interests affecting trade and colonial power was further complicated by the hegemony of former slaves in St Domingo where the Spanish half of the island had also fallen prey to risings, the leaders of which warred between themselves. In April 1798 the weakness of British land forces maintaining toe-holds in the west of the island prompted their commander to surrender these enclaves to the forces of the former slave, General Toussaint L'Ouverture. Early in May British and royalist colonial forces were evacuated from Port-au-Prince, St Marc and l'Arcahaye to Cape Nicolas Mole and Jeremie, which were also surrendered to Toussaint in August under an agreement between the two parties to respect the territories of the other, a treaty especially important for Britain on account of the necessity to secure Jamaica against attack.

The relative weakness of British forces in the Caribbean compared to the territories they held incited the Spanish that August to attack the British settlements in the Bay of Honduras with over 2000 troops in about twenty schooners and sloops. Early the following month several attempts were made to force passages through shoals north of Belize but all were beaten off by British gunboats and schooners, supported by a 16-gun sloop. It was an attempt that was not repeated, partly because, after navigation marks were removed, the few settlements along the coast became difficult of access.

In spite of the weakness of British forces, a Dutch-British conspiracy between diplomats in Europe gave rise in August 1797 to an attack on the Dutch colony of Surinam on the northern coast of South America. A little over 1000 men, in two line of battle ships and four frigates only had to make a demonstration off the island for the governor, after due prevari-

cation, to surrender the island. Negotiations were made delicate owing to currents having swept a quarter of the British force five miles along the coast from the rest of the expedition off the mouth of the Surinam river. The governor of the island was nevertheless able to represent British occupation as preferable to that of the French from neighbouring Cayenne.

In September 1800 the Dutch island of Curaçao also surrendered to the British when visited by the 36-gun frigate *Nereide*. Thirteen French privateers from Guadaloupe, intent on restoring their own island to prosperity, had landed under false pretences and, having a force 1200 strong, demanded a ransom to depart. Summoning reinforcement from Jamaica, the commander of the *Nereide* and the Dutch governor agreed to British occupation on the same terms as Surinam, whereupon the French privateers, realising the island was not now easily subjected, departed in fewer vessels than those in which they arrived.

Further islands were seized by the British in 1801 following reinforcement from Europe, where the Armed Neutrality of the North suddenly presented the potential need for bargaining counters in the event of need to negotiate with the Baltic powers. That March, the Swedish island of St Bartholomew, the Danish islands of St Thomas, St Johns and St Croix, and the island of St Martin, divided between France and Holland, were all seized in quick succession. The almost simultaneous dissolution of the Armed Neutrality, however, resulted in a settlement with Russia in June which returned the Danish and Swedish islands.

Meanwhile in the east, British commercial interests were enlarged by territorial gains in India. The new governor-general, Richard, Marquis Wellesley, who arrived in 1797 to direct the territories managed by the East India Company, regarded India as a theatre of a world war against France. In 1799 hostilities were opened against Tipu Sultan, ruler of the south Indian principality of Mysore, who had lost territory in his war of 1791-92 with the British. In 1798 he opened negotiations with the French at Mauritius and, encouraged by Napoleon's invasion of Egypt, he recruited a number of French agents and military volunteers. But in February and March 1799 British land forces from Madras, Bombay and Bengal closed on the fortress capital of Mysore, Seringapatam, and,

after a brief siege, stormed the city. Tipu Sultan was killed in the fighting, and the state was divided between the British, the Nizam of Hyderabad and the former ruling Hindu dynasty, whose representative welcomed the protection offered by the East India Company.

By its own annexations, the British cut Mysore off from the sea and themselves gained control of most of the Malabar coast of southern India. On the eastern side of the Indian peninsula, in 1799 Wellesley also took over the administration of the principality of Tanjore. Further annexations followed. Evidence of Tipu Sultan's conspiracy with the ruler of the Carnatic supplied reason to take control of that state too in 1801. With a vague threat from Afghanistan, which might have been linked to French influence, Wellesley also established a British protectorate over Oudh in the very north of India. To pay for the troops that had to be stationed in this border state, further territories were ceded.

All these acquisitions of territory vastly enlarged the power and influence of the East India Company. Needless to say, it also enlarged the market for British goods, especially those of the Lancashire cotton industry. Hitherto bullion had been exported to the east to pay for imports from India and China, and for the troops that garrisoned British settlements. Henceforth exports to the sub-continent, especially cotton cloth, would grow by leaps and bounds. The shipping required would also grow, eventually bursting the constraints imposed by the monopoly of the East India Company.

It was part of a process of economic growth that was actually stimulated by a war waged against enemy trade and colonies. The British shipping industry was a major growth sector, for it was also stimulated by wartime demands for transports, for naval stores from the Baltic, as well as by the maintenance of the coastal and oceanic trades. Fed by new building and captures of enemy shipping, between the beginning of 1798 and the end of 1801, the merchant naval strength of Britain rose from 14,631 vessels to 17,207, representing a growth in total tonnage of more than 20 per cent. Few other periods of warfare had equal benefits for British trade and shipping. It was an acceleration of growth, moreover, that was to be continued throughout the Napoleonic War.

1

West Indies 1798

1. 'Vue du Port au Prince, Isle St
Dominique', engraving and etching
by Nicolas Ponce after an original by
Perignon, 1795.
NMM ref PAH2988

2. 'Vue de la Ville de Jérémie, Isle St
Dominique', engraving and etching
by Nicolas Ponce after an original by
Ozanne, 1795.
NMM ref PAH3002

BY 1798 the expense in both men and money was making the British occupation of Saint Domingue increasingly difficult to sustain, given the outbreak of war with Spain and the need to divert troops to Jamaica and the Bahamas, threatened from Cuba. The struggle between the British and the republicans on the island itself was deadlocked, and on 23 April the British commander-in-chief, Lieutenant-Colonel Maitland, opened negotiations with Toussaint L'Ouver-

ture, offering withdrawal of British forces to St Nicolas Mole and Jeremie in return for guarantees of the safety of the colonists who chose to remain. Toussaint, whose forces had been unable to decisively defeat the British, accepted these terms and the withdrawal began in early May, Port au Prince (1) being evacuated on the night of 7-8 May. The bulk of British forces moved to Jeremie (2), but Maitland came to feel that the cost of maintaining this garrison in the face of renewed pressure was prohib-

2

itive. The republicans were building roads through the mountains around the town, depriving it of its natural defences, and even to hold just Jeremie and the Mole would cost in excess of £800,000. Maitland was able to negotiate a successful withdrawal with the various republican leaders, Toussaint being given St Nicolas Mole (3) and his rival, Rigaud, Jeremie. He was also able to obtain an agreement from Toussaint not to attack Jamaica or foment slave revolt on the island in return for a partial lifting of the blockade of Saint Domingue to allow trade with Jamaica. This deal was finalised on 31 August, Maitland writing, 'Thank God I have at length got Great Britain rid of the whole of the incumbrance of this Island'. With the defences of Jamaica having been recently increased and the agreement with Toussaint, direct occupation of Saint Domingue was no longer essential to the security of Britain's most valuable West Indies possession. The evacuation of St Nicolas Mole was finally completed on 3 October, bringing the whole costly venture to an end.

In September 1798 the Spanish attacked the British possessions in the Gulf of Honduras (4) in considerable force, attempting to enter the approaches to Belize with twenty armed sloops and schooners, many carrying a single 24pdr in the bow, and eleven transports, carrying 2000 troops. The only Royal Navy vessel in Belize at the time was the 16-gun sloop *Merlin*, but the locals had fitted out a squadron consisting of three armed sloops, *Towzer, Tickler* and *Mermaid*, two schooners, *Swinger* and *Teazer*, and

3

eight gun launches, manned by a mixture of merchant seamen and volunteers from the troops ashore. This force prevented the first Spanish attempt to cross the shoals at the river mouth on 3 September with five ships which had been unloaded as far as possible to reduce their draught, and then removed all the navigation marks from the channel, making it impossible for the larger ships of the Spanish squadron to enter. Further attempts were similarly defeated on the next two days, and a final concerted attack on the 10th was beaten off with no casualties on the British side. The shoals prevented the *Merlin* pursuing the Spanish, and the other gunboats could not have faced them alone, so they were able make their escape, returning to Mexico. The Spanish never again attempted to attack the British in Honduras.

3. 'Platform Bay, near Cape Nicolas Mole, St Domingo', aquatint engraved by Hall after an original by William Hamilton, published by Joyce Gold, 30 July 1808.
NMM ref PAD5591

4. 'A View of Truxillo Bay and City on the Coast of Honduras', coloured engraving and etching by T Bowen, published by Robert Wilkinson, 4 June 1796.
NMM ref PAH2959

4

1

The birth of a new naval power

FOR A decade after independence the United States had no professional military forces. This was one manifestation of a deeply ingrained antipathy to the trappings of a centralised state, born out of the country's struggle against what it considered oppressive government. However, without the protection of the Royal Navy American trade was vulnerable to the depredations of even the weakest seapower, the problem becoming acute when the Barbary state of Algiers turned its rapacious attention to American merchantmen after its conflict with Portugal was settled in October 1793.

After some debate Congress passed a Naval Act on 27 March 1794, authorising the construction of six frigates, four of 44 guns and two of 36. Considerable thought was given to the design, since a navy of so few ships would need to have the very best, and the final concept was radical. Because of their outstanding showing in the War of 1812, most attention has been focused on the 44s of the *Constitution* class (1), huge vessels for their day, with the size and scantlings of a 74-gun line of battle ship and a main battery of thirty 24pdrs beneath a flush spar deck that could carry a second complete tier of guns. However, even the so-called 36s were larger than European 18pdr frigates, and for her first cruise *Constellation* actually mounted 24pdrs (2).

Construction proceeded in fits and starts, subject to material shortages and the vicissitudes of international relations. The Algerine crisis was resolved by a treaty of September 1795, whereupon the Naval Act of 1796 authorised the completion of only the three most advanced, but there was no funding even for these until March 1797. *United States, Constitution* and *Constellation* were launched in the fall of 1797, and deteriorating relations with France resurrected the remainder of the 1794 programme. From the spring of 1798 further Acts provided for the construction (and purchase) of more warships to meet the crisis, but there were already some doubts about the size of the existing frigates and most of the purpose-built ships were relatively small, like the 850-ton *Essex* (3), and armed with 12pdrs. By 1799 the ambitions of the administration extended to a programme of six ships of the line, but these were never completed.

Material shortages were largely confined to metalwork. Copper sheathing for the early frigates was supplied from Britain but by the time exports were halted in 1799 Paul Revere had forged the first US copper spikes, and his mill was able to roll sheets by 1801. It was a similar story with guns, where shortages required that about 300-400, mainly carronades, had to be imported from Britain during 1797-1801.

There were other problems, partly due to inexperience. As fitted by Truxton, for example, *Constellation* was oversparred, overarmed and unable to stow more than three months provisions; she was so crank that in her fight with the *Insurgente* she had to take the lee station in order to open her gunports with safety. Despite delays and the shortcomings of the officer corps, the rapid rise in the numbers of ships the new navy sent to sea in pursuit of what it called the 'quasi-war' with France reflects to the credit of the new naval administration, under its first Secretary, Benjamin Stoddert. Eleven ships in September 1798 had become twenty-four a year later and peaked in July 1800 with thirty-two ships operational. He also made progress in establishing proper regulation for the service, while the degree of professionalism in the officer cadre was further honed by seagoing experience in the conflict with France.

---

1. 'US Frigate Constitution of 44 guns', engraving and etching by Abel Bowen after an original by William Lynn, published by the artist, no date. *NMM neg 522*

2. An unidentified American frigate, possibly the *Constellation*, entering a French port, watercolour by Ange-Joseph Antoine Roux, undated but possibly about 1805. She is wearing a commodore's broad pendant and the cutter and frigate astern are also American. *Peabody Essex Museum, Salem MA neg 14508*

3. The American frigate *Essex* in the Mediterranean, watercolour attributed to Joseph Howard (1780-1857). The ship made a number of deployments to the Mediterranean, the first in 1801, her first commission being devoted to a long voyage to Batavia. *Peabody Essex Museum, Salem MA neg 11764*

2

3

America's 'quasi-war' with France

1. *'Constellation & L' Insurgente* - the Chace', engraving produced and published by E Savage, Philadelphia, 20 May 1799.
Beverley R Robinson Collection, Annapolis ref no 80.26.5

2. 'Action between the *Constellation* and *L' Insurgente* on the 9th February 1799', engraving produced and published by E Savage, Philadelphia, 20 May 1799. It follows Truxton's less than candid claim that the French ship carried 40 guns to his own vessel's 36, ignoring the vast difference in calibre.
Beverley R Robinson Collection, Annapolis ref no 80.26.6

3. 'A View of the American Merchant Ship Planter beating off a French National privateer of 22 Guns July 10th 1799', produced and published by John Fairburn, London, 1 October 1800.
Beverley R Robinson Collection, Annapolis ref no 51.007.0183

4. 'The *Mount Vernon*', watercolour by Michele-Felice Corné, dated Naples 1799. This one of a series of ten shows the ship racing between a pair of French lateen rigged privateers towards the safety of Gibraltar and the British fleet.
Peabody Essex Museum, Salem MA neg 11769

FOR A neutral trading nation, war between its commercial rivals offers both opportunities and dangers, and the new republic of the United States walked a narrow line between the belligerents for the first five years of the European war. France was America's first ally, but Britain was a more important trading partner and the more powerful naval power. As a result of America signing the Jay Treaty of 1794, a pro-British commercial agreement, the French Directory stepped up measures against US trade, including an insistence that each ship carry a complete *rôle d'équipage* — elaborate documentation that was almost impossible to comply with. These measures were introduced without notice, rendering the vast majority of American ships liable to capture.

In 1798 the US government protested: 'The result of these regulations has been the most extensive and universal devastation of the American commerce.' Over 300 ships had been seized in Caribbean alone since July 1796 and during 1797 300 of the 5000 vessels in foreign trade fell to French privateers. Insurance rates quadrupled and trade fell off rapidly, but last-minute diplomacy failed, and America had no alternative but to take armed action. War was never declared, however, and the conflict in which 2309 vessels were involved by time agreement was reached in September 1800 is known as the 'Quasi-War'.

The crisis finally secured a navy for the United States,

a proper Department being established in April 1798, with the capable Benjamin Stoddert as its first Secretary. The Naval Act of 1 July 1797 authorised the commissioning of the *United States, Constitution* and *Constellation*, but the first naval vessels to put to sea were eight purchased merchantmen. Initial operations were purely defensive, protecting merchant ships off the US coast, but in the fall of 1798 the decision was made to send a squadron to the West Indies to convoy and protect shipping in the area of its greatest danger.

If America was not quite at war with France, it was not quite in alliance with Britain either, and there were a number of embarrassing clashes with high-handed officers of the Royal Navy over those traditional bones of contention, impressment and the rights of search. Eventually some degree of co-operation evolved, and the mutual recognition signals adopted in August 1798 prevented the worst misunderstandings.

The new navy's operations in the West Indies were a great success and between 1797 and 1798 losses in the Caribbean fell from 280 to 105 ships. Merchants appreciated the greater security and falling insurance rates, but public enthusiasm for the war was finally secured by the US Navy's first victory over a major enemy warship when Truxtun's *Constellation* pursued, overwhelmed and forced the surrender of the French frigate *Insurgente* on 9 February 1799 (1, 2). The American ship, with its 24pdr

main battery, was clearly far more powerful than her 12pdr-armed opponent, and Truxtun spoiled his achievement by claiming the opposite. This rebounded on him the following year when *Constellation* failed to take the equally matched *Vengeance*. In fact, during both battles the American frigate proved to be better handled and fired faster and more accurately, so it augured well for the future of the navy.

Outside the West Indies, American trade was more or less left to its own devices, and a letter in the London *Star* for 18 July 1799 described a typical experience. The London-bound merchantman *Planter* beat off a 22-gun French privateer a week earlier after a fierce fight of nearly three hours. Obviously inspired by the ship's gallant defence, Fairburn published a print which quoted the main details of the report in the caption – *Planter* with twelve 9pdrs, six 6pdrs, and 43 men, lost four dead and eight wounded; two lady passengers were much praised for carrying ammunition during action (3).

At the Peabody Museum in Salem there is a splendid series of ten paintings celebrating an even more heroic exploit by the 355-ton *Mount Vernon* which survived not only privateers but the whole of Bruix's Franco-Spanish fleet. The story is told in a letter to his father from the ship's master, Elias Derby, dated Gibraltar 1 August 1799. Having run into a fleet estimated at 50 sail on 28 July, he reasonably assumed they must be British, but having realised his error, he outmanoeuvred and fought off a French corvette, and although he escaped he suffered 'constant brushes' with the enemy until his arrival at Gibraltar. The expected British fleet was not off Cadiz (Keith had been led on a wild-goose chase around the Mediterranean) so *Mount Vernon* made for Gibraltar, arriving on the 30th after 'popping at Frenchmen all the fore noon'. In a clash with a large lateener off Algesiras, Derby claimed the privateer surrendered but *Mount Vernon* was carrying too much sail to stop (4). With understandable pride, he goes on to say, 'It was however a satisfaction to lick the rascal in full view of the English fleet who were to leeward . . .' Even as he wrote he could see two US ships captured by privateers, but he was also witness to St Vincent's temporary flagship, the *Argo*, retaking one.

Derby, carrying letters for Nelson, went on to Naples to sell his sugar cargo, where he met an émigré painter from Elba called Michele-Felice Corné who returned to America on his ship. Corné recorded *Mount Vernon's* incredible escapades in watercolours, and went on to decorate the new East India building in Salem, which, to complete the story, now houses the Peabody Museum, where his *Mount Vernon* series resides.

The 'Quasi-War' meanwhile drifted to a close. After the coup of 18 Brumaire (9 November 1799), the French Consulate moved to improve relations with America in an attempt to isolate Britain, and in April 1801 orders to cease operations were sent to all US warships in the West Indies. It had been a considerable achievement to improvise a fleet with an effective strength of over thirty ships in little more than eighteen months, but even more so to produce a navy of such potential. As the historian of the conflict summed it up: 'Between 1798 and 1801 the United States Navy had scored a double victory, defeating both the French enemy and the memory of the service's own Continental precursor.'

4

1

West Indies 1799-1801

DESPITE THE evacuation of Saint Domingue and the scaling-down of military activity in the West Indies, the last three years of the war saw several acquisitions of territory by the British, fortunately at little expense to the government.

On 19 March 1799, the British envoy at Hamburg reported that he had been approached by a representative of the governor of the Dutch colony of Surinam, a M De Frédéric, offering the surrender of that colony to the British in return for a knighthood for himself and £100,000. It would be necessary for there to be a considerable military force sent to the island nonetheless, so that he could appear justified in capitulating. His offer was accepted, since a rich colony could be obtained at relatively little cost and the ships and troops required for the demonstration of force could be provided from those already on the Windward Islands station.

On 31 July, a squadron under the command of Vice-Admiral Lord Hugh Seymour (1) sailed from Martinique for Surinam, having been preceded by a Dutch intermediary. Seymour had with him the *Prince of Wales*, 98, as his flagship, the *Invincible*, 74, four frigates, a sloop and a gunbrig, and approximately 1000 troops, arriving off Surinam on 11 August. It was fortunate that no real fighting was intended, as there were considerable problems, shallow water preventing the larger ships from coming close to shore, and three ships carrying a quarter of Seymour's

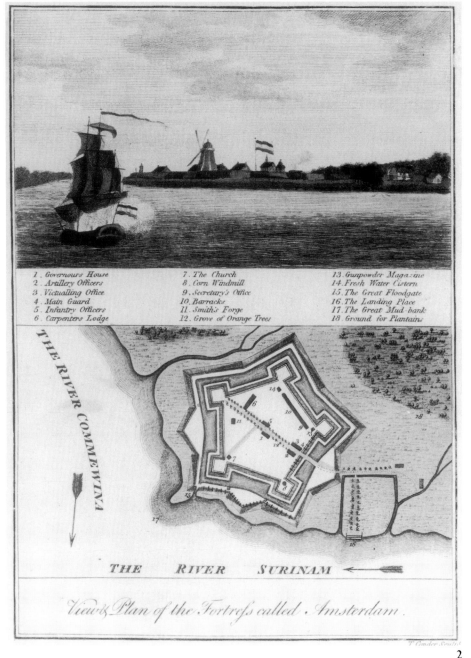

2

troops missed the correct landfall due to strong currents and ended up several miles down the coast from the fort at New Amsterdam (2) which was their objective, taking five days to rejoin the main force. There was some doubt as to whether Frédéric would feel himself able to surrender to this weakened force, but after a face-saving delay of two days, he agreed to terms on 18 August. The British were then able to sail up river to the capital Paramaribo (3) which was entered on the 22nd.

Similarly, just over a year later, the Dutch island of Curaçoa (4) came under British control, quite by chance. In July 1800, 1000 French privateers from Guadeloupe had landed on the island, accusing the colony of harbouring enemies of the French Republic and demanding financial compensation. The Dutch

1. 'Vice-Admiral Lord Hugh Seymour 1759-1801', mezzotint engraved by Samuel William Reynolds after an original by John Hoppner, no date. *NMM ref PAG9402*

2. 'View and Plan of the Fortress called Amsterdam', coloured engraving by T Conder, published by J Johnson, 1 December 1791. *NMM ref PAD2049*

3

3. 'View of the town of Paramaribo, with the Road & Shipping from the Opposite Shore', coloured aquatint published by J Johnson, 1 December 1794.
NMM ref PAH3049

4. 'Curaçao Anno 1786', anonymous watercolour c1786.
NMM ref PA10334

governor Lauffer had insufficient men at his disposal to drive the privateers off, and on 6 September the French began to loot the colony. Three days later the British frigate *Nereide*, 36 (5), commanded by Captain Frederick Watkins, arrived off the island looking for the French frigate *Vengeance*, and Lauffer offered to place the colony under British rule in return for help against the French. Watkins agreed and sent messages to Vice-Admiral Seymour for more ships and troops. Seymour was unable to raise many troops quickly as military forces were under the control of the governor of Jamaica who,

fearing attacks from Cuba and Saint Domingue, would not spare the men. However, on 13 September Lauffer formally capitulated to Watkins, who landed marines to bolster the defences of the capital. Seeing this, the privateers left without a fight ten days later.

In 1801, as part of the war against the League of Armed Neutrality, the British decided to seize the West Indian islands held by Denmark and Sweden, and all shipping in the region owned by those two countries and Russia, and 5400 troops were sent out from Britain for this purpose. On 16 March a squadron from the Windward

4

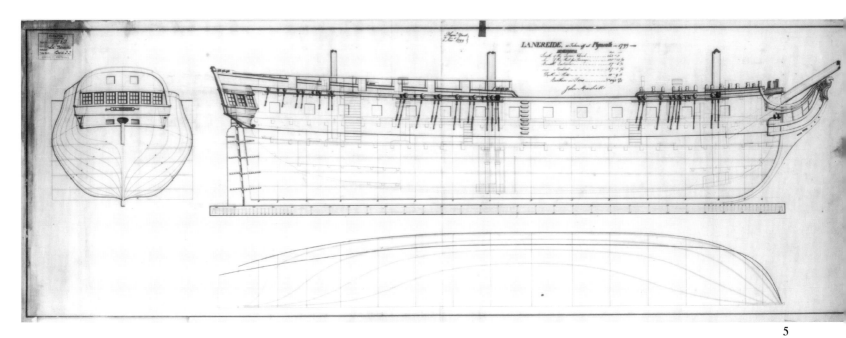

5

Islands commanded by Admiral Sir John Thomas Duckworth arrived off the Swedish island of St Bartholomew, which was totally undefended and surrendered on the 20th. Having received reinforcements of 200 men, the British then attacked the neighbouring island of Saint Martin, held jointly by the Dutch and the French. The landing was made on 24 March, and after a brief skirmish, the island capitulated. Twelve ships were taken in the harbour of the French capital of the island, including a 12-gun privateer.

Since any delay would permit French help to arrive,

the British immediately re-embarked for an attack on the Danish islands of St Thomas and St Johns which capitulated without a fight on 28 March. On 3 March, the Danish brig *Lougen*, 18, had fought an indecisive action with the *Arab*, 22, and the *Experiment*, 20, from which she was able to escape (6). The relative lack of opposition encountered should not detract from what was an efficiently-executed campaign. All the conquests in the West Indies during this war were returned to their original owners at the Peace of Amiens, only Trinidad (taken in 1797) being retained by the British.

5. *Nereide*, lines and profile draught as taken off at Plymouth 1799. *NMM neg DR1789*

6. 'Briggen Lougen under Capitain Jessens Comando angribes ved St Thomas af 2de Engelske Fregatter den 3die Marty 1801', engraving and etching by F M Dodt, no date. *NMM ref PAG9007*

6

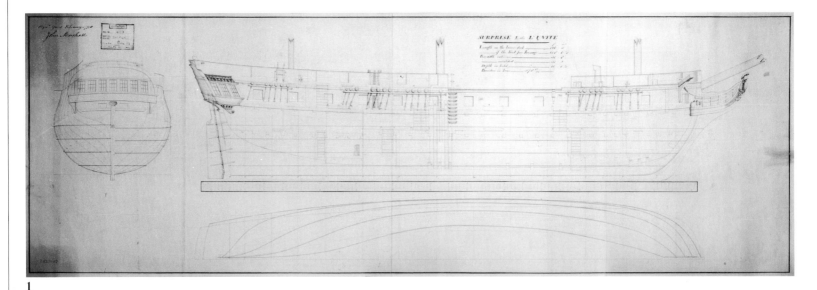

1

The Black Ship

1. Lines and profile of the Surprize as captured.
NMM neg D8700

2. 'The cutting out of HMS Hermione', oil painting by Nicholas Pocock (1740-1821).
NMM ref BHC0519

2

O N 21 September 1797, the crew of the 32-gun frigate *Hermione* rose up against their captain, Hugh Pigot, in the bloodiest mutiny in the history of the Royal Navy, and then handed their ship over to the Spanish.

The *Hermione*, based at St Nicholas Mole in Saint Domingue as part of Vice-Admiral Sir Hyde Parker's command, had sailed on 16 August 1797 to patrol the Mona Passage between Spanish-held Santo Domingo and Puerto Rico. Pigot, a tyrannical and cruel commander, had already done much to alienate his crew by both the number of floggings he had ordered in his seven months in command of the ship, and the inconsistency of these punishments, with varying numbers of lashes given for the same offence. On 20 September, while the crew were aloft reefing topsails, Pigot was unsatisfied by the performance of the mizzen topmen, and threatened to flog the last man down off the yard. In their rush to escape punishment, three men fell to the deck and were killed. Captain Pigot was then heard to say, 'Throw the lubbers overboard'. This caused murmurings amongst the maintopmen, and Pigot lost his temper completely at such insubordination. The Bosun's Mates were ordered to 'start' all the maintopmen, and the next morning six of them were flogged.

These events seem to have been the last straw for the crew of *Hermione*, and at 11 o'clock that night a number of men overpowered the marine sentry outside Pigot's cabin, burst in and stabbed him repeatedly, finally throwing him out of the stern windows. There seems to have been little if any resistance to the mutiny and the ship was taken over in minutes. A night of drunken slaughter followed, with eight other officers and warrant officers following the captain over the side. The mutineers then sailed the ship to the Spanish port of La Guayra, in present-day

Venezuela, and surrendered her to the authorities there, telling them that they had set their officers adrift. *Hermione* was taken into Spanish service under the name *Santa Cecilia*.

A mutiny such as this was every naval officer's worst nightmare, and great efforts were made to hunt down *Hermione*'s crew and recover 'the Black Ship'. When mutineers were taken, they received swift punishment, a total of twenty-four being hanged, the last in 1806. Soon after they took possession of her, the Spanish moved the frigate up the coast to the well-defended harbour of Puerto Cabello where it was planned to refit her. However, the colonial authorities' shortage of money and, more importantly, shortage of seamen to man her, meant that it was nearly two years before the *Santa Cecilia* was fit to go to sea.

Aware of this, Hyde Parker sent the 28-gun frigate *Surprise* (1), under the command of Captain Edward Hamilton, to cruise off the Spanish Main in September 1799, in the hope of recapturing the ship. Hamilton had suggested that, rather than wait for the *Santa Cecilia* to come out, he could send his ship's boats into Puerto Cabello to capture her, but Hyde Parker refused to allow it, given the strength of the harbour's defences. Nevertheless, after cruising without success for some time, Hamilton decided to try cutting out the frigate, and on the night of 24 October 1799 he set out in six boats with just over 100 men to capture a ship with a crew of 392 seamen and soldiers, lying in a harbour defended by 200 guns. The odds were heavy, but Hamilton had planned meticulously, right down to the construction of special platforms over the stern of the boats to allow a proper swing to the the axemen detailed to cut the substantial anchor cables.

In the event the *Surprise*'s boats were spotted by Spanish patrol craft which raised the alarm, the *Santa Cecilia* clearing for action and opening fire; but it seems that the men aboard the frigate were unaware that a cutting-out expedition was in progress and were firing more or less blindly at the harbour entrance (2). With most of the Spanish crew below manning the guns, some of Hamilton's boats were able to get alongside and the boarding parties clambered aboard, while others set about cutting the ship's anchor cables (3). A ferocious hand-to-hand battle followed, in which Hamilton himself was badly wounded, but despite the British being outnumbered – some of the boats detoured to attack the guardboats, and were late in arriving (4) – the ship was taken control of and sailed out of the harbour under heavy fire, exploiting a fortuitous offshore breeze.

When the Spanish felt the ship under way, they surrendered. Casualties amongst the defenders were very heavy, Hamilton reporting 119 Spanish killed and 231

4

captured, but amazingly none of his own men had been killed and only eight had been wounded. Hamilton was knighted for his daring exploit, and the recaptured *Hermione* was taken back into the Royal Navy, initially as the *Retaliation*, but she was later renamed *Retribution*, under which name she served until she was broken up at Deptford in 1805.

Dudley Pope, the historian of the *Hermione* mutiny, described this incredible achievement as 'among the bravest, best-planned and most successful operations in British naval history. There were plenty of actions of a similar nature during the war against Revolutionary France. Most were gallant; few were so completely successful; none provided such vindication for the Royal Navy and its officers and men.'

3. 'The Boarding and Capturing of His Majesty's late ship Hermione (now Retribution) of 32 guns, by the Boats of the Surprize frigate, under the batteries of Harbour of Porto Cavallo . . . Oct 25th 1799', engraving and etching by Roffe after an original by Elms, no date. *NMM neg B3820*

4. 'British Sailors Boarding a Man of War. Hermione 25 Oct 1799', coloured aquatint engraved by Fry and Sutherland after an original by John Augustus Atkinson, published by Edward Orme, 4 June 1815. *NMM ref PAD5628*

1

The Caribbean commerce war

THROUGHOUT THE final years of the French Revolutionary War, the naval conflict in the West Indies was typified by single-ship actions, with Royal Navy vessels hunting down French privateers and warships which menaced the Caribbean trade.

On 26 January 1798, HMS *Babet*, 20, was cruising between Martinique and Dominica when she sighted the French armed schooner *Désirée* of 6 guns. Almost immediately,

2

the wind died away and the *Babet* was becalmed. Seeing the French schooner making off under sweeps (long oars), Captain Jammett Mainwaring sent his ship's launch and pinnace in pursuit of her, commanded by his First Lieutenant Samuel Pym. After a chase of three hours, Pym and twelve men in the pinnace boarded the *Désirée* (1) and carried her at the loss of two men. The French lost three men killed, eight drowned and fifteen wounded out of a crew of forty-six. The *Babet*'s launch was not able to reach the *Désirée* before she had already struck her colours.

The war against privateers was unrelenting, but the actions were too commonplace to interest historians, even if they warranted a contemporary print. An example otherwise lost to history, from John Fairburn's series of minor West Indies battles (2), is the action of 26 December 1798 between the *Perdrix*, 24, and the large privateer *Agréable*, 24. Although the ships were of similar size, the British vessel's 6pdrs and 140 men made her victory over a 9pdr-armed opponent with 250 men a creditable achievement.

At the other end of the cruiser scale the big French frigate *Vengeance*, 36, which had been a menace to the West Indies trade for some years, was finally brought to battle by HMS *Seine*, 38, in the Mona Passage between Santo Domingo and Puerto Rico on 20 August 1800. After a chase lasting most of the day, the *Seine* was forced to drop back due to damage to her masts, but was able to resume the action at close quarters the following morning. After a hard fight of three hours, the *Vengeance* had lost all her masts and was badly damaged in her hull, and she struck her colours, an officer hailing the *Seine* from her bowsprit (3). The French had lost 35 men killed and 70 wounded to *Seine*'s 13 killed and 31 wounded. *Vengeance* was towed to Jamaica, with 9ft of water in her hold, and purchased for the Royal Navy but she was so badly damaged that she never sailed again.

In late 1800 the French fitted out a small squadron at Cayenne consisting of the brigs *Curieux*, 18, and *Mutine*, 16, and the schooner *Esperance*, 6, to attack the outward-bound West Indies convoy. On 29 January 1801 this squadron was cruising off Barbados when it sighted the British Sixth Rate *Bordelaise* and moved to attack her. Unfortunately for the French, twenty-two of the *Bordelaise*'s twenty-four guns were 32pdr carronades and at her first broadside into the *Curieux* at a range of 10 yards, the other two French ships fled (4). After 30 minutes the *Curieux* surrendered, and was so badly damaged that she sank that evening, many of her wounded being lost with her despite the best efforts of the *Bordelaise*'s crew to save them. In fact, two British midshipmen and five seamen went down with the *Curieux*, while there had only been one fatality aboard the *Bordelaise* during the battle.

3

1. 'The Boarding and Capturing La Desiree near Martinique, Janr 16th 1798', coloured aquatint engraved by William Elmes after his own original, published by John Fairburn, 1 September 1798.
NMM ref PAD5590

2. 'The Perdix capturing the Agreeable French Frigate in the West Indies, Decr 26th 1798', aquatint engraved by William Elmes after his own original, published by John Fairburn, no date.
NMM ref PAD5618

3. 'Capture of Le Vengeance', coloured aquatint engraved by Thomas Sutherland after an original by Thomas Whitcombe (born c1752), published 1 December 1816.
NMM ref PAD5639

4. 'The Bordelaise Corvette, sinking a French man-of-war', brown pen and wash by John Cantiloe Joy (1806-1866), no date.
NMM neg X1452

4

Ships of the Royal Navy: the Sixth Rate

AT THIS period the Sixth Rate was the smallest rank of ship commanded by a Post Captain. They carried between 20 and 28 guns, and were often referred to as frigates, although strictly speaking those of 24 guns and below were 'post ships'; all usually carried a main armament of 9pdr guns.

28-gun frigates

The very first British frigates, the *Unicorn* and *Lyme* of 1748, were armed with twenty-four 9pdrs on the upper deck, and later had four 3pdrs added to the quarterdeck. Apart from upgrading the latter to 6pdrs in 1780, there was little growth in the armament (or size) of 28-gun frigates during the four decades during which they were

1

2

built; survivors acquired additional carronades in later life (1). During the American Revolutionary War it was decided that they were too small and no more should be built, but it was impossible to find enough competent builders for larger ships so in 1782 a programme of nine further 28s was put in hand. Eight of these were eventually completed, the last of their line to British order, but it meant that there were significant numbers available on the outbreak of the French Revolutionary War—twenty-three in 1793 and twenty-one in 1797. The fleet list shows a steady decline in numbers—eleven in 1801, and only three by 1812—and the type had effectively disappeared by the end of the war. France had ceased building 8pdr frigates, their equivalent of British 28s, in the mid-1770s, but large French quarterdecked corvettes were sometimes rated as 28s on capture (2). They had a poor reputation in the Royal Navy, being regarded as crank and sluggish sailers.

As a cruising class the 28-gun Sixth Rate was in rapid decline, the few survivors being largely banished to far-off and minor stations; those nearer home were usually converted to auxiliaries—mainly troopships, but some were rearmed with 24pdr or 32pdr carronades on the upper deck to became floating batteries during the invasion scare of 1803.

Post ships of 20 and 24 guns

Although no longer considered proper frigates by the 1790s, in many ways the post ship bore the same relationship to the frigate as the 50-gun ship did to the line of battle. Both were descendants of more important types of the same gun power, neither was built in large numbers, but both retained minor roles for which there was no apparent substitute.

When the frigate-form cruiser replaced the old two-decker 24s, new Sixth Rates of both 20 and 24 guns (9pdrs) were introduced shortly afterwards. They adopted the frigate's unarmed lower deck and were very similar in layout, apart from the absence of an orlop platform amidships (3). With a full quarterdeck and forecastle, these ships were relatively high for their length, and were never regarded as fast or weatherly. However, they were seaworthy, and in peacetime found favour for long overseas voyages, the best known being *Pandora*'s mission to hunt down the *Bounty* mutineers. Just as 50-gun ships were cheaper than bigger two-deckers to commission in peacetime, so the post ship was often employed as a frigate substitute, particularly on the more distant stations. Their wartime utility was more questionable, and only a handful had been built after France's entry into the American War in 1778. As a result there were only twelve fit for service in 1793.

The rise in numbers to twenty-three during the French Revolutionary War and twenty-nine by 1814 was largely the result of captures. These were mainly faster and more weatherly flush-decked ships, some of which were large privateers, but Holland provided a few quarterdecked ships like their British equivalents. Not surprisingly, in the 'big ship' era of the 1790s no new post ships were ordered, but in the numbers-obsessed Napoleonic War these small cruisers again found limited favour, twelve being ordered in 1805 (4).

In the first phase of the war some post ships posed as cruisers, but the capture of *Hyaena* in the West Indies in 1793 — easily overhauled by the 40-gun *Concorde* — emphasised how vulnerable they were to big frigates. *Eurydice*, a notoriously dull sailer, nearly cost Saumarez the whole of his cruiser squadron in June 1794, and only a miniature version of Cornwallis's famous retreat saved the day (see page 51 of *Fleet Battle and Blockade* in this series). In general their poor sailing qualities put them in the 'can neither fight nor run away' category: significantly, when recaptured *Hyaena* was found to have had her quarterdeck and forecastle removed by the French and was much faster (or at least, far more weatherly) in consequence. Peter Cullen, who served in the *Squirrel*, said the ship '... though a good sea boat, was not a fast sailer,' and this more or less summarised their virtues and their vices.

Post ships continued to perform some cruising functions — particularly chasing small privateers in the West Indies — but nearer home they were mainly consigned to convoy duties, often specifically as flagships of coastal convoys. Even this had its dangers, and *Daphne* was taken in 1795 while so employed. With a mean draught of about 15ft the post ship offered the same advantages over a frigate as the 50 did over a real battleship, and as a result developed a number of similar roles during the

3

course of the war. They were especially useful on anti-invasion duties, because they could back up the small craft in shallower waters than a frigate could be risked, and because they were commanded by post captains they could be used as leaders for flotillas of sloops and gunbrigs which would be in the charge of more junior officers — commanders and lieutenants respectively. Thus in 1805 both *Champion* and *Ariadne* were to be found commanding detachments of gunbrigs harrassing the invasion preparations in the Channel ports — and the twelve-ship programme of 1805 was probably a response to this requirement.

Similar duties resulted from the war with Denmark. Five post ships went with Parker to the Baltic in 1801 — *Jamaica* leading the gunbrigs at the battle of Copenhagen — and after 1807 they were often to be found supporting small craft in the hit-and-run fighting in the skerries and fjords. Their suitabilty for inshore work was confirmed by warfare in the Adriatic, where *Porcupine*'s exploits in 1807-8 may stand as a prime example.

4

1. 'Corvette Anglaise de 30 Canons', coloured engraving by Gio Maria Merlo after an original by Emeric, 1794. It actually depicts a 28-gun Sixth Rate before carronades were added; the crew are shown far too small which exaggerates the size of what was actually a rather small ship.
NMM ref PAH9405

2. 'Corvette française, se touant dans une passe les vergues brassées au vent', Plate 59 of *Collection de Toutes les Especes de Batiments* (third edition, Paris 1826), engraving by J J Baugean after his own original.
NMM ref PAD7423

3. 'British frigate in three positions', etching by Robert Pollard after an original by T Mitchell, published by William Mitchell 7 February 1806. It is actually a 24-gun post ship of the 1780s.
NMM neg A3212

4. Design draught for the new 22-gun Sixth Rates of the *Laurel* class, dated 25 March 1805.
NMM neg DR2796

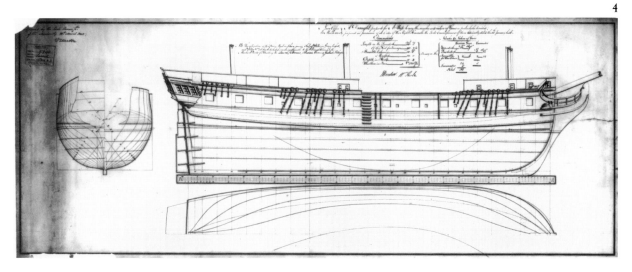

1

East Indies 1798-1801

1. 'View taken on the Esplanade, Calcutta', coloured aquatint engraved and published by Thomas Daniell after his own original, August 1797. *NMM neg A6279*

2. 'View of Penang from the sea', anonymous coloured etching, no date. *NMM neg A6799*

3. 'The Arrogant, Intrepid and Virginie chasing French and Spanish squadron off coast of China, 27th January 1799', watercolour by Thomas Buttersworth (1768-1842), 1804. *NMM ref PAH9508*

4. 'A view of Batavia the Capital of the Dutch settlements in India', brown aquatint engraved and published by J Wells after an original by Drummond, 25 February 1796. *NMM ref PA10233*

2

DURING 1797 the attention of the East Indies squadron under Admiral Peter Rainier had been directed towards the Spanish-ruled Philippines, but plans to attack Manila had been abandoned on news of the treaty of Campo-Formio, which potentially released French forces for intervention in India. The threat was enhanced by Bonaparte's invasion of Egypt, which looked like the first stage of an advance on the sub-continent, and naval forces had to sent to the Red Sea to block any eastward moves. In the event, the storming of Seringapatam in May 1799 and the death of France's most powerful local ally, Tipu Sultan, effectively terminated French intrigues in India.

This still left the naval threat of the French raiding squadron, and its base on Mauritius was usually under blockade. However, Calcutta (1) – the administrative and trading centre of British India – and the whole Bay of Bengal was vulnerable during the north-east monsoon to forces based to the east, as Suffren had proved in 1782 when he had based his fleet in Sumatra. This had prompted the British in 1786 to establish a fort on Prince of Wales Island in the Malacca Straits, through which much of the China trade usually passed; this grew to become the important settlement of Penang (2), which offered a good anchorage and shipping facilities.

Perhaps in emulation of Suffren, Rear-Admiral Sercey's French squadron was indeed in the Dutch East Indies in 1798, proposing to co-operate with the Spanish Manila squadron. The homegoing China fleet was always a major source of concern to the British naval commander – 'a convoy of the largest merchantmen in the world, richly laden and adhering to a time-table (fixed by the monsoons and tea crop) which was known, in outline, to everyone', as Northcote Parkinson pointed out. Knowing of the French presence, Rainier sent the 74-gun *Arrogant* and the *Virginie*, 38 to join the single 64 detailed to protect the China fleet. After a remarkably quick passage, although both suffered storm damage, the reinforcement arrived at Macao on 21 January 1799. A week later, to their mutual astonishment, a Franco-Spanish squadron appeared off the port. They were the Spanish 74s *Europa* and *Montanes*, frigates *Lucia* and *Fama* (Spanish), and *Preneuse* and *Brûle-Gueule* (French).

What followed is given in the official British report:

Captain Hargood of the *Intrepid* [64 guns], the senior officer, slipped his cables per signal and sail'd imedi-

3

ately in pursuit of them, being followed by the other two ships. Both squadrons were obliged to anchor among the Ladrones in the night, and in the morning to their surprise the Enemy were not seen. – the ships of the enemy appeared in very good order, and the Spanish Admiral's ship sail'd remarkably fast – their running away from a force so much inferior to their own is no otherwise to be accounted for, but from their dread of a conflict that would in all probability have terminated in their disgrace . . .

This little-known incident is depicted in a dramatic watercolour by Thomas Buttersworth (3), with the British squadron making sail into the evening twilight, with the *Virginie* accurately shown without the mizzen she lost in the previous week's storm. After this failure, the Franco-Spanish squadron broke up and there were no further attempts on the China trade during the remainder of this war, although the campaign was revived after 1803.

The fall of Seringapatam had released British troops in India for further expeditions, and an attack on Java was mooted but Manila and Mauritius were alternatives dis-

cussed. In May 1800 Rainier actually received orders to capture Java and Surinam, and Batavia (4), the capital of the Dutch Indies, was blockaded as a preliminary to invasion. However, when the expulsion of the French from Egypt was made a priority, the available troops were redirected to the Red Sea.

4

1. 'Attaque de Kosseir par les Anglais', from C de la Jonquière, *L'Expedition D'Égypt 1798-1801,* Vol V (Paris 1907). *Chatham collection*

2. 'View of Jiddah taken from the West', lithograph engraved by W Walton after an original by Captain C Head, printed by Charles Joseph Hullmandel, no date. *NMM ref PAH2852*

3. 'Aden', tinted engraving after an original attributed to Leighton, 1850. *NMM neg C52*

4. 'A New chart of the Red Sea or Arabian Gulf, by Sir Home Popham K.M., F.R.S., Commanding His Majesty's Vessels on that Station in the Years 1801, 1802', published by W Faden, 13 July 1804. *British Library SEC. II. (7)*

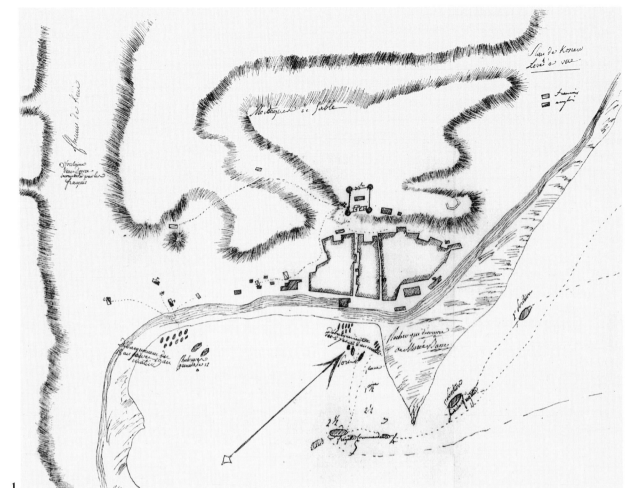

1

Red Sea operations

THE FRENCH invasion of Egypt posed an obvious threat to India, especially if they could link up with the anti-British Sultan Tipu of Mysore; but if the unlikely scenario of an overland march is dismissed then the only practical alternative would be to transport an army by ships sent to Suez at the head of the Red Sea. Since the French had a convenient base in Mauritius, this was not impossible, and of the British Cabinet Henry Dundas seemed most exercised by the possibility. As a result of his urgings, a small squadron, comprising *Leopard*, 50 and the frigate *Daedalus* and sloop *Orestes* under

Commodore Blankett, was dispatched direct to Suez from Britain. After a very difficult passage Blankett arrived at Mocha, at the entrance to the Red Sea, in April 1799 to find that the commander of the East Indies station, Rear-Admiral Rainier, had anticipated the need for a Red Sea force. The *Centurion*, 50 and *Albatross*, 18 with some Company vessels had already been sent up to the head of the gulf to reconnoitre Suez, leaving Blankett to wonder if his journey was really necessary.

The Red Sea was unfamiliar waters to the Royal Navy at that time, and not only was it uncharted but its

2

weather conditions were unhelpful to sailing ships—winds were fickle for part of the year, followed by the northern Monsoon which almost prohibited square riggers from working northwards. In any event, Suez proved impossible to attack from seaward because of shallows and sandbars that extended far out to sea.

As an interim measure of security, Company troops seized the island of Perim in May 1799 to close the straits of Bab-el Mandeb to an enemy squadron. The French occupation forces, which had only reached Suez in the previous December, went on to garrison Kosseir in May. The possession of this port further down the Red Sea allowed the French to intercept reinforcements to their Mameluke enemies and facilitated negotiations with the Shereef of Mecca, whose port of Jiddah was the nearest source of shipping. Therefore, the frigates *Daedalus* and *Fox* were sent to Kosseir in August—a considerable achievement in the teeth of the northern Monsoon—to destroy the French defences. A three-day bombardment did little significant damage, to either side, but the operation was primarily designed as a demonstration of seapower to impress Arab opinion (1).

In the meantime, Blankett had learned of the death of Tipu Sultan and Bonaparte's escape from Egypt, which effectively spelled the end of the danger to India. It remained to put as much pressure as possible on the French occupying forces, so he took his squadron to Jiddah (2) and persuaded the Shereef to embargo all communication with Suez. In September by the invitation of the governor, British forces moved from Perim to occupy Aden (3), a far more satisfactory base, but its value was not yet fully appreciated and it was later evacuated on the orders of the Indian Government.

The Red Sea was a backwater for most of 1800, but when it was decided to invade Egypt from the Mediterranean the Red Sea squadron was ordered to cooperate. Blankett was based on Jiddah, and after the French abandoned Suez, it was quickly occupied by the British on 22 March 1801, Blankett sending his small Indian Army force of 300 men across the desert to join General Hutchinson's operations in lower Egypt. The British government also sent a force direct from Britain under Commodore Home Popham (who also replaced Blankett in command). These rendezvoused at Kosseir with 6000 troops from Bombay under General David Baird, but despite a rapid water-borne advance down the Nile, they did not arrive until after the surrender of Alexandria.

Popham was partly chosen for the command because of his amphibious experience, but also because he was a formidable hydrographer, and he was to fill his hours during the eighteen months *Romney* was in the Red Sea making the first reliable British charts of the area (4).

3

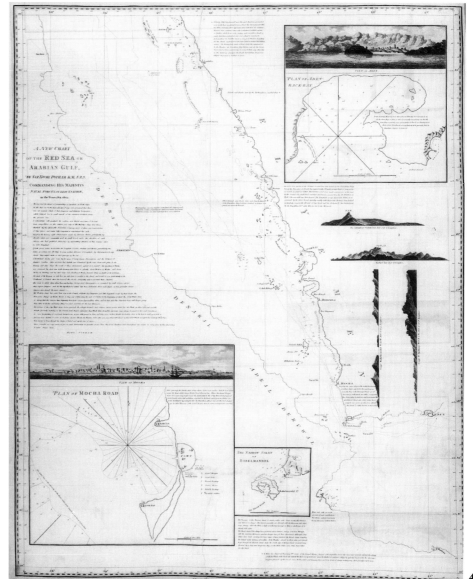

4

'Dangers of the sea': dismasting

THE MOST vulnerable feature of any sailing warship was undoubtedly its top-hamper, the masts and rigging which not only provided propulsion but also control. The loss of masts and spars, therefore, threatened the safety of the ship and all on board. The main reasons for damage aloft—apart from battle, which in terms of the naval prayer was more a result of 'the violence of the enemy' than the 'dangers of the sea'— could be divided into incompetence, stress of weather, or equipment failure. Serious accident occasioned by poor seamanship was very rare in the Royal Navy, a force which regularly spent more time at sea than its enemies, but spars and rigging were frequently lost or

damaged by carrying too much sail in heavy weather. This was a matter of fine judgement, and in certain circumstances—particularly in chase of an enemy—British captains would take chances.

Of all events classed by insurance companies as 'Acts of God', the most unusual was lightning strike, but there were several well-documented instances in the Royal Navy, even after Benjamin Franklin's lightning conductor was adopted. However, the frigate *Thisbe* (1) was probably unique in that she was struck twice in rapid succession, losing all except her fore and mizzen lower masts to the strike and resulting fire.

Far more common was simple storm damage, from

which there was no recourse if the weather was heavy enough – even in a sheltered anchorage like Spithead. In November 1800 a great gale hit the south coast, driving a number of ships from Spithead, and the brig *Requin*, schooner *Redbridge*, Sixth Rate *Bourdelais*, and the big frigate *Hussar* were badly damaged. They were all saved and brought into Portsmouth three days later, an excellent portrait surviving of *Hussar* in this condition (2). She lost all her topmasts and the mizzen, and judging from the water gushing from the scuppers, must have suffered hull damage as well. Most importantly, she also lost her rudder, which would have made her unmanageable, and the dockyard hoy astern is probably acting as a temporary rudder, exerting leverage via the cables through the cabin lights.

If a storm could wreck a well-found ship in a safe anchorage, what could similar weather do to worn-out vessels on an exposed coastline like the Bay of Biscay? The experience of the 74-gun *Montagu* early in 1801 provides one answer. She was an old ship, built in 1779, and had seen much action with the Inshore Squadron off Brest in the previous year, a service that was stressful for both ships and men. While part of Rear-Admiral Calder's squadron of seven ships of the line, on 13 February the ship began to split sails and lose spars, which were quickly replaced, as the weather started to deteriorate. A strong gale with violent squalls followed, the ship being pooped by a heavy sea, and as the ship laboured some of the shroud bolts were drawn through the ship's rotten sides. The shrouds provided the main lateral support to the masts, and a running battle began to replace and reinforce the shrouds and backstays with runners and tackles to take the strain.

At a quarter past midnight on the 15th, off Cape Ortegal, the battle was dramatically lost when the main, mizzen and fore topmast went overboard (3): in the telegraphic style of the captain's log, 'the ship rolling heavy, obliged to cut all away and bear up, to preserve the foremast, and get clear of the wreck. Fired several guns as signals of distress. ½ past 6 none of the squadron in sight'. The *Montagu* was located by the frigate *Diamond*, but after the weather abated on the 16th the ship was able to make her own way into the Tagus, crossing the bar two days later. The facilities at Lisbon did not compare with a British dockyard, and while the *Hussar* had been refitted and undocked in two weeks at Portsmouth, it took over a month to rerig the *Montagu*, which did not sail until 31 March.

It is a remarkable feature of most dismastings that not only did the ship survive, but that the ship was largely responsible for its own salvation. The wooden sailing ship with a well-trained crew was very self-sufficient by modern standards and capable of a degree of self-repair

3

undreamed of in the age of maintenance-by-replacement. Ships carried spare spars – although they could not replace lower masts – and officers and crews became very skilled in improvising 'jury' (a contraction of 'injury') rigs. Whereas contriving a jury rudder was difficult and a number of patented systems were published, there was no standard pattern to a jury rig, which necessarily depended on which spars and sails survived. The *Theseus*, for example, when dismasted in a hurricane off San Domingo in 1804, first set the main royal on the bowsprit in an attempt to wear ship; this failed and extra boat sails were set from the bowsprit, and even from the catheads before it was achieved. The crew then got up a topgallant mast and sail in place of the foremast to give the ship some steerage.

This was a temporary jury rig while the storm still blew, but when the wind moderated, over a period of four days the ship got up and rigged a jury mainmast and bent on a fore topsail, employed sheers to set up a fore topmast for a foremast, to which a jury topmast was added, and set a mizzen on the ensign staff, as shown in (4). In company with the similarly damaged *Hercule*, the ship made Jamaica safely on 15 September, a week after losing all her lower masts except the bowsprit.

Some ships were not as fortunate as these examples, but such were the skills of the seamen of this period that dismasting was by no means inevitably followed by wreck or foundering.

4

Indian Ocean raiders

THE EFFECTIVENESS of the French squadron under Rear-Admiral Sercey in the Indian Ocean was seriously eroded by the unco-operative political regime in power on the Isle de France (modern Mauritius), where they were based; and both supplies and seamen were hard to come by. At the beginning of 1798 there were seven frigates available, but their number was to be reduced rapidly during the year. In need of major repair, *Vertu* and *Régénérée* were sent home as escort to a consignment of Spanish treasure; *Seine*, with a less valuable cargo of 300 refractory troops, followed, only to be captured in sight of the French coast (see pages 127-128); the *Prudente* was then sold on the orders of the colonial assembly, and was captured in February 1799 acting as a privateer. This left only the 44-gun *Forte* (Sercey's flagship), the 36-gun *Preneuse* and the *Brûle-Gueule*, 32.

A prime target for these commerce raiders was the East Indiaman, the largest and usually most valuably

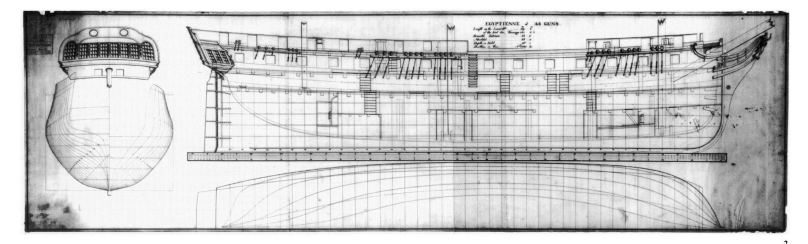

3

freighted type of merchant ship in the world (1). *Preneuse* was lucky enough to capture two on 8 March 1798 at Tellicherry, emphasising the impossibility of protecting every ship. The far more powerful *Forte* was let loose in the Bay of Bengal at the beginning of 1799, snapping up half a dozen vessels in quick succession, although these were mainly 'country' ships engaged in local trading. Low morale was a major problem in Sercey's ships, the *Preneuse* having suffered a serious mutiny the previous summer, and one of the captains of the captured British ships was scandalised by the state of *La Forte*:

> As for the discipline of the ship, it was very slack. It was not at all unusual to see one of the foremast men, with his beef in his hands, eating it while walking the quarter-deck, and claiming an equal right to do it with the commanding officer, thus, I suppose, demonstrating the claims of liberty, equality and brotherhood. Nor was any scruple made of playing cards on the quarter-deck. The lieutenants generally came on deck with only trousers and an open shirt, often a check one, so that it was almost impossible to distinguish them.

He did admit, 'The men, however, went through their duty with alacrity, and were obedient to orders.'

But she was a slack ship and the events of the night of 28 February proved it. In the moonlight a large vessel was seen approaching, but it caused no concern to *La Forte*'s officers, who were expecting another fat

4

Indiaman. The stranger was HMS *Sybille*, 38 guns, and she had put two full broadsides into her astonished opponent before the Frenchman could reply. Despite the surprise, *La Forte* was an immensely powerful ship, and it took the British frigate nearly two hours to force her surrender (2). With her sister-ship *Egyptienne* (3), *La Forte* was the largest frigate in the French navy, carrying thirty 24pdrs, twelve 8pdrs and ten 36pdr carronades in this battle, yet her outgunned antagonist with 18pdr main batteries had only a few shots in hull and some damaged rigging. By contrast *La Forte* was entirely dismasted, with her topsides wrecked by over 300 hits, her casualties amounting to 93 dead and 80 wounded (20 of them mortally); the British ship lost 5 killed and 17 wounded, both captains, Cooke of *Sybille* and Beaulieu le Loup of *La Forte*, being among the dead. The prize should have been an important addition to the strength on the station, but unfortunately she ran aground two years later in the Red Sea and had to be abandoned.

The *Brûle-Gueule* having been sent home, where she was to be wrecked in the approaches to Brest, the sole survivor of Sercey's squadron was the *Preneuse*. Under Captain L'Hermitte, she had been both the most active

and most successful of the frigates, but after an eventful cruise off the African coast in which she had clashed with a British storeship and sloop, and beat off a pursuing 50-gun ship (*Jupiter*) in high seas, she was finally trapped against the coast of Mauritius by the *Tremendous*, 74 and *Adamant*, 50. On 11 December 1799 the *Preneuse* was run ashore and surrendered (4), where the British set her on fire. Sercey himself, who had been ashore all year, witnessed this final extinction of his squadron and, now lacking a command, he returned to France.

The last French attempt to interfere in the Indian Ocean during the war was to send out the frigate *Chiffonne*, 36. Rainier had suspected that some effort might be made to interrupt communications with the Red Sea squadron, and that any such operation would have to come from the Seychelles, so he sent the *Sybille* to counter any such move. Having overcome the mighty *Forte*, the *Sybille* had no difficulty taking the 12pdr-armed *Chiffonne*, although her anchored position in Mahé harbour was not easy to approach (5). She was added to the Royal Navy as a 12pdr 36-gun frigate under her original name.

5

UNTIL 1800 Britain's relations with the northern powers—Russia, Prussia, Denmark and Sweden—had been cordial, if not actually warm, owing to mutual interest in Britain's trade with the Baltic and a common concern to maintain the stability of northern Europe in the face of France's attempts to advance the Jacobin cause and French imperial ambitions. However, the ambivalence of that relationship was demonstrated in 1800-1 when the northern powers opposed British interests in the region, and threatened to lend their weight to the advantage of France.

Compared to that of the East India and West India trade, the value of British trade to and from the Baltic was relatively small. In the year ending on 5 January 1798, for example, imports from the Baltic into the port of London were valued at about 2.2 million pounds, while those from the two former regions were valued at 6.5 million and 7.1 million. However, apart from corn from Prussia and linen from Russia, these imports mainly consisted of naval stores: iron from Stockholm, hemp from Riga and St Petersburg, pitch and tar from Sweden and Archangel, tallow from Russia, oak from Stettin, Hamburg, and Danzig (modern Gdansk), fir timber and deals from Norway, masts and yards from Riga, St Petersburg and Norway.

These stores were consumed by the growing merchant shipping industry as well as by the Royal Navy. In 1801, for example, the total quantity of Russian hemp imported was 36,000 tons, of which the Royal Navy only consumed 13,000 tons, but enough to manufacture 15,260 tons of cordage. Nevertheless, the largest single consumers were the Royal Dockyards. Their consumption may be judged from the quantities required by the Royal Navy in 1801 alone: they needed 36,000 loads of timber (two such cartloads providing a little over one ton of shipping), 1400 tons of iron, 5500 barrels of pitch, 18,800 barrels of tar, 371,000 deals, and at

least 900 masts greater than 21 inches diameter, of which at least 500 were expected to be from Riga. The importance of these stores to the Navy as well as to merchant shipping increased markedly during the last quarter of the eighteenth century; indeed it would be fair to claim that British maritime power was partly built on imports from the Baltic states, which escalated from a value of £1.6 million in 1772-73, to £2.5 million in 1789-90, and £3.3 million in 1797-98.

This trade was vital to the wealth of the northern states, for, though replete with natural resources, they had few manufactures to export. St Petersburg, for example, though exporting over forty different commodities to London, apart from iron, hemp and tallow, sent only flax, diapers (cloth), linen, linseed, horsetails and bearskins in noteworthy quantities. Mutual interest thus kept the trade going in spite of a strong French influence, especially at the court of St Petersburg. British subsidies and naval power helped in this respect, for Britain financed Russian armies in the field until 1799, while the Royal Navy, convoying British trade to the Sound between Denmark and Sweden had a far higher profile at the mouth of the Baltic than the French navy, which was largely confined to port and rarely ventured north. Russian amity with Britain kept the other Baltic states in line, for divergence would have placed them between two dangerous powers.

Denmark, Sweden and Russia each had their own navies, developed principally to defend their own interests in the Baltic against one another: Russia fought both Sweden and Turkey prior to the outbreak of the French Revolutionary War. But the navies of Denmark and Sweden—at twenty-three and eighteen ships of the line in 1801—were relatively small, while that of Russia, split between the Baltic and Black Sea, was large but not as effective as its size suggested it might have been: in 1801 it had eighty-two ships of the line, of which only

thirty-one were available for service. Nevertheless, the Danes and Swedes were enterprising seafarers, while in 1795 and 1798 respectively Russian squadrons had joined the British navy in the North Sea and Mediterranean. Separate, these powers were known quantities, no match for the British navy. United, however, they were a very different proposition.

The danger they presented only became apparent in 1800. Russia, the key power in the north, was defeated by France at Zurich in 1799. Napoleon's repeated defeats of Austria in 1800 laid the new Tsar, Paul I, who succeeded Catherine the Great in 1796, open to diplomatic advances from Paris. In September the exclusion of Russia from the retaking of Malta by British forces offended Paul I, irritation complemented by that of Denmark and Sweden with Britain's protracted insistence on the exclusion of France from the Baltic trade in naval stores. Neutral shipping was everywhere stopped and searched by the Royal Navy for cargoes destined for enemy territories or belonging to enemy owners. All such cargoes were liable to confiscation. The neutral shipping was simply diverted to an allied port and the offending part of the cargo unloaded, subjected to adjudication, and sold as prize goods. Cargoes of war, munitions or naval stores were automatic confiscations. Not unnaturally, to avoid such interference, neutrals adopted every form of documentary disguise of cargo ownership and destination, an effort that simply enhanced and aggravated policing by the British navy.

Resentment of this interference came to a head in July 1800 when a British frigate squadron fell in with a Danish convoy, exchanged shots with its escort, and took the convoy into the Downs. Diplomatic settlement of the issue at Copenhagen agreed repair of the Danish frigate but maintained the British right to search, especially in the Mediterranean. However, the British envoy was escorted to Copenhagen by four sail of the line and three 50-gun ships, a show of force in the Baltic which angered Russia. At the beginning of September 1800 Tsar Paul I sequestered all British property within the Russian empire and mobilised his armed forces. The sequestration was lifted three weeks later, but the Russian army and navy remained on a war footing. Furthermore, following news of the British capture of Malta, an embargo was placed on British shipping in Russian ports, affecting about 200 vessels. That December, Russia signed a defensive pact with Sweden, which also embargoed British vessels. Prussia and Denmark also joined and, to enforce recognition of the interests of the Armed Neutrality, their armies occupied Hanover.

These acts of the northern powers removed all pretence of neutrality. The occupation of Hanover was a direct attack on the British crown. The embargo on British shipping threatened both the supply of grain to England, then in the throes of food riots, and the supply of naval stores. The response in London was immediately offensive. By mid-March a fleet under Sir Hyde Parker was hastily assembled and despatched to the Baltic with Nelson as second-in-command to perform the fighting part. The whole fleet comprised fifty-three vessels including fifteen of the line, later increased to eighteen. In effective ships, they faced perhaps ten of the line at Copenhagen,

eleven at Karlscrona, and twenty spread between St Petersburg, Archangel, Kronstadt and Reval.

Parker's instructions were to appear before Copenhagen and demand the Danes withdraw from the Armed Neutrality, and to enforce this either by 'amicable arrangement or by actual hostilities'. He was then to proceed northeast to make 'an immediate and vigorous attack' on the Russian fleet at Reval and Kronstadt. In the event, preliminary diplomatic negotiations with the Danes failed and, as the British passed through the Sound, fire was exchanged at long range with Elsinore Castle. Anchored north of Copenhagen, Parker was inclined to impose a blockade of the Baltic to bring the Danes to terms; however, Nelson was for destroying each of the fleets of the Armed Neutrality before they could concentrate. To have attacked the Russian fleet first would have left the Danes in the British rear. Parker was thus persuaded to allow Nelson to take ten ships of the line and two 50-gun ships and attack the Danish fleet, drawn up in defence of Copenhagen, from the south, by which means a British fleet was kept between the Danes and the Russians and the powerful guns of Copenhagen's Trekroner fortress were avoided.

The attack took place on 2 April 1801. It was terminated three hours later, not without severe damage to the British ships, after Nelson

submitted an ultimatum to 'set on fire all the floating batteries he has taken without having the power of saving the brave Danes who have defended them'. A ceasefire was extended the following day by Nelson himself going ashore to conduct British diplomacy. In a series of meetings, he extended it to a 14-week truce, time enough for the British fleet to engage the Russians.

Secure in his rear, on 12 April Parker took his fleet into the Baltic to carry out his instructions with regard to the Russian fleet. Hearing of a Swedish squadron at sea, which thereupon took refuge in Karlscrona, Parker steered to the north of Bornholm island, from where he opened negotiations with the Swedish crown. This resulted on 22 April in an agreement to seek settlement of all differences. The following day Parker received news of the assassination of Tsar Paul I on 24 March by a group of dissident Russian officers. Unsure now how to proceed, especially with the Swedish fleet still operational, Parker returned to the Danish coast where he received instructions to transfer command of the fleet to Nelson and to return to England, which he did on 6 May.

Nelson's immediate objective was to ensure the pacification of the Russian fleet. Leaving six of the line off Kronstadt, with an intimation to the Swedish court that if a Swedish squadron was found at sea it would be destroyed, he sailed for Reval at the mouth of the Gulf of Finland with eleven of the line where he anchored on 14 May. The Russian fleet was missing. The ice had melted in the Gulf over the previous two weeks and the Russians had withdrawn to concentrate at Kronstadt. The new Tsar, Alexander, declined to negotiate while British ships remained in sight off the Russian coast. Diplomatically, Nelson withdrew on 19 May.

Two days later both the Russian and Swedish crowns lifted the embargoes each had placed on British ships, the former since 5 November 1800. Danish and Prussian troops had already been withdrawn from Hanover. The Armed Neutrality of the North was effectively dissolved. In June 1801 Russia and Britain signed a convention in which the latter maintained her right to search neutral ships and to seize the hostile cargoes they carried. Nelson was relieved on 18 June, and British trade in the Baltic resumed its interrupted pattern.

A contribution to the growing tension between Britain and Denmark: the detention of the frigate Freja *and her convoy in the Channel, 25 July 1800, after a scuffle with three British frigates, a sloop and a lugger. The damaged* Freja *was later repaired at Britain's expense, but relations with Denmark could not be so easily mended.* NMM neg 220

Forcing the Sound

2

1

ALTHOUGH APPOINTED to the Baltic fleet, in St Vincent's words, to 'act the fighting part', Nelson was prevented from forming any specific strategy or tactics for dealing with the Armed Neutrality of the North until summoned to a council of war on board Sir Hyde Parker's flagship off the Koll, at the southern end of the Kattegat on 23 March, eleven days after the fleet had sailed from Yarmouth Roads. Hyde Parker (1), commanding the fleet of fifteen of the line and two 50-gun ships, had received his instructions shortly after sailing, and was directed to force the Danes to withdraw from the Armed Neutrality either by 'amicable arrangement or by actual hostilities'. The diplomat, Nicholas Vansittart, was also present at the council of war, having just received Denmark's refusal to withdraw. In consequence, Hyde Parker was commissioned to destroy Copenhagen's arsenal with all the shipping in that port.

Hitherto Hyde Parker's proceedings had been characterised by caution. Having had some of his ships scattered by gales, he had been anchored at the Koll to regroup and because he feared the guns of Kronborg castle, at Elsinore, commanding the northern end of the Sound, might severely damage his fleet should he attempt to push through without the Danes' permission. Nelson, on the other hand, in the dark as to their instructions, was for the demonstration of a powerful British force before Copenhagen even while they considered the British ultimatum.

At the council of war, Hyde Parker was still for considering all options, including the blockade of the Baltic from where they lay, or sailing through the Great Belt to the west of the island of Zeeland, so as to avoid the guns of Kronborg castle. Nelson impatiently stressed the lateness of the year, which might free the Russian fleet from ice to concentrate, possibly even with the Danes or Swedes, and urged Hyde Parker to force the Sound and to leave a token force off Copenhagen in order to attack the Russians, the main threat, without delay. To Nelson's frustration, the council of war reached no firm decision; he returned on board his ship, the *St George*, still uncertain what they were to do.

Moreover, when the fleet weighed on the 25 March, Hyde Parker directed the fleet towards the Great Belt. Unbeknown to Nelson, however, pressure was immediately brought upon Parker by William Domett, his flag captain, who had become alarmed at the prospect of a passage through the Great Belt permitting the British ships of the line reaching Kioge Bay, south of Copenhagen, and southerly gales combined with shallow waters then preventing them from approaching the Danish capital. Nelson was again summoned and further consulted. He had been drafting a letter to Parker,

3

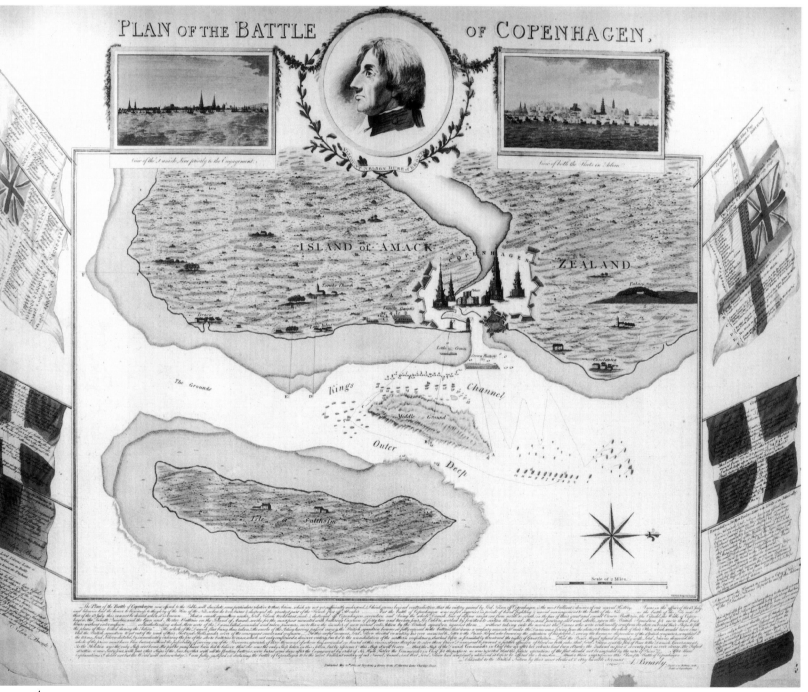

emphasising the essence of time and the fact that the Danes would be taking advantage of their delays to strengthen their own defences. He now read his letter to Parker, offering to take a portion of the fleet to attack the Russians. Parker reacted against this possible division of his fleet, but, almost in compromise, acceded to the risk of navigating the Sound. The fleet was put about and that evening moored a few miles south of their previous anchorage.

The fleet nevertheless proceeded by the smallest stages. Off Elsinore on 29 March, Parker entered negotiations with the governor of the Kronborg, raising again the prospect of Denmark acceding to Britain's ultima-

4

5

tum, a suggestion that was predictably rejected, and accompanied by the threat of bombardment from the castle if the British fleet attempted to pass through the Sound. Only with this threat of unavoidable hostilities, Parker agreed that Nelson should make an attack on the Danish fleet with the ships of more shallow draft; in the evening of 29 March Nelson consequently transferred to the *Elephant*, a 74 of less draft than his current three-decker *St George*.

Next morning Nelson commanded the van division of the British fleet as it entered the Sound in line ahead. The batteries of Elsinore and the Kronborg opened fire at 7am (2). The Sound at Elsinore is only three miles wide, and the batteries on the Danish side were matched by batteries in Helsingborg on the Swedish side. The latter, however, did not open fire; later they were known to have mounted only eight guns of light calibre; the Swedes had also begun to reconsider their position in the Armed Neutrality. The British fleet was thus able to keep towards the Swedish shore, so that not a Danish shot reached home (3).

Above the island of Huen, twelve miles from Copenhagen, the fleet anchored while Nelson, Domett and Rear-Admiral Graves, third in command, reconnoitred the Danish defences. The Sound off Copenhagen was divided by a middle ground. An approach by sea was limited to the north-south channel to the west of this middle ground. This was three-quarters of a mile

wide, known as the King's Deep, and lined along its western banks by mud flats. The Danes had lined this channel, close to the mud banks, with their fleet of eighteen vessels, some hulked, its northern end shielded by the Trekroner battery and Crown batteries at the entrance to the city's harbour, its southern end shielded by a battery on the island of Amak (4). That evening, on 30 March, there was another council of war at which Nelson offered to attack the Danish fleet with ten British ships. Parker accepted the offer, adding two 50-gun ships to the ten he requested.

That night Nelson went in the fleet's boats to re-buoy the outer channel, to the east of the middle ground. The operation opened the option of attacking the Danish fleet from the south. Next morning the wind changed to permit Nelson's force to negotiate this outer channel. On 1 April, after a final examination of the Danes' anchorage, leaving Hyde Parker with eight of the line, Nelson took his ships south down the outer channel to anchor that night at its southern extremity. It was then 8pm, but Nelson summoned his captains and gave them verbal instructions. Captain Hardy, a volunteer, was sent to sound the channel in the King's Deep. The rest of that evening until 1am, Nelson dictated written instructions for copying that night and distribution the following morning at 8am; from exhaustion, he finished dictating these instructions from his cot on the floor. At 9.30am, next morning, the attack began (5).

1. 'Admiral Sir Hyde Parker [1739-1807]', stipple engraving, produced by John Chapman, 1 May 1796. *NMM ref PAD4282*

2. 'Passo della Flotta Inglese per il Sund nel Baltico il 30 Marzo 1801', engraving by Poggioli after an original by Allezard, no date. *NMM ref PAG9008*

3. 'Den Engelske Flaade naermende sig Kiobenhavn Morgen den 30te Marti 1801', anonymous coloured etching, no date. *NMM ref PAD5656*

4. 'Plan of the Battle of Copenhagen (with, inset , View of the Danish Line prior to the Engagement: Portrait of Nelson; View of both the fleets in Action)', coloured etching by Samuel John Neele, published by John Bryden, 20 May 1802. *NMM ref PAH7985*

5. 'To Admiral Sir Hyde Parker . . . His Majesty's Baltic Fleet . . . The Danish Line of Defence off Copenhagen with . . . Nelson approaching to the attack', coloured aquatint and etching by J Wells and Robert Pollard after an original by Nicholas Pocock (1740-1821), published by William Jeffryes, 1 October 1801. *NMM ref PAH7979*

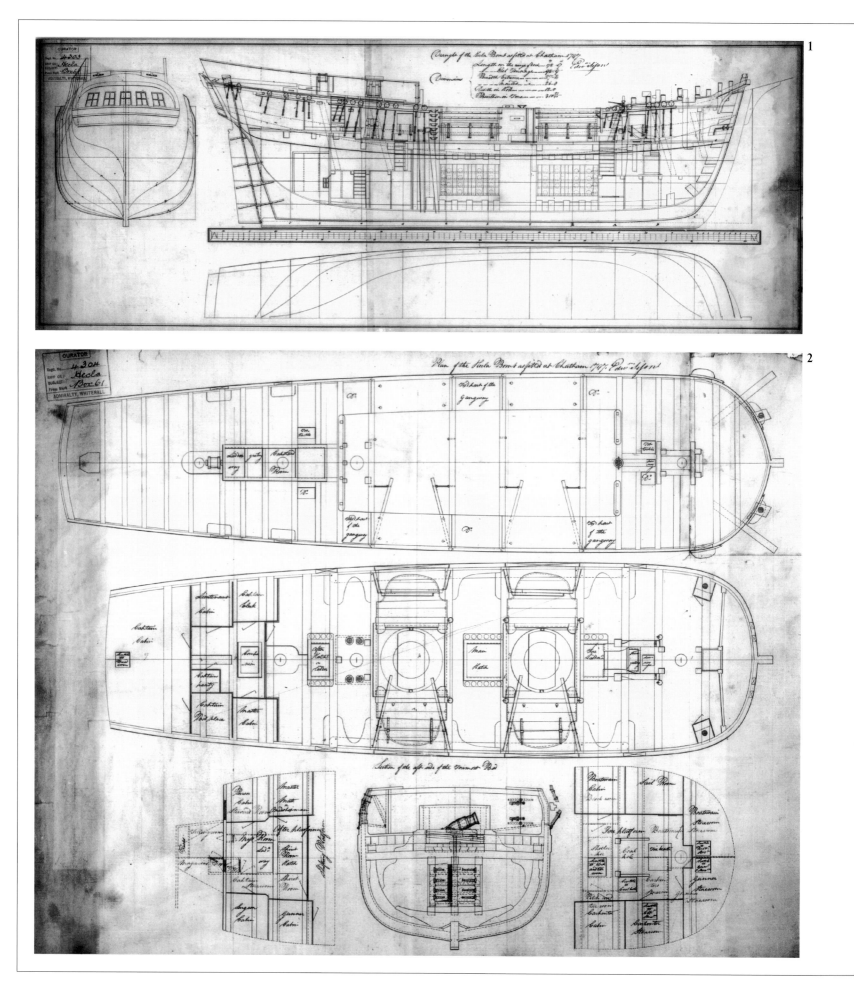

Ships of the Royal Navy: bomb vessels

THE BOMB vessel, a French invention of the 1680s, was one of the first specialist 'weapon systems' of modern naval warfare, being purely intended for the role of bombarding stationary targets with explosive shells or incendiary carcasses. For this the usual British bomb vessel had two mortars, one 13in and one 10in calibre, in traversing mountings on the centreline. The recoil was enormous and so the ships had to be very strongly built and very stable, which made them slow and often uncomfortable sea-boats. When not required for bombardment they often cruised with the rating of 'sloop', a role compromised by their poor sailing qualities.

There were only two purpose-built bombs available in 1793, both of which saw some action in the West Indies early in the war, in the traditional British role for bombs of supporting amphibious attacks on enemy colonies. However, in 1797-98 eight merchantmen (1, 2) and four warships were converted to bombs. The ex-mercantile bombs were fitted with a novel and elaborate system of folding bulwarks to facilitate low-angle firing (at 15 degrees elevation), devised by Colonel Congreve of the Royal Laboratory at Woolwich. It was tested in April 1797 in the *Vesuvius* and although correspondence relating to its function has disappeared, it was probably intended as an anti-invasion measure, for use at short range to disable packed troop transports. It is clear that this was never attempted and the complex hinged screens were eventually removed (3). However, even if the method of operation remained the same, the strategic aim was different. Hereafter, bombs were mainly used on anti-invasion duties, in attacks on concentrations of shipping intended for landings, and on the ports which constructed and harboured them.

In May 1798 *Tartarus* and *Hecla* supported Home Popham's Ostend expedition; a number took part in Nelson's abortive attacks on Boulogne in 1801; and in 1803 there was a series of bombardments of Channel ports carried out by *Perseus, Explosion, Sulphur* and *Terror*. All were frustratingly ineffective, partly through the inherent inaccuracy of mortars and their tendency to burst after prolonged firing, but also because the ports concerned were protected by shallow waters and sandbars that made it difficult to get close enough. Small 8in mortars were fitted in ships' launches—and later in some gunbrigs (4)—and a few experimental shallow-draught classes like the *Convulsion* and *Destruction* were

3

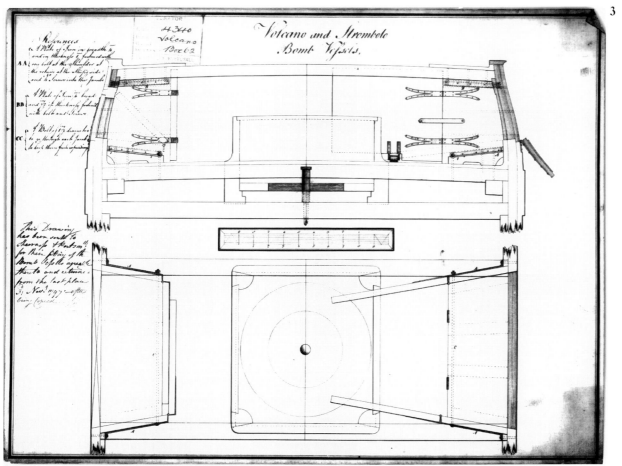

1. Lines and profile draught of the ex-mercantile *Hecla* as fitted at Chatham 1797.
NMM neg DR4303

2. Decks plan of the ex-mercantile *Hecla* as fitted at Chatham 1797.
NMM neg DR4304

3. *Volcano* and *Stromboli* details of embrasures for low-angle fire. All the 1797 conversions were similarly fitted.
NMM neg DR4340

4. Draught for fitting the bomb beds of the mortar brigs *Charger, Indignant, Desperate* for an 8in brass mortar, dated 3 July 1809.
NMM neg DR3773

5. Lines and profile of the two shallow-draught mortar boats of the *Convulsion* class, dated 12 June 1804.
NMM neg DR6852

6. 'The Battle of Copenhagen April 2d 1801', steel engraving by James Fittler after an original by Nicholas Pocock (1740-1821), published by Thomas Cadell and William Davies, 15 November 1808. The bombs are in the left foreground, and the trajectory of shells from two of them can be seen arcing into the air towards the city.
NMM ref PAD5662

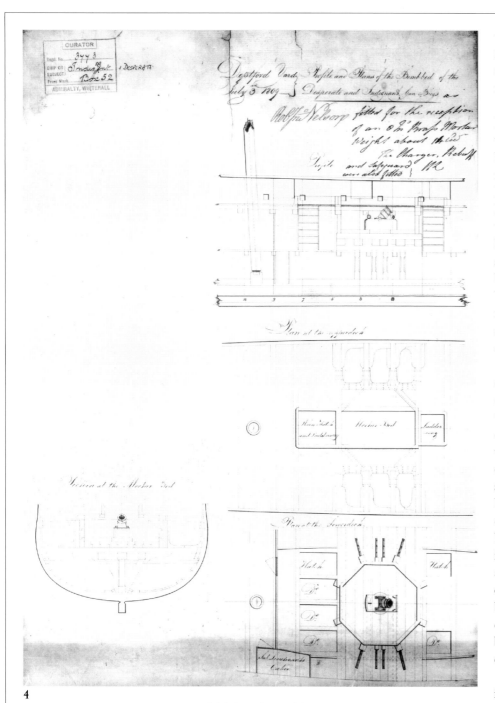

4

tried (5), but the problem was never really solved.

A related issue, which after Trafalgar replaced the concern with invasion, was how to destroy elements of the blockaded French fleet. A foretaste of the problem was afforded in 1799 when a Spanish squadron of five ships of the line trapped in Basque Roads was attacked by a British force that included the bombs *Sulphur, Explosion* and *Volcano*. A French mortar battery kept the British ships beyond range, and the bombs achieved nothing. On a more famous occasion in 1809 in the same venue, the British attacked a French squadron with every conceivable inshore weapon – gunbrigs, fireships, bombs, explosion vessels and rockets. Five bombs were promised but only *Aetna* (and eventually *Thunder*) arrived in time to

take part; the absence of the others was partly blamed for the relative failure of the attack, but the bomb vessel's record of accuracy suggests that they would have made little difference.

Bombs could be effective against area targets on shore, however, and the biggest set-piece scenario of this kind was the attack on Copenhagen in 1801 when seven bombs went into action (6). Gambier's repeat performance in 1807 included only four bomb vessels, but he had the advantage of the new Congreve rockets; these last seem to have been conceived in the Navy as a substitute for incendiary carcasses rather than explosive shells, but since they imposed no reactive force on the firing ship they strongly hinted that the day of the specialist bomb vessel might be nearing a close. Indeed, for the Walcheren expedition of 1809, the sloop (ex-merchantman) *Galgo* was fitted out as a 'rocket ship', in a primitive anticipation of the Second World War rocket-firing amphibious fire support ships.

Although bombs were in action relatively frequently during this war, it still left them plenty of time to act as cruisers 'between engagements'. Their disadvantages in this role were well understood, so they tended to draw convoy escort duties. Even here they were vulnerable, as was demonstrated by the epic, and justly celebrated defence of her convoy by the *Acheron* and Benthamite sloop *Arrow* in February 1805: the sloop was sunk and the bomb so badly damaged that she had to be burnt by her captors, two large French frigates. Unfortunately, the bomb's main armament, the mortars could not be used in ship-to-ship combat, although there is one recorded attempt: in June 1808 the *Thunder* and three gunbrigs, escort to a large convoy from the Baltic, were attacked by Danish gunboats when becalmed; one gunbrig was captured by the manouevrable oared craft, but the bomb kept them at bay by firing charges of 1lb balls and conventional shells from her mortars.

Seven more merchant ships were converted to bombs in 1803 and between 1807 and 1812 a handful of warships (themselves mainly ex-mercantile) were similarly taken up. The mercantile bombs were not entirely satisfactory, not least because their bomb rooms were above water: the crews of *Lucifer* and *Meteor* must have had a very nervous time during Duckworth's passage of the Dardanelles, when they came under heavy Turkish fire. A combination of the inadequacies of existing ships and the arduous service so many had seen, suggested to the Admiralty that it was time to design a new class, which was duly undertaken in 1812.

The *Vesuvius*, and the slightly improved *Hecla* class of 1813, were more like merchant vessels in hull form than previous Navy-built bombs and were designed for greater self-sufficiency. They came into service just in

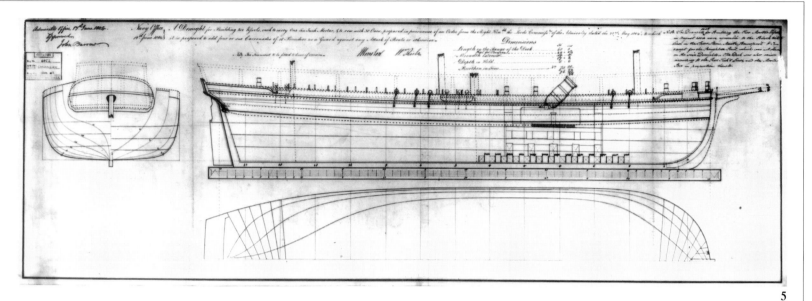

5

time, in Sir John Borlase Warren's apposite phrase, 'to annoy the coast of America' during the War of 1812. Although used for nuisance rather than serious conquest, their efforts – along with the Congreve rockets often employed at the same time – obviously impinged on the American conscience, immortalised in a line of the national anthem: 'the rockets' red glare and the bombs in the air'.

Postwar, some bombs, most notably *Erebus* and *Terror*, found a more pacific glory in their exploits as polar expedition vessels, a role for which their strongly constructed hulls made them ideal.

6

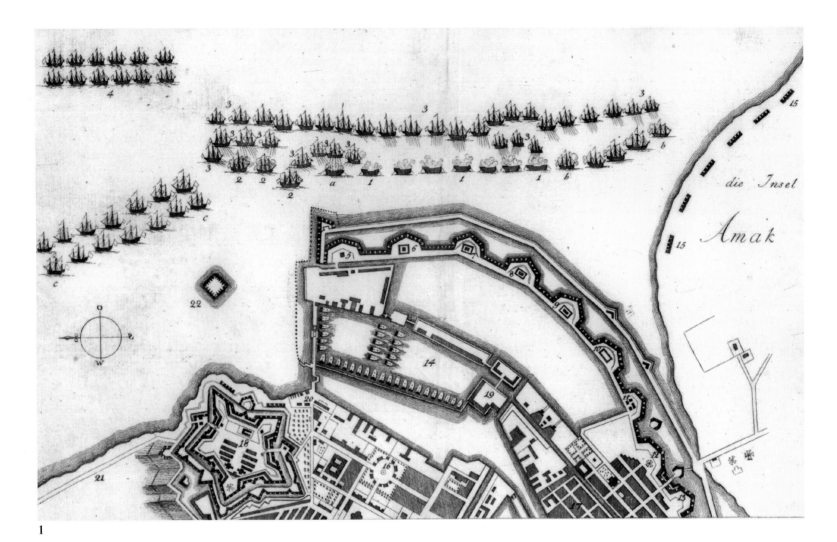

1

The Battle of Copenhagen

WHEN NELSON took stock that night of 1 April 1801, he planned to engage the line of Danish vessels two miles to his north consisting of nine vessels larger than 50 guns, two of 48, ten frigates, and numerous armed brigs and schooners. He himself commanded ten ships of the line of 64 or 74 guns, two of 50 and 54, with five frigates, two sloops and seven bomb vessels. On paper his own force was stronger. But the Danish line was interspersed with pontoons and floating batteries, and its northern end was reinforced by the batteries on the Crown islands mounting eighty-eight 24pdrs and the Trekroner fortress mounting sixty-eight 36pdrs and 24pdrs (1). Nelson had with him 600 men of the 48th Regiment who could be put into flatboats to storm these batteries when suitably subdued. But there was no doubting the resolution of the Danes to resist assault. The Danish vessels were fully manned with crews who fought to defend their homeland and national pride.

Nelson planned that his leading ship, the 74-gun *Edgar*, should pass the first four ships in the Danish line before anchoring beside the 64-gun *Jylland*. His two succeeding ships, *Ardent*, 64 and *Glatton*, 54, would then pass *Edgar* on her disengaged side to anchor and engage respectively the frigate *Kronborg*, 22 with a battery, and the 64-gun *Dannebroge*. *Isis*, 50 and *Agamemnon*, 64, supported by a frigate, would anchor opposite the first three vessels in the Danish line which would have already received the fire of the preceding three British ships. The remaining British ships were to sail up the disengaged side of their predecessors to anchor in turn beyond the *Glatton*. When all had done so, the final British ship, *Polyphemus*, should have reached the head of the Danish line. *Ardent* and *Agamemnon*, after subduing the first four Danes, were to proceed up the line to engage the Trekroner fortress, supported by the remaining frigates and sloops, with the flatboats for soldiers should an opportunity be presented for storming the fort. Seven bomb vessels were detailed to take stations close to the Middle Ground where they might throw shells over the British ships at the Danish vessels and into the Danish arsenal on shore.

4

5

That night the wind veered to the south, favouring the British attack. At 9.30am on 2 April, the signal was made to weigh in succession, and *Edgar* led north (2). She held her fire though passing and receiving the fire of the first four Danish vessels, watched by those following with trepidation as she manoeuvred to engage the *Jylland*, which she did at 11am. Thereafter, however, the plan started to go awry. *Glatton* could not get past *Edgar* and had to pass between her and the Dane, while the *Agamemnon* was unable to get round the end of the Middle Ground against wind and current and had to anchor where she was. *Bellona* and *Russell* then also grounded on the Middle Ground, their pilots believing the deeper water was closer to the central shoal than to the Danish defence line. However, by 11.30am the principal British ships were engaged (3, 4), while the frigates made their way past them towards the Trekroner, and the bombs began firing (5).

About 1pm, Hyde Parker made his now famous signal 'to discontinue the action'. He could see at long distance from the north–where his portion of the fleet had remained when Nelson proceeded south outside the Middle Ground the night before–the signals of distress from the mastheads of the *Bellona* and *Russell*, with that of 'inability' from the *Agamemnon*. Thinking that Nelson

might feel his force insufficient to maintain the attack, he made the signal to facilitate Nelson's withdrawal. Nelson acknowledged Parker's signal, but kept that for 'close action' hoisted at his own masthead. When Parker's signal continued flying, Nelson became quite agitated and angry. It was then that he put his telescope to his eye with the reported words: 'I have only one eye; I have a right to be blind sometimes; I really do not see the signal'. However, Parker's signal did have the effect of inducing the British frigates to withdraw from the Trekroner batteries where Captain Riou had placed them under intense fire. Their withdrawal thus probably saved them from being soon destroyed, but cost Riou his life.

Half an hour later the fire of the Danes slackened; by 2.30pm their fire had ceased. Those vessels which had struck their flags would not, however, permit boarders. Indeed the *Glatton* and *Elephant* had to resume firing, which was taken up again on both sides. The continued resistance irritated Nelson, who sent a message under a flag of truce to the Crown Prince of Denmark (6) pointing out that, if Danish fire did not cease, he would be obliged 'to set on fire all the prizes that he has taken, without having the power of saving the men who have so nobly defended them'. Some of the Danes were still of the view that a British victory was still not complete,

6

and a Danish messenger returned questioning the intention of the message. However, Nelson's subsequent declaration of intended humanity had the effect of bringing about a complete ceasefire.

Because of their damage aloft, several British ships had difficulty extricating themselves from their positions of engagement. But over the next five days all the Danish prizes were removed and all burned except for the 60-gun *Holstein*. The battle had lost the Danes 370 killed and 665 wounded (7). According to the official figures, the

7

British fleet had lost 253 killed and 688 wounded, though slight wounds and later deaths were said to have enlarged these official figures to 350 and 850 respectively.

Though beaten, the Danes did not willingly acknowledge their submission. At sunset on 2 April, the Danish Crown Prince sent to inquire what terms Parker demanded. The latter sent back a copy of those demanded by the British government. No immediate reply was forthcoming—only an offer by the Crown Prince to mediate with Russia—so on 3 April Nelson was deputed to go on shore to settle the terms of the Danish surrender (8). Over the course of the next five days, at the end of which he again returned in person, Nelson was praised by observers for diplomatic acumen previously unnoticed. However, the Danes did not agree to abandon the Armed Neutrality, as required by the British government, and only under the blunt threat of renewed hostilities was Nelson able to negotiate a fourteen-week truce. This gave the British fleet time enough to attack both the Russian and Swedish fleets if necessary.

Yet, in this form, the armistice favoured the Danes as much as British interests. On 8 April, as negotiations were being concluded, the Danes appear to have learned what was kept from Parker and Nelson, that Tsar Paul I of Russia had been assassinated on 24 March by a group of dissident Russian officers. The event foretold the break up of the Armed Neutrality of the North and ren-

8

dered further hostilities ultimately unnecessary, especially as Sweden and Prussia, the other partners, were weakening in their commitment to the alliance. Parker was not to learn of the assassination for another two weeks, by which time, his rear secure, on 12 April he had taken the bulk of his fleet into the Baltic with the intention of subjecting the Swedes (9) and Russians to what had just been inflicted on the Danes.

9

1. 'Darstellung des am 2n April 1801 Zwischen der Danischen und Englischen Floote bey Copenhagen vorgefallene Seetrestens', anonymous etching, no date.
NMM ref PAD5655

2. 'The Battle of Copenhagen 2 April 1801', black and watercolour pen and ink by J Bang, 1803. The artist appears to be compressing various stages of the battle in to one view, with the British fleet simultaneously sailing south (as on the night of 1 April) and having turned north engaging the Danish line.
NMM ref PAH5238

3. 'The Battle of Copenhagen, fought on the 2nd April 1801 under the Command of Admiral Sir Hyde Parker', brown aquatint and etching by Lieutenant William Ramage and Thomas Whitcombe (born c1752), published by B B Evans, 22 April 1801.
NMM ref PAH7976

4. 'Bataillen d. 2 April 1801, paa Kiobenhavns Reed', engraving and etching by Johan Frederick Clemens after an original by Christian August Lorentzen, no date. A view of the Danish lines from the city.
NMM ref PAH7975

5. 'The Bombardment of Copenhagen', anonymous engraving, no date. It shows the small craft and (left) the bombs at the northern end of the British line.
NMM ref PAD5663

6. 'A message sent ashore', anonymous Danish black and watercolour pen and ink, no date. It represents Nelson's message to the Crown Prince, and is annotated: 'D' is the Trekroner (right background); 'B' the blockships *Elephanten* and *Mars* (left background); while the burning vessel left of the Trekroner, 'C', is the *Dannebrog*; the anchored ships, left to right, are marked *Nidelven, Sarpen, Dannemark, Trekroner* and *Iris*.
NMM ref PAH4321

7. 'Danish Commanders at the Battle of Copenhagen 2 April 1801', lithograph published by Baerentzen & Co, no date.
NMM ref PAH5659

8. 'L'Amiral Nelson Offre un Armistice au Prince Royal de Dannemarck', anonymous engraving, no date.
NMM ref PAD5674

9. 'Frégate Suedoise vue par le travers au mouillage', Plate 31 *of Collection de Toutes les Especes de Batiments*, (third edition, Paris 1826), engraving by J J Baugean after his own original. Besides proper battleships the Swedish navy also possessed a number of powerful frigates, like this one, originally designed by the great F H Chapman with a 24pdr battery so they could stand in the line of battle in an emergency.
NMM ref PAD7407

Postscript

WHILE BRITISH land forces were proving their ability to stand up to the formidable fighting qualities of the French army in Egypt, and British naval forces were reducing the Armed Neutrality of the North to terms, the war against France in central and southern Europe had come to a virtual stalemate. Early in 1801 the conclusion of the Peace of Lunéville between France and the defeated Austrians left Britain without a major continental ally. Also early in 1801, France's ally Spain invaded Portugal and, by the treaty of Badajos in June, forced the Portuguese government to agree to exclude British shipping from the port of Lisbon. Deprived of a valuable refuge for the blockade of the coast of Spain, the loss of Lisbon was more inconvenient than crippling to the British navy while it held Gibraltar. Nevertheless, the difficulties of waging the naval war on that coast were enhanced since Gibraltar had neither water nor victuals in sufficient quantity.

Meanwhile in England Pitt's long ministry, dating back to 1783, came to an end. The failure of the 'protestant ascendancy' to keep Ireland loyal was proved by the succession of risings culminating in that of May-June 1798. Pitt's alternative was a constitutional union of Ireland with the remainder of the United Kingdom, which was achieved in 1800. But while Pitt had indicated his own willingness to admit Irish catholics to full political participation in the election of MPs to Westminster, George III remained obdurate against it and, on rejection of his advised policy, Pitt resigned in February 1801. His successor, Henry Addington, succeeded to peace negotiations with France driven on the French side by Bonaparte, who, having become First Consul and virtual dictator in 1799, took advantage of Britain's increasing isolation in 1801 to impose terms recognising France's predominant position on the continent.

The preliminaries of the peace were signed in October 1801. Britain abandoned virtually all her overseas conquests from France, Spain and

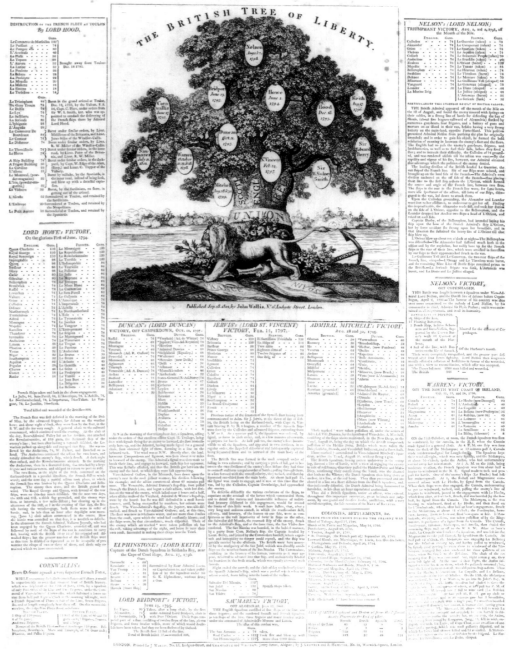

The British tried to persuade themselves that the Peace of Amiens represented victory and was a product of the Royal Navy's supremacy at sea: the allegorical Tree of Liberty produces naval victories as fruit. 'Peace!! The Result of our Naval Victories . . . From the Commencement of the War to the signing Preliminaries, Oct 1 1801', etching published by John Wallis, 28 September 1801. NMM ref PAH7487

Holland. In the Caribbean Britain retained only Spanish Trinidad; in the Indian Ocean, only the Dutch settlements of Ceylon. Even key strategic positions, like Tobago in the Windward Islands, and the Cape of Good Hope, the southern gateway to the Indian Ocean, were given up to their former occupants. Similarly, Addington and his foreign secretary, Lord Hawkesbury, undertook even to withdraw from Malta and return it – under certain conditions – to the Knights of St John, surrendering a vital barrier to the Near East and the western approach to India.

The spirit of appeasement no less permitted the annexation by France of Savoy, control of the Cisalpine Republic, and a French military presence in Holland. Although to Austria at Lunéville, France had agreed to recognise the independence of the Dutch, the Swiss, and the Ligurian Republic, Lord Hawkesbury secured no confirmation of these. Indeed, when the final terms of the Peace were signed at Amiens in 1802, they were more adverse than the preliminaries. For example, whereas the latter had laid down that Cape Town should be a free port, open to both British and French commerce, the actual treaty conceded full sovereignty back to Holland, leaving no pretext for protest in the event of French annexation. Nor was a trade agreement arranged, leaving France free to close all the ports of her colonies to British trade as soon as she regained control of them.

British critics of the terms of the Peace of Amiens thus had much about which to complain. Lord Grenville, the former Foreign Secretary, regarded the treaty as a disgrace and attacked its terms vehemently in Parliament, where he moved firmly into opposition. To the credit of Addington and his colleagues, however, the government never regarded the treaty as any more than a truce. Napoleon was soon attempting to bring the resources of Europe firmly under his control, and the government were quick to respond to mounting French threats to what remained of the balance of power – impatience that precipitated a declaration of war by the Addington government within twelve months. Indeed, it was a measure of that government's clear concern for British interests that as early as October 1802, in anticipation of an early resumption of hostilities, Lord Hawkesbury sent instructions to the governor-general at Calcutta to delay the for-

mal restitution of Pondicherry to France.

The respite from hostilities nevertheless had its impact on the British armed forces. Both the army and the navy were subject to measures of varying efficacy. Present security dictated that 130,000 men be retained in the regular army, about 50,000 of whom were stationed overseas; while for the future, military reforms sponsored by the Duke of York gave rise to a small staff college in 1801, which was followed in 1802 by the establishment of the Royal Military College.

Less cautious were measures adopted for the Navy by the new First Lord of the Admiralty, St Vincent. Determined to rid the dockyards of inefficient men and distrustful of contractors, he ran down the labour force in the dockyards, failed to maintain timber reserves, and refused to build new ships of the line in merchant shipyards. At the same time, against Cabinet approval, in 1802 he obtained the parliamentary commission of inquiry into abuses in the naval departments that produced a number of damning reports before being succeeded in 1805 by the commission for revising and digesting the civil affairs of the navy. What began as

an attempt to punish malefactors thus evolved into a vehicle for overhauling the organisation of the Navy. The alarms created by St Vincent's refusal to deal with contractors led also to a firm rejection of this policy. His peacetime policies thus ironically helped to steady confidence in the institutions of the Navy until the very end of the Napoleonic War.

For Britain the Peace of Amiens consequently brought gains as well as losses. The terms of the peace aside, it had direct benefits in laying foundations and gathering resources for a renewal of hostilities. Above all it demonstrated that peace with conscience was impossible while French imperial ambitions were given credence through Napoleon's military genius. The French Revolutionary War had taught that peace would not be forced on Britain while economic growth, closely linked to her commercial and naval power, facilitated the funding of continental allies along with the seizure of enemy colonies and the suppression of enemy trade. While Napoleon consolidated his claim to further elevation as first emperor of France, Britain rallied herself for a war that would be stubbornly maintained until Napoleon was dethroned.

If France had its Napoleon, Britain's hero by 1801 was definitely Nelson. This plate shows, with a fair degree of individual portraiture, the twenty-six ships of the line – a medium-sized navy – in which Nelson had a hand in capturing between 1793 and 1801. A coloured etching by P Roberts after an original by Thomas Buttersworth (1768-1842), published by Buttersworth and Roberts, 16 March 1802.   NMM ref PAG8678

Sources

Introductions

M Acerra and J Meyer, *Marines et Revolutions* (Rennes 1989)

I R Christie, *Wars and Revolutions: Britain 1760-1815* (London 1982)

Julian S Corbett and H W Richmond (eds), *Private Papers of George, Second Earl Spencer, First Lord of the Admiralty, 1794-1801*, 4 vols (London 1913-24)

W S Cormack, *Revolution and Political Conflict in the French Navy, 1789-1794* (Cambridge 1995)

R P Crowhurst, *The Defence of British Trade, 1689-1815* (Folkestone 1977)

———, 'The voyage of the *Adelaide*. A Swiss owned privateer at Nantes, 1798', *The Mariner's Mirror* 72 (1986)

Michael Duffy, *Soldiers, Sugar and Seapower: The British Expeditions to the West Indies and the War against Revolutionary France* (Oxford 1987)

William James, *The Naval History of Great Britain from the declaration of war by France in 1793 to the accession of George IV*, 6 vols (London 1837)

A G Jamieson (ed), *A People of the Sea: The Maritime History of the Channel Islands* (1986).

H J K Jenkins, 'Privateers, Picaroons, Pirates: West Indian Commerce Raiders, 1793-1901', *The Mariner's Mirror* 73 (1987)

Brian Lavery, *Nelson's Navy. The ships, men and organisation, 1793-1815* (London 1989)

Piers Mackesy, *British Victory in Egypt, 1801: the end of Napoleon's conquest* (London 1995)

Roger Morriss, *The Royal Dockyards during the Revolutionary and Napoleonic Wars* (Leicester 1983)

———, 'St Vincent and Reform, 1801-4', *The Mariner's Mirror* 69 (1983)

C Northcote Parkinson, *The Trade Winds: a study of British overseas trade during the French Wars, 1793-1815* (London 1948)

Tom Pocock, *A Thirst for Glory: the life of Admiral Sir Sidney Smith* (London 1996)

———, *Horatio Nelson* (London 1987)

Richard Saxby, 'The Blockade of Brest in the French Revolutionary War', *The Mariner's Mirror* 78 (1992)

D Bonner Smith (ed), *Letters of Admiral of the Fleet the Earl of St Vincent whilst First Lord of the Admiralty, 1801-4*, 2 vols (London 1922 & 1927)

D J Starkey, *British Privateering Enterprise in the Eighteenth Century* (Exeter 1990)

J S Watson, *The Reign of George III, 1760-1815* (Oxford 1960)

The *élite* of the navy of England

Julian S Corbett (ed), *Private Papers of Earl Spencer*, Vol II (London 1914)

Sir H Nicolas (ed), *The Dispatches and Letters of Lord Nelson*, Vol III (London 1845)

Ludovic Kennedy, *Nelson and his Captains* (London 1975)

Bonaparte's oriental adventure

Napoleon Bonaparte, *Campagnes d'... Égypte et de Syrie 1798-1799: Mémoires ... Napoleon dictés par lui-même ... et publiés par le Général Bertrand* (Paris 1847)

J Christopher Herold, *Bonaparte in Egypt* (London 1962)

C de la Jonquière, *L'Expédition en Egypt, 1798-1801*, 5 vols (Paris 1899-1907)

Malta and the Knights

Roderick Cavaliero, *The Last of the Crusaders: The Knights of St John and Malta in the Eighteenth Century* (London 1960)

W Hardman, *A History of Malta during the Period of the French and British Occupations 1798-1815* (London 1909)

The French landings in Egypt

Philip J Haythornthwaite, *The Napoleonic Source Book* (London 1990)

J Christopher Herold, *Bonaparte in Egypt*

C de la Jonquière, *L'Expédition en Egypt, 1798-1801*

Nelson's pursuit of Bonaparte

Ludovic Kennedy, *Nelson and his Captains*

Sir H Nicolas (ed), *The Dispatches and Letters of Lord Nelson*, Vol III

Battle of the Nile – the attack
The destruction of *L'Orient*
Pressing home the victory

Brian Lavery, *Nelson and the Nile* (forthcoming)

Christopher Lloyd, *The Nile Campaign: Nelson and Napoleon in Egypt* (Newton Abbott 1973)

Oliver Warner, *The Battle of the Nile* (London 1960)

The Hero of the Nile

Christopher Hibbert, *Nelson. A personal history* (London 1994)

Roger Morriss, *Nelson. The life and letters of a hero* (London 1996)

Leander* and *Généreux

James Hewitt (ed), *Eye-Witnesses to Nelson's Battles* (Reading 1972)

William James, *Naval History*, Vol 2

The capture of Minorca

Jonathan Coad, *The Royal Dockyards 1690-1850* (Aldershot 1989)

Quentin Hughes, *Britain in the Mediterranean and the Defence of her Naval Stations* (Liverpool 1981)

William James, *Naval History*, Vol 2

Nelson and Naples

William James, *Naval History*, Vol 2

Sir H Nicolas (ed), *The Dispatches and Letters of Lord Nelson*, Vol III

Jack Russell, *Nelson and the Hamiltons* (London 1969)

The Neapolitan navy

Jan Glete, *Nations and Navies*, 2 vols (Stockholm 1993)

Otto von Pifka, *Navies of the Napoleonic Wars* (Newton Abbot 1980)

Sir H Nicolas (ed), *The Dispatches and Letters of Lord Nelson*, Vol III

The Cadiz station 1798-1799

William James, *Naval History*, Vol 2

Christopher Lloyd (ed), *The Keith Papers*, Vol II (London 1950)

Russo-Turkish operations 1798-1800

Piers Mackesy, *Statesmen at War: The strategy of overthrow 1798-1799* (London 1974)

A B Rodger, *The War of the Second Coalition, 1798 to 1801* (Oxford 1964)

Defence of Acre

J Christopher Herold, *Bonaparte in Egypt*

Lord Russell of Liverpool, *Knight of the Sword: the life and letters of Admiral Sir Sidney Smith* (London 1964)

The French stranded in Egypt

Mary Dorothy George, *Catalogue of Political and Personal Satires preserved in the Department of Prints and Drawings in the British Museum*, Vol VII 1793-1800 (London 1942)

J Christopher Herold, *Bonaparte in Egypt*

William James, *Naval History*, Vol 2

Rev Cooper Willyams, *Voyage up the Mediterranean ...* (London 1802)

The siege of Malta

Roderick Cavaliero, *The Last of the Crusaders*

W Hardman, *A History of Malta*

The Mediterranean Fleet under Keith

Christopher Lloyd (ed), *The Keith Papers*, Vol II

Piers Mackesy, *War without Victory: the downfall of Pitt 1799-1802* (Oxford 1984)

The loss of the *Queen Charlotte*

William James, *Naval History*, Vol 3

Christopher Lloyd (ed), *The Keith Papers*, Vol II

The invasion of Egypt – an opposed landing
Victory in Egypt

Aeneas Anderson, *A Journal of the Forces which Sailed from the Downs, in April 1800 ...* (London 1802)

J Christopher Herold, *Bonaparte in Egypt*

Commander Inglis, 'Operations on the Egyptian Coast, 1801', in *The Naval Miscellany II* (London 1912)

Piers Mackesy, *British Victory in Egypt, 1801*

Thomas Walsh, *Journal of the Late Campaign in Egypt* (London 1803)

Ships of the Royal Navy: the 44-gun two-decker

R N Buckley (ed), *The Napoleonic War Journal of Captain Thomas Henry Browne 1807-1816* (London 1987)

Robert Gardiner (ed), *The Line of Battle*, Ch 3 (London 1992)

David Lyon, *The Sailing Navy List* (London 1993)

Thomas Walsh, *Journal of the Late Campaign in Egypt*

The Battle of Algesiras
Saumarez's revenge

William James, *Naval History*, Vol 3

Ludovic Kennedy, *Nelson and his Captains*

Cochrane and the *Speedy*

Thomas Cochrane, *Autobiography of a Seaman* (second edition, London 1860)

David Hepper, *British Warship Losses in the Age of Sail* (Rotherfield 1994)

William James, *Naval History*, Vols 2 & 3

David Lyon, *Sailing Navy List*

Donald Thomas, *Cochrane: Britannia's last sea king* (London 1978)

Mars* versus *Hercule

Sir William Laird Clowes, *The Royal Navy: a History*, Vol 4 (London 1899)

William James, *Naval History*, Vol 2

Ships of the Royal Navy: experimental vessels

Robert Gardiner (ed), *The Line of Battle*

John C Dann (ed), *The Nagle Journal, 1775-1841* (New York 1988)

Rehearsing the invasion: attack on St Marcouf

M Acerra and J Meyer, *Marines et Revolutions*

Sir William Laird Clowes, *The Royal Navy: a History*, vol 4 (London 1899)

William James, *Naval History*, Vol 2

French naval bases: Le Havre

M Acerra and J Meyer, *Marines et Revolutions*

Popham's attack on Ostend

Julian S Corbett (ed), *Spencer Papers*, Vol II

Mary Dorothy George, *Catalogue of Political and Personal Satires*, Vol VII

Hugh Popham, *A Damned Cunning Fellow: The Eventful Life of Rear-Admiral Sir Home Popham, KCB, KCH, KM, FRS 1762-1820* (Tywardreath, Cornwall 1991)

The destruction of Bompart off Lough Swilly

Sir William Laird Clowes, *The Royal Navy: a History*, Vol 4

William James, *Naval History*, Vol 2

Ships of the Royal Navy:
the Second Rate
William James, *The Naval History of Great Britain*, 6 vols
Brian Lavery, *The Ship of the Line*, Vol 1 (London 1983)

Anglo-Russian invasion of the Netherlands, 1799
H W Richmond (ed), *Private Papers of George, second Earl Spencer*, Vol III
William James, *Naval History*, Vol 2
Piers Mackesy, *Statesmen at War*
A B Rodger, *The War of the Second Coalition*

Tightening the blockade, 1799-1800
Piers Mackesy, *Statesmen at War*
C Northcote Parkinson, *Britannia Rules: the classic age of naval history 1793-1815* (London 1977)

Watching the Biscay ports
William James, *Naval History*, Vols 2 & 3

One against the odds
Sir William Laird Clowes, *The Royal Navy: a history*, Vol 4
William James, *Naval History*, Vol 2
Michael Lewis, *A Social History of the Navy, 1793-1815* (London 1960)

Captain Schank's Q-ship
Sir William Laird Clowes, *The Royal Navy: a History*, Vol 4
William James, *Naval History*, Vol 2

The wandering army
Piers Mackesy, *Statesmen at War*

C Northcote Parkinson, *Edward Pellew, Viscount Exmouth* (London 1934)

Cutting-out attacks in the Channel
Sir William Laird Clowes, *The Royal Navy: a History*, Vol 4
William James, *Naval History*, Vol 2

Invasion threat
Sir William Laird Clowes, *The Royal Navy: a History*, Vol 4
William James, *Naval History*, Vol 2

West Indies 1798
West Indies 1799-1801
Sir William Laird Clowes, *The Royal Navy: a History*, Vol 4
Michael Duffy, *Soldiers, Sugar and Seapower*
William James, *Naval History*, Vol 2

The birth of a new naval power
Howard Chapelle, *The History of the American Sailing Navy* (New York 1949)
R G O'Connor, *The Origins of the American Navy* (Lanham, Maryland 1994)

America's quasi-war with France
D W Knox (ed), *Naval Documents related to the Quasi-War between the United States and France*, Vol III (Washington DC 1936)
Michael A Palmer, *Stoddert's War: Naval Operations During the Quasi-War with France, 1798-1801* (Columbia, South Carolina 1987)
Edgar Newbold Smith, *American Naval Broadsides: A Collection of Early Naval Prints* (New York 1974)

M V and Dorothy Brewington, *Marine Paintings and Drawings in the Peabody Museum* (Salem, Massachusetts, 2nd ed 1981)

The Black Ship
Dudley Pope, *The Black Ship* (London 1963)

The Caribbean commerce war
Sir William Laird Clowes, *The Royal Navy: a History*, Vol 4
William James, *Naval History*, Vols 2 & 3

Ships of the Royal Navy:
the Sixth Rate
Robert Gardiner, *The First Frigates* (London 1992)
—— (ed), *The Line of Battle*, Ch 2

East Indies 1798-1801
C Northcote Parkinson, *War in the Eastern Seas 1793-1815* (London 1954)

Red Sea operations
Piers Mackesy, *British victory in Egypt, 1801*
C Northcote Parkinson, *War in the Eastern Seas*
Hugh Popham, *A Damned Cunning Fellow*

Dangers of the sea: dismasting
Naval Chronicle, Vols III (London 1800) and XII (London 1804)
Captains' Logs, Public Record Office, Adm 51

Indian Ocean raiders
C Northcote Parkinson, *War in the Eastern Seas*

Forcing the Sound
William James, *Naval History*, Vol 3

Tom Pocock, *Horatio Nelson* (London 1987)
Dudley Pope, *The Great Gamble: Nelson at Copenhagen* (London 1972)

Ships of the Royal Navy:
the bomb vessel
Chris Ware, *The Bomb Vessel: shore bombardment ships of the age of sail* (London 1994)

The Battle of Copenhagen
William James, *Naval History*, Vol 3
Nicholas Tracy, *Nelson's Battles. The art of victory in the age of sail* (London 1996)
Oliver Warner, *A Portrait of Lord Nelson* (London 1958)

Artists and printmakers
E H H Archibald, *Dictionary of Sea Painters* (Woodbridge 1980)
E Bénézit, *Dictionnaire critique et documentaire de Peintres, Sculpteurs, Dessinateurs et Graveurs* (Paris 1976)
Maurice Harold Grant, *A Dictionary of British Etchers* (London 1952)
Ian Mackensie, *British Prints: Dictionary and Price Guide* (Woodbridge 1987)
Lister Raymond, *Prints and Printmaking* (London 1984)
Ronald vere Tooley, *Tooley's Dictionary of Mapmakers* (New York and Amsterdam 1979)
Jane Turner (Ed), *The Dictionary of Art* (London 1996)
Ellis Waterhouse, *The Dictionary of 18th Century Painters in Oils and Crayons* (Woodbridge 1980)
Arnold Wilson, *A Dictionary of British Marine Painters* (Leigh-on-Sea 1967)

Notes on Artists, Printmakers and their Techniques

These brief notes cover most of the artists and printmakers who appear in the volume, as well as the principal printing techniques. They are intended only to put the artists in context with the period and readers wanting further information on their art and lives should turn to the sources; in many cases there is little more to tell.

Alexander, William *(1762-1816)* English watercolourist and architectural illustrator known mainly for his series on China which he visited in 1792. In 1807 he was appointed Professor of design at the Military College at Great Marlow.

Anderson, William *(1757-1837)* Scottish marine painter who trained as a shipwright. He is known principally for his small river and estuarine scenes around Hull, but he also executed large-scale set pieces such as 'The Battle of the Nile' and 'Lord Howe's Fleet off Spithead'. The British Museum hold sketchbooks of the battles of the Nile and Copenhagen.

Aquatint A variety of etching (*qv*) invented in France in the 1760s. It is a tone rather than a line process and is used principally to imitate the appearance of watercolour washes. The process involves the etching of a plate with acid through a porous ground of powdered resin. The acid bites small rings around each resin grain and gradations of tone are achieved by repetition of the biting process and the protection of areas of the plate with varnish.

Atkinson, John Augustus *(1775-c1833)* English history painter who worked at the Court at St Petersburg before returning to London in 1801. He painted any number of Russian subjects, but is particularly remembered for his depiction of the battle of Waterloo which he painted first-hand.

Baugean, Jean-Jérôme *(1764-1819)* French painter and prolific engraver best known for his collection of shipping prints, *Collection de toutes des Especes de Batiments,* which went through numerous editions in the early nineteenth century. Also well known is his depiction of 'The Embarkation of Napoleon onboard *Bellérophon*'.

Bayard, Marc-Henri *(fl nineteenth century)* French publisher and engraver who, in

1891, published some twenty-five studies of Neapolitan ships and fortifications.

Bendorp, Carel-Frederik (*fl mid-late eighteenth century*) Flemish painter and engraver who worked at Rotterdam and produced topographical views and historical and naval subjects.

Bowen, Abel (*1790-1850*) American painter and wood engraver.

Bowen, Thomas (*fl late eighteenth century*) English engraver who worked for his father, the publisher and printseller Emanuel Bowen. He died in Clerkenwell Workhouse.

Bowles, Carington (*fl late eighteenth century*) London engraver and publisher of decorative and allegorical subjects and topographical views.

Bowles, John (*fl mid-late eighteenth century*) English draughtsman and line engraver of topographical views.

Bowyer, Robert (*1758-1834*) English miniaturist and watercolour painter who became particularly popular at the Court of George III. His portraits were used to illustrate a *History of England*.

Boydell, John (*1752-1817*) English engraver, publisher and printseller who was patron of most of the painters of his day whose works he engraved and supplied to every European market. This export market made him a considerable fortune and in 1790 he became Lord Mayor of London.

Brown, Mather (*1761-1831*) American portrait and history painter who settled in England in 1781 where he became a pupil of Benjamin West. As well as portraits of members of George III's Court, he also painted military and naval subjects such as his depiction of 'Howe on the Deck of the *Queen Charlotte*'.

Buttersworth, Thomas (*1768-1842*) English marine painter who served in the Royal Navy from 1795 until he was invalided out in 1800. His vivid watercolours of the battle of St Vincent and the blockade of Cadiz, painted while he was at sea, suggest first-hand experience. After leaving the Navy he devoted himself full-time to his painting and created a very considerable body of work.

Cadell, Thomas (*1742-1802*) London publisher and bookseller, amongst whose publications was *Cook's Voyages, 1773-77*.

Carpenter, Francis-Bicknell (*1830-1900*) American portraitist who painted the the leading personalities of his day such as Abraham Lincoln and James Russell Lowell.

Cartwright, Joseph (*1789-1829*) English landscape and marine painter and member of the Society of British Artists who was also a naval paymaster. He was made marine painter to the Duke of Clarence and painted a number naval scenes particularly of actions in the Mediterranean including 'The Battle of the Nile' and 'The *Euryalus* Frigate Becalmed in the Channel of Corfu'.

Cauvin, Thomas (*1762-1846*) French geographer and archaeologist.

Chesham, Francis (*1749-1806*) English draughtsman and engraver, principally of topographical views and naval subjects.

Conder, Thomas (*fl the late eighteenth century*) English engraver and cartographer whose works included *Maritime Survey of Ireland* (1775) and *Moore's Voyages* (1778).

Cook, Henry R (*fl the first half of the nineteenth century*) English engraver, mainly of portraits.

Corné, Michèle-Félice (*1752-1832*) American painter, born on Elba, who lived and painted on the East Coast.

Crepin, Louis Philippe (*1772-1851*) French marine and history painter who studied under Joseph Vernet as well as the history painter the Baron Regnault.

Daniell, Thomas (*1749-1840*) English landscape painter who spent six years in the East Indies before returning to London in 1790 where he became a member of the Royal Academy in 1799

Dodd, Robert (*1748-1815*) English marine and landscape painter and successful engraver and publisher, best known for his portrayals of the naval battles of the Revolutionary American and French wars. He is also known for his formal portraits of ships in which three views are included in a single image.

Drummond, Samuel (*1765-1844*) English landscape painter and portraitist who served in the Royal Navy for seven years. Self-taught, and with first-hand experience of naval warfare, he painted a small number of naval subjects including the well-known 'Death of Lord Nelson'.

Drypoint Intaglio (*qv*) engraving (*qv*) technique in which the image is scratched into a copper plate with a steel needle which is held like a pen. Ridges—burr—are created around the lines which give drypoint its characteristic fuzzy effect. The burr is delicate and quickly wears away during the printing process so that print runs are short.

Duplessi-Bertaux, Jean (*1747-1819*) French engraver and painter whose principal body of work depicted the events of the French Revolution.

Elmes, William (*fl late eighteenth and early nineteenth centuries*) English draughtsman and engraver who made caricatures much in the manner of Cruickshank, including two of Napoleon, published between 1811 and 1816.

Emeric, F J (*fl late eighteenth century*) French naïve ship portrait painter.

Engraving The process of cutting an image into a block or metal plate which is used for printing by using a number of techniques such as aquatint (*qv*), drypoint (*qv*), etching (*qv*), or mezzotint (*qv*). An engraving is a print made from the engraved plate.

Etching An intaglio (*qv*) process by which the design is made by drawing into a wax ground applied over the metal plate. The plate is then submerged in acid which bites into it where it has been exposed through the wax. An etching is a print made from an etched plate.

Faden, William (*1750-1836*) English cartographer and publisher, and the partner of Thomas Jeffereys, whose business he ran in the Charing Cross Road after the latter's death in 1771. He is best known for his *North American Atlas*, published in 1777, *Battles of the American Revolution* and *Petit Neptune Français*, both of 1793.

Fairburn, John (*fl late eighteenth and early nineteenth centuries*) London publisher and geographer and map seller whose works include *North America* (1798) and *Spain and Portugal* (1808).

Francia, François Thomas Louis (*1772-1839*) French watercolourist and marine painter who spent most of his life in England before returning to Calais at the end of his life. He was made painter to the Duke of York and his style was considerably influenced by Bonington

Gillray, James (*1757-1815*) English draughtsman and engraver of caricatures and satirical works, mainly after his own designs. His first political satires appeared in the late 1770s. He was amongst the first satirists to exaggerate subjects' features while at the same time retaining a likeness, and by the mid-1780s he was regarded as the leading British satirist. After 1789 he produced a number of anti-republican designs and his skills were turned against Napoleon after the resumption of war in 1803; during this period his work was widely copied by his contemporaries. By the time of his last print, dated 1811, he had become quite insane.

Gold, Joyce (*fl early nineteenth century*) English printer and publisher whose works included Rowe's *English Atlas* (1816). Also the publisher of the *Naval Chronicle*.

Hamilton, William (*1751-1801*) English history and landscape painter, many of whose works were used for book illustration.

Hoppner, John (*1758-1810*) English portrait painter and engraver of German descent, regarded in his time as the foremost portraitist and the natural successor to Sir Joshua Reynolds. Throughout the 1770s, when his reputation was at its highest, he painted ever more distinguished sitters. His vibrant use of colour and almost abstract brushwork, shown to good effect in *A Gale of Wind*, look forward to Turner.

Hullmandel, Charles Joseph (*1789-1850*) English printer and publisher of landscapes and topographical scenes, and one of the first practising lithographers (*qv*) in England. He is credited with a whole range of lithographic developments in the twenty years after his first plate was produced in 1818, and was a central figure in early nineteenth-century lithography.

Jeakes, Joseph (*fl early nineteenth century*) English engraver of aquatints (*qv*), notably of topographical scenes and naval engagements after his contemporaries, particularly Thomas Whitcombe (*qv*) and his own designs.

Jones, George (*1786-1869*) English history painter, particularly of battle scenes of the Napoleoenic Wars, for example 'Nelson Boarding the *San Josef* at the Battle of St Vincent'.

Joy, John Cantiloe (*1806-1866*) English marine painter and brother of William Joy (*qv*).

Joy, William (*1803-1866*) English marine painter who worked mainly in collaboration with his brother John Cantiloe, and the two are often referred to as the 'brothers Joy'. As well as paintings of naval incidents they were commissioned by the Government in the 1830s to record and make drawings of fishing craft.

Jukes, Francis (*1747-1812*) English painter and etcher of aquatints. As well as his popular 'Views of England' and his sporting prints he was a prolific exponent of marine subjects.

Langendyk, Dirk (*1748-1805*) Dutch painter and engraver mainly of military subjects.

Lee, John Theophilus (*fl early nineteenth century*) English marine painter.

Lithograph A print made by drawing a design on porous limestone with a greasy material. The stone is then wetted and ink applied to it which adheres only to the drawn surfaces. Paper is then pressed to the stone for the final print. Lithography was discovered only at the very end of the eighteenth century but quickly developed into a highly flexible medium.

Livesay, J (*fl late eighteenth and early nineteenth centuries*) English marine watercolour painter.

Lorentzen, Christian August (*1749-1828*) Danish portraitist and history and landscape painter.

Melling, Antoine Ignace (*1763-1831*) French topographical painter who travelled to Egypt and the Near East. He illustrated and published between 1809 and 1819 the *Voyage pittoresque de Constantinople et des rives du Bosphore*.

Mezzotint A type of engraving (*qv*) in which the engraving plate is first roughened with a tool known as a rocker. The rough surface holds the ink and appears as a black background and the design is then burnished onto it by scraping away the rough burr to create lighter tones and by polishing the surface for highlights. Thus the artist works from dark to light, creating a tonal effect which was particularly suited to reproducing paintings and had its heyday in eighteenth-century England.

Milton, Thomas (*1743-1827*) English aquatint (*qv*) engraver of landscapes and protraits after his own designs and those of his contemporaries, and son of a marine painter.

Neele, Samuel John (*1758-1824*) English line engraver of military subjects and topographical views, mainly after his contemporaries.

Northcote, James (*1746-1831*) English portrait and history painter, engraver and writer. His portraiture was much influenced by Reynolds' style and, indeed, he repaid the debt by publishing his *Memoirs of Sir Joshua Reynolds* in 1813, one of a number of works devoted to the theory and practice of art.

Orme, Daniel (*fl late eighteenth and early nineteenth centuries*) English aquatint (qv) engraver of decorative, military and naval subjects after his contemporaries.

Ozanne, Nicholas Marie (*1728-1811*) French draughtsman and painter of marine subjects and brother of Pierre Ozanne (*qv*). He was made draughtsman to the Navy in 1762 and is remembered chiefly for his accurate recording of maritime and naval events.

Ozanne, Pierre (*1737-1813*) French marine painter and the pupil of his brother Nicholas Marie Ozanne (qv) whom he succeeded as draughtsman to the Navy after the elder's death. As well as his paintings he completed and published a series of sixty engravings of ship types.

Pickersgill, Henry William (*1782-1875*) Prolific English portrait painter who continued to work until his ninetieth year. He also painted a number of seascapes of the Thames and Medway.

Pocock, Lt William Innes (*1783-1863*) English marine painter and a son of Nicholas Pocock (*qv*). Like his father he went to sea in the merchant service before spending ten years in the Royal Navy from 1805 to 1814, during which time he recorded incidents in sketchbooks, many of which are held by the National Maritime Museum. His oil paintings are very much in his father's style and suggest that he spent time as his pupil.

Pocock, Nicholas (*1740-1821*) Foremost English marine painter of his day. He was apprenticed in the shipbuilding yard of Richard Champion in Bristol before being appointed to command the barque *Lloyd*, setting sail to Charleston in 1768. This was the first of a number of voyages for which there are illustrated logbooks, some of which are at the National Maritime Museum. He was present at the West Indies campaign in 1778 or '79, and completed an oil painting in 1780, receiving helpful criticism from Sir Joshua Reynolds. Thereafter he devoted himself to his art and painted numerous depictions of the struggles with Revolutionary France

Pollard, Robert (*1755-1838*) English line and aquatint (*qv*) engraver of naval and historical subjects, as well as of portraits and architectural scenes. He set up business in London in 1781 and is known to have collaborated with Francis Jukes (*qv*).

Ponce, Nicholas (*1746-1831*) French publisher and engraver to the Count of Artois, based in Paris.

Reynolds, Samuel William (*1773-1835*) English painter and engraver of landscapes, topographical views and portraits. Though not related to Sir Joshua Reynolds, he engraved many plates after that artist's work. Under the patronage of Samuel Whitbread he expanded his interests to include architecture, landscape gardening and collecting.

Ridley, William (*1764-1838*) English engraver of bookplates and portraits, mainly after his contemporaries.

Roux, Joseph Ange Antoine (*1765-1835*) French marine painter of naval battles, and ship portraitist.

Rowlandson, Thomas (*1756-1827*) English humorous draughtsman, caricaturist and engraver of scenes on urban and country life. He also did a number of topographical scenes. The images were charaterised by much picaresque detail and were well suited to such contemporary novels as those by Lawrence Sterne which they illustrated.

Schouman, Martinus (*1770-1838*) Dutch marine painter who is credited with reviving the tradition of marine painting in Holland in the nineteenth century. As well as dramatic seascapes, he painted a number of naval subjects.

Serres, John Thomas (*1759-1825*) English marine painter and elder son of Dominic Serres, the elder. Though he painted a number of dramatic naval battle scenes in the manner of de Loutherbourg whom he greatly admired, his main activity was drawing the coasts of England, France and Spain in his capacity as Marine Draughtsman to the Admiralty. A selection were subsequently published in *Serres Little Sea Torch* (1801). He died in debtors' prison as a result of the pretensions and wild extravagances of his wife, the self-styled 'Princess Olive of Cumberland'.

Smirke, Robert (*1753-1845*) English subject painter and illustrator who specialised in depicting scenes from literature and the theatre; he worked for Boydell's Shakespeare Gallery.

Spilsbury, Francis B (*fl late eighteenth and early nineteenth centuries*) English painter and engraver and naval surgeon. He recorded the topography, costumes and customs of the many countries he visited including Syria and west coast of Africa.

St John, Georgina (*fl mid nineteenth century*) English land- and seascape painter.

Stadler, Joseph Constantine (*fl late eighteenth and early nineteenth century*) Prolific aquatint engraver of marine, military and topographical subjects.

Sutherland, Thomas (*fl late eighteenth and early nineteenth centuries*) English aquatint (*qv*) engraver of sporting, naval and military subjects and portraits after his contemporaries.

Swaine, John (*1775-1860*) English engraver and draughtsman of scenes from antiquity.

Turner, Charles (*1773-1857*) English aquatint (*qv*) and mezzotint (*qv*) engraver of portraits, military and sporting subjects and topographical views. His engraving of J M W Turner's 'A Shipwreck' in 1805 was the first one after a Turner painting.

Vinkeles, Reinier (*1741-1816*) Dutch engraver of portraits and landscapes.

Vivares, Thomas (*fl late eighteenth and early nineteenth centuries*) Engraver, born in London and son of the French engraver François Vivares. He mainly did landscapes and architectural views.

Wells, J G (*fl late eighteenth and early nineteenth centuries*) English aquatint (*qv*) engraver of landscapes and topographical views and naval and military subjects after his own designs and those of his contemporaries.

Whitcombe, Thomas (*born c1752*) English marine painter who, like Pocock (*qv*) and Luny, was celebrated for his huge output of paintings depicting the French Revolutionary Wars. He contributed some fifty plates to the *Naval Achievements of Great Britain* and also painted numerous works for engravings. There is no record of his death.

Willyams, Rev Cooper (*fl late eighteenth and early nineteenth centuries*) English amateur engraver who made illustrations for his books on his foreign travels.

INDEX

All ships are British unless otherwise indicated in brackets following the name

Abbreviations
Cdr = Commander
Cdre = Commodore
Den = Denmark

Fr = France
GB = British merchant ship
Lt = Lieutenant
Lt-Col=Lieutenant-Colonel

Lt-Gen=Lieutenant-General
Neths = Netherlands
R/A = Rear-Admiral
RM=Royal Marines

Sp = Spain
USA=United States
V/A = Vice-Admiral

Abercromby, General Sir Ralph
16-17, 69, 74, 78-82, 98-9, 120
Aboukir Bay 26
  battle of (1798) see Nile, battle of
  British landing at (1801) 16-17,
  79-82
Acheron 176
Acre, siege of 16, 61-5
  see also Copenhagen, battle of
Acton, John 51
Adamant 106, 168
Addington, Henry 12, 184-5
Aden 163
Aetna 176
Afghanistan 143
Africa 95, 108, 168
Agamemnon 178, 181
Agréable (Fr) 156
Aix Roads 98
Albania 14, 61
Albatross 162
Alceste (Fr) 56
Alerte (Fr) 56
Alexander I, Tsar 170
Alexander 18, 30, 33, 35-6, 67
Alexandria 13, 15-17, 26-7, 30, 33,
  65-6, 81-3, 163
Algeciras Bay 150
  battle of 17, 88-93
Algiers 146
Alliance 61
Amboyna 141
Ambuscade 130-1
Amelia 112-14, 127
Amfitrite (Neth) 122
Amiens, Peace of 11, 17, 45, 53, 70, 75,
  153, 185
Ancona 59-60
Andromeda 137
Anémone (Fr) 65
Anson 98, 112-15
Aquilon (Fr) 33
Arab 153
Ardent 178
Argo 56, 85, 87
Ariadne 159
Arrogant 160
Arrow 102, 133, 176
Artémise (Fr) 36, 38
Athénien (Fr) 21, 69
Atlas 117
Audacious 89, 91-3
Aurora 45
Austria 10-11, 18, 97-9, 123, 184-5
  in Italy 9-10, 15-16, 49-50, 60, 73, 76,
  120
  in Netherlands 9, 185
Aventurier (Fr) 136

Babet 123, 156
Badger 106

Bahamas 144
Baird, General David 163
Baird, John 76-7
Ball, Captain Alexander John 13,
  18-19, 67-9
Baltic Sea 11-12, 58, 102-3, 119, 141,
  143, 169-71, 176, 183
  see also Copenhagen, battle of
Banda 141
Bantry Bay 9, 97-8
Barbados 156
Barbary States 24, 146
Basque Roads 176
Bastia 13
Batavia (East Indies) 161
Batavian Republic 120-2
Bayonnaise (Fr) 130-1
Beaulieu 137
Beaulieu le Loup, Captain 168
Belize 143, 145
Belleisle 74, 78, 97, 99, 134-5
Bellerophon 33, 35, 38
Belliard, General 83
Bellona 181
Bellone (Fr) 113-14
Bengal 143, 160, 167
Bentham, Samuel 102, 133, 176
Berry, Captain Sir Edward 18-19, 42-3
Bertrand, General 21, 80
Biche (Fr) 113-14
Biter 137
Black Joke (GB) 98, 124
Black Sea 58, 169
Blackwood, Captain 69
Blankett, Cdre 162-3
Blenheim 117
Blonde (Fr) 133
Boadicea 112
Bombay 143, 163
bomb vessels 175-7
  see also individual ships
Bompart, Cdre Jean 98, 112-13
Bon, General 26-7
Bonaparte, General Napoleon 11, 18,
  94, 150, 184-5
  and capture of Malta 13, 20-1, 23,
  25, 67
  Egyptian campaign and Acre 9-11,
  13, 15-18, 20-2, 26-7, 30, 39, 61-2,
  65-6, 97, 124, 160, 163
  and invasion of British Isles 9, 13,
  20, 97, 99, 105, 138
  Italian campaign 10-11, 16-17, 20,
  73, 78
Bonne Citoyenne 18, 61
Boorder, Cdr 123
Boulogne 97, 108-9, 133
  British raid on 99, 138-9, 175
Bounty 158
Bourdelais 156, 165

Boxer 137
Boyne 77, 119
Bravoure (Fr) 75
Brenton, Captain Jahleel 91
Brest 9, 11, 15-16, 18, 74, 91, 97-100,
  115, 168
  British blockade of 11, 97-8, 124-5,
  127, 165
Brilliant 54, 135
Brisbane, Captain Charles 137
Britain
  Army 9-10, 16-17, 44-6, 68, 73-4,
  78-84, 86, 98, 120-3, 134-5, 143,
  163, 178, 185
  blockades 11-12, 14-16, 18, 44-5, 56,
  97, 124-6, 141, 160, 171
  see also under Cadiz, East Indies,
  France, Malta
  convoys 97, 141-2
  crew conditions and losses 12, 38,
  43, 50, 52, 77, 90, 93-5, 101, 114,
  117, 119, 131, 137, 155-6, 165, 168,
  183
  diplomatic position 9-12, 18, 61,
  169-70, 184-5
  dockyards 12, 18, 52, 169, 185
  French invasion attempts 9, 13, 20,
  97-9, 105-9, 138, 159
  gunnery 33, 42, 101, 175
  mutinies 154-5, 158
  privateers 141-2
  shipbuilding and ship types 12,
  85-7, 102-4, 117-19, 158-9, 175-7
  see also Nelson, *individual battles and
  ships, and under* Egypt,
  Guadeloupe, Malta
Britannia 118
Browne, Captain Henry 86
Brueys, Admiral 13, 20, 26-7, 31-3, 35,
  38, 82
Bruix, Admiral Eustache 15, 49, 55,
  68, 97-8, 124-5, 150
Brûle-Gueule (Fr) 160-1, 166, 168
Brune, General 122-3
Buttersworth, Thomas 56-7, 161

Cadiz 17, 91-2
  British blockade of 11, 13, 15, 18,
  44, 54-7, 88, 93, 98, 125, 150
  British raid on 74-5, 78, 97, 99, 135
Caesar 17, 89, 91-3
Cairo 17, 27, 81-3
Calabria 49
Calais 108
Calcutta 160, 185
Calder, Admiral 165
Calpe 88, 93
Camel 86
Campbell, Captain 53
Camperdown, battle of 9

Campo-Formio, Treaty of 160
Canada 113-14
Canary Islands 54
Canopus see Franklin
Cape of Good Hope 16, 86, 185
Cape St Vincent, battle of 9, 117
Cape Town 141, 185
Capri 49
Capua 15, 50
Caraccioli, Prince Francesco 15, 50
Carlotta 93
Caroline 18, 56-7
Carrère (Fr) 17, 66, 75
Cartagena 54, 98
Cartaginoise (Fr) 69
Caruana, Canon Saverio 67
Casa Bianca, Captain de 35
Cayenne 143, 156
Centurion 162
Champion 159
Channel Islands 124, 142
Chapman, F H 102, 105
Charles Emmanuel, King of
  Piedmont-Sardinia 15
Charles V, Emperor 24
Charon 86
Chatham, Earl of 11
Cherbourg 97, 105, 107-8
Chesme, battle of 58
Chevrette (Fr) 137
Chiffonne (Fr) 168
Childers 136
China 143, 160-1
Chouan revolt 99, 134
Church, Lt Thomas 93
Cisalpine Republic 185
Civita Vecchia 13, 15, 50
Clyde 127
Cochrane, Captain Alexander 80
Cochrane, Captain Thomas 94-5
Colpoys, Admiral 97
Comet 137
Concorde (Fr) 159
Confiante (Fr) 98, 107, 109
Congreve rockets 175-7
Conquérant (Fr) 33
Constellation (USA) 146, 148f9
Constitution (USA) 148
  class 146
Convulsion 175
Cooke, Captain 168
Coote, General Sir Eyre 17, 82-3, 111
Copenhagen, battle of 11, 41, 119,
  138, 159, 170, 176, 178-83
Coquille (Fr) 113-14
Corfu 14, 20, 43, 55, 59, 68, 124
Cormorant 45
Corné, Michèle-Félice 150
Cornwallis, Admiral Sir William 97
Cornwallis, General Charles 78, 159

Coron 30
Corréjou 136
Corsica 13, 45
Courageuse (Fr) 56
Crete 24
Crimea 58
Cuba 141, 144, 152
Cullen, Peter 159
Culloden 13, 33
Curaçao 143, 151
Curieux (Fr) 156
Curtis, Sir Roger 18
Cynthia 102, 134-5
Cyprus 23, 66

Daedalus 162-3
Daendals, General 121
Danae (Fr) 128
Dannebroge (Den) 178
Daphne 159
Dart 102, 111, 137
d'Auvergne, Captain Philip 124
Davison, Alexander 40
Defence 33
de Frédéric, M. 151
Dégo (Fr) 21, 69
de Louthbourg, Philip 80
Denmark 11-12, 94-5, 119, 143, 152-3,
  159, 169-73, 176, 178-83
  see also Copenhagen, battle of,
  Kronburg, Trekroner
Derby, Elias 150
Desaix, General 26-7
Desaix (Fr) 88-9
Désirée (Fr) 137, 156
Destruction 175
Diamond 106, 165
Diane (Fr) 16, 38, 67, 69
Diomede 87
dismasting 164-5
Djezzar Pasha 61-2
Dolphin 86
Domett, William 171, 173
Dominica 156
Donegal see Hoche (Fr)
Doris 114, 137
Draak (Neths) 133
Dreadnought 118-19
Duckworth, Cdre Sir John 14, 44-5,
  153, 176
Duke 119
Dumanoir le Pelley, Admiral 88, 91,
  93
Duncan, Admiral 40
Dundas, Henry 97, 135, 162
Dundas, Lt 77
Dunkirk 9, 98, 136
Dupetit-Thouars, Captain 36

Earl of St Vincent 56

190